THE
ARTIST'S
GUIDE

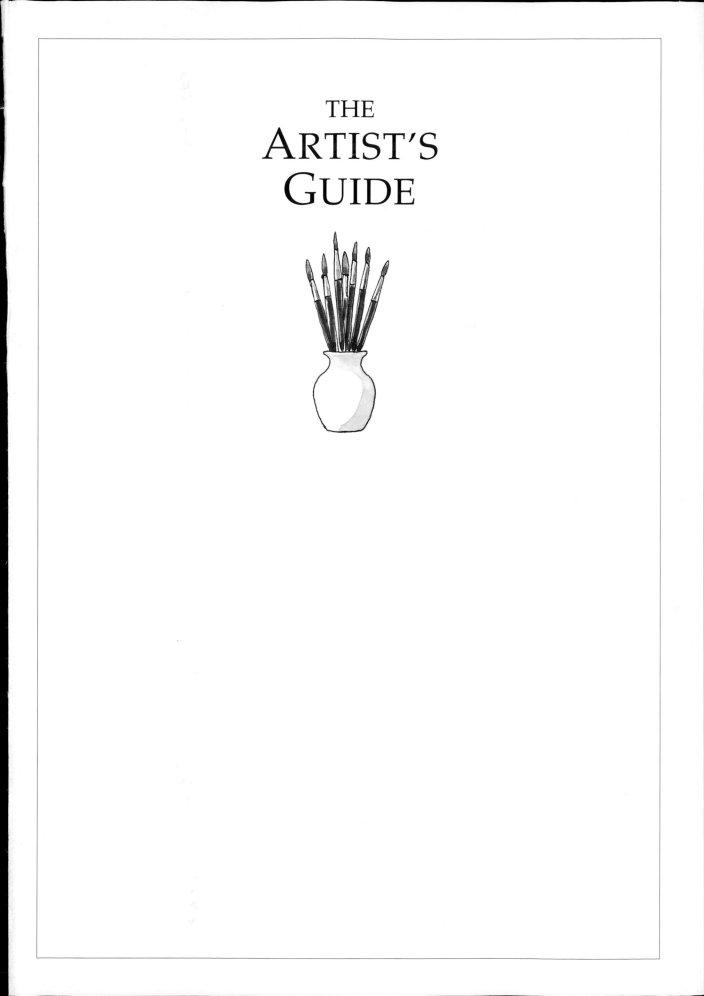

THE ARTIST'S GUIDE

John Wilkinson

DORLING KINDERSLEY

LONDON • NEW YORK • SYDNEY • MOSCOW

A DORLING KINDERSLEY BOOK

First published in Great Britain in 1998
by Dorling Kindersley Limited,
9 Henrietta Street, London WC2E 8PS

Visit us on the World Wide Web at http://www.dk.com

ISBN 0 7513 0496 4

A CIP catalogue record for this book is available from the British Library

Printed in Slovenia

CONTENTS

Introduction 6

─────────────── HOW TO SEE 8 ───────────────

─────────────── THE COLOURS 88 ───────────────

─────────────── THE MEDIA 110 ───────────────

Suppliers 252

Further Reading 252

Index 253

INTRODUCTION

Making a painting or drawing with your own eye and hands gives considerable satisfaction, the more so as one gets better at it. This book sets out to show how to do this, and for that reason it is chiefly a book of technique. Fortunately the mastering of technique is itself an enjoyable process.

The question is often asked, especially by those with no artistic training themselves, whether in fact art can be taught at all. This idea, the suggestion that inborn talent is all, an indispensable element without which it is not worth painting anything, has discouraged many people from even trying to make the most of their own underestimated abilities. In practice, as with learning most other human skills, persistence and hard work are what matter most. With my own pupils I try to show that the essentials of painting can be quite easily learned by anyone, of whatever age, providing they really want to learn and are prepared to work at it.

Art is often separated into two parts: technique and vision, although in practice they are closely intertwined. A work of art, successful or not, brilliant or banal, arises from the artist's perception of the world (actual or remembered) and from his or her interpretation of that vision. What is now-adays called creativity (see pages 42-3) is no more than a flattering term for this ability to look and think for oneself, and then to convey one's vision to others through words, paint, music or any other medium.

The ability develops over time with practice and in tune with the artist's personality, experience, and – yes, eventually – native skill or genius. This book aims to help you with the vital first step: acquiring the means, or technique, of realising and conveying your visions.

To start with, don't bother as to whether or not you feel "creative". Just learn the techniques! Paint what you feel like painting, knowing that your pictures will at least be unique. Do not worry about mistakes or failures: errors are an inevitable part of the process and one learns from them. Learn how to handle materials, to get the best out of them and to make them follow your wishes. As one improves with that, painting becomes increasingly fascinating and a pleasure.

HOW THE BOOK IS SET OUT
There are three main sections; the first part deals with "seeing" as the foundation of drawing and painting; the second considers the colours and their characteristics; the third describes in turn the materials and techniques of each of the major media.

HOW TO SEE
Painting what you see involves accurate and clear observation: in my experience as a teacher, many problems arising simply from careless observation are blamed on a supposed lack of technique. All artists find that drawing, in particular, enhances and improves their powers of observation. They also benefit from analysing the tones, lighting and colouring of the subject. This section concludes with a necessarily long section on the important subject of perspective, hoping to throw light on it even for the less mathematical. It contains an outline of how to find the position and shapes of cast shadows for both natural and artificial light.

THE COLOURS USED IN PAINTING
The paints and pigments common to all media, except drawing, are described and illustrated.

MATERIALS
It is strongly recommended that you use the best, or "artist's" quality, grade whenever possible. Materials such as canvas, paper, oils and resins that are mostly specific to a particular medium are included in their respective sections. Some colours work better in one medium than another, so suggestions are offered as a guide for each. The paints have a section to themselves, clarifying the differences or similarities among the huge range provided by the makers, and a list of suppliers given on p. 252.

MEDIA AND TECHNIQUES

The last section begins with Drawing, the foundation of almost all painting as well as a complete and satisfying medium in its own right. Although pencil and cartridge paper are found everywhere, they are by no means the only drawing materials, neither are they always the most appropriate, so it is worth considering charcoal, conté crayon on toned paper or line-and-wash, among others. The four water-based media, Watercolour, Acrylics, Gouache and Egg Tempera are described and compared. Egg Tempera is a very old medium that has had a revival, and its materials are now much easier to obtain through the suppliers of dry pigments.

Oil painting is the most flexible and comprehensive medium, and probably the easiest to use - if handled correctly - as there is plenty of time to manipulate the paint, and the opportunity to work towards both light or dark. The final section on Pastels completes the circle as there is a strong element of drawing in pastels. Pastels differ from any other medium in the desirability of collecting as many pastels as possible, as except for a certain amount of blending, colour mixing is rarely practical.

The different media are compared in more detail on pages 110-11, where convenience and cost are taken into account. Many artists have taken up watercolours or oils by accident, through being given them or being introduced to them by a friend. It may be worthwhile to consider whether your medium is the right one for the way you work.

Many new variations of the media are appearing at the present time. Some of these, like the acrylic inks and liquid watercolours, can be incorporated into watercolour or acrylic paintings, and the oil-bars into oil paintings; try them if they could solve particular problems. Some manufacturers of acrylic and gouache paints, and Sennelier pastels, now include iridescent colours in their ranges.

Finally the Further Reading list includes a sample of the wide range of inspirational and instructive books that can assist your progress and increase your enjoyment as an artist.

Lily Pond Cat. Acrylic.

WHERE TO BEGIN

Start with drawing, the basis of all that follows. Just pick up a pencil and paper and start to draw whatever appeals to you. Don't worry if it seems to fall short of your hopes, most things do at first. Many claim, after a brief try, to be unable to draw, but so far I have never met anyone who can't draw once they have been shown how to do it, and then practised for a while. Once you have a reasonable technique to convey your message, a style your own will inevitably emerge, but while you are learning new things, don't be afraid to copy or follow some admired painter; copying is one of the quickest ways of learning how to draw and paint, and has been the practice of most of the great painters.

HOW TO SEE

Painting can be said to consist of two main processes: the first is the "seeing" and visualising of an intended picture, and the second is the technique, which is the process of applying the paint. In my teaching experience I have noticed the crucial role that accurate observation plays in an artist's progress. Limitations in this field often remain unrecognised, causing difficulties that are blamed on technique; this section of the book shows a way of observing more closely.

Observation is the habit of seeing and recognising all the features and details of the scene in front of you. From the whole, a selection can be made. Of the elements described in the following pages, those below are especially important:

■ **Shape**, or form
■ **Tone**, the range of tonal values from light to dark, is fundamental to interpreting both reality and paintings.

■ **Lighting**, with tone, reveals form.
■ **Colour**, an attractive addition to tone.

Your eyes record everything in complete detail, but from this mass of information the mind selects only those items it considers necessary. The act of drawing itself sharpens the vision, and this in turn exercises the memory, which is useful when finishing a painting based on earlier sketches. There is rarely enough time to do a complete picture in front of the subject, especially out of doors. In daily life, simple identification of an object is usually enough: a book is "seen" so it can be moved, or picked up and read, and for these purposes there is no need to study its proportions or the colour of the cover. But if you wish to draw it rather than read it, then you need to see it in a different way, beginning by converting three dimensions into two, and estimating the apparent area occupied by the subject in front of you.

Belshazzar's Feast by Rembrandt. Oil.
At about the age of thirty, Rembrandt produced one of his most spectacular paintings. From the thin transparent shadows to the thickly encrusted paint of the jewellery and clothing material, the textures of the paint mirror the subject matter. The dramatic lighting is characteristic of a time before electric light eliminated heavy indoor shadows.

Giotto, **Lamentations**. Fresco.

Claude Yvel, **Baseball/Strike One.** Oil.
Giotto was the new realist of his time, (1276-1337), breaking away from restrictive symbolism, but keeping to acceptable subject matter. Modern realism has reached new levels of close observation and accuracy in depicting everyday subjects. As time passes, these subjects are likely to gain just as much historic interest.

The great paintings of the past give a good idea of the way artists saw and interpreted the world. The advent of photography in the 1850s was a turning point, and some artists have used it since to expand their range of subjects. By permanently fixing fleeting effects, photography has brought lighting effects formerly attained only by masters like Cuyp and Claude within the range of many.

Examining the work of master painters – in galleries, but also in books – improves our powers of observation, and judgement of shape, tone, lighting and colour. We learn from noting how artists have converted their observation into actual paintings.

Rembrandt lived during the high tide of great painting when artists possessed the highly developed oil technique perfected by Rubens in the north and the Italian masters in the south. Over the centuries, all paintings have gradually darkened through the accumulation of grime and the yellowing of oils and varnishes, and many have undergone extensive cleanings, repairs and re-varnishings in the past.

The evidence of modern cleaning and restoration, in the cases of the ceiling of the Sistine Chapel by Michelangelo, and The Ambassadors, by Holbein, in the London National Gallery, shows that many paintings were lighter and brighter than they now appear. But restoration is still a matter of controversy, with disagreement over how much lighter and brighter, and the danger of accidentally removing subtle and almost transparent paint films without realising that they were there. Furthermore, certain pigments may have altered or faded, and restorers today are sensibly cautious over trying to restore lost colourings.

Old watercolours have generally faded as even their soundest pigments lack the protection against daylight and the atmosphere afforded by a coating of oil and varnish; nowadays they are usually exhibited in subdued light.

Women in the Garden by Manet. Oil.
Manet painted at a time when the conventions of realism and design had begun to be loosened, and his work represents a transitional period towards a greater freedom of expression. The rise of the Impressionists was not a single event but a gradual change in painting methods and vision.

OBSERVATION

Although the eye impartially records everything in front of it, the brain is selective in its scrutiny, as noted on p. 8, and may ignore anything irrelevant to the matter in hand; a conscious effort is needed at first to question and re-think the way we see things.

The brain itself has no direct viewing screen like the eye's, but builds up its picture from the messages sent along the optic nerve – if it didn't, we would see the world just like the tiny image on the retina, upside down, reversed and in miniature. But however well long-term habits of interpretation and observation work in daily life, artists need to improve and refine them.

We start with the most obvious elements which may have been taken for granted, concentrating on the larger scheme of things rather than the details.

Size is deceptive – apparent size and real size can be unexpectedly different – because objects are interpreted in their real, or natural size, rather than by how much of the space in front of you they occupy. Many drawing difficulties arise from this, so it will be returned to from time to time, and the first of the elements considered separately on the following pages is size.

In learning to see more analytically, two steps are especially useful:

■ Avoid preconceptions about appearance – the unexpected is everywhere.

■ Look at your subject as if you had never seen it before, starting with the most obvious main features, then gradually to the lesser detail.

Realism over the centuries. The heightened accuracy of our vision eventually led some artists to break free from its constraints and seek freedom in abstraction.

The apparently unremarkable greys and browns of the familiar mallard reveal a wealth of fine feather detail on closer inspection; even the plainest feathers are covered with reticulated patterning, and show fine gradations of tone.

The ability to see is more important than manual dexterity with pencil or brush, although each reinforces the other, for your powers of observation are the key to a solid technique based on accurate placing of tone and colour.

Simplified head and eye

Complete eye detail

Plain grey at a distance, a pattern becomes apparent when near enough.

Fine feather detail

Representation of this tree-like shape corresponds to the way objects are identified, labelled and forgotten. Even the outline conveys a lot of information that has been carefully observed, as each tree has very characteristic outlines that say a lot about it even when no interior detail or colour is present.

The painting of an aloe shows detail noted after a lengthier observation.

Red Oak

The flowers form out of the initial confusion of similar yellows and convoluted shapes, and become individuals that can be analysed further. Complex forms can almost always be broken down into simpler elements.

Many difficulties experienced by artists arise from a failure to see the difference between what is actually there and what is assumed; more of my time as a teacher has necessarily been spent in explaining what things really look like rather than in teaching how to handle the paint. A significant saving of time and worry is an immediate benefit of accurate observation. Although technical skill is essential, it is the artist's interpretation of what is seen that creates art, and what is seen depends on the depth and richness of observation.

Aloe ferox

AGASSIZ ON OBSERVATION

It takes time to train yourself to keep looking at something when you think you have already seen it all, as there is always more than is at first apparent, and the great French scientist Louis Agassiz, (1807-1873), taught this to his students in a concentrated and effective way. He would leave his pupil alone in a room to study a single preserved specimen, to observe and draw it for many hours, until Agassiz was satisfied on one of his periodic visits that everything to be seen had been seen. Painful though this experience could be, its value to the students was enormous.

WHAT TO LOOK FOR

SIZE

Think of size in relation to surroundings, as well as actual size. Psychological factors often influence one's idea of size, so that "important" things are seen as larger than they really are – notice the size of the head compared to the body on many life-drawings.

Size comparisons can be made with familiar everyday objects.

PROPORTION

The simplest is length compared to height. Proportion is particularly subject to erroneous preconceptions, so check carefully. A grasp of true proportions gets your drawing on to the right track straight away. When judging proportions, ignore detail and the smaller shapes, at first working progressively from large to small.

Compare length to height and area of head and neck to the body.

By first suppressing all interior detail, the big shapes become apparent. When these are right, it is relatively easy to place the eyes, nose and other features.

SHAPE

The most variable attribute and without limit. Overall shapes are often different from what we expect, but can nearly always be analysed to reveal simpler forms. Recognition of the simpler basic forms is the foundation of all drawing.

Some simpler shapes are shown. Complex shapes can often be broken down into an assemblage of simpler ones, see "Recognising the Basic Shapes" on p. 130. This process needs the practice and imagination that come with experience – learning to draw is largely devoted to learning to do this.

ANGLES, DIRECTION

Angles give direction and movement, and are another area in which preconceptions can lead us astray. The angles to notice are those that are close to the vertical or horizontal; these can play a big part in gauging the directions of many other lines.

Angles are usually clear to see, but the expectation of seeing them in a pre-conceived way sometimes leads to their being overlooked.

Notice how the shore on the far side of a lake or wide river approximates to the horizontal, where distant lines are flattened by the perspective.

This only affects lines at ground level and close to the horizontal.

Outside angles

Directional angles

The ducks are sitting and moving at many angles, mainly seen in the bends of their necks as they casually look around. Few lines here are either horizontal or vertical, but there are some right-angles where the forms touch or overlap. Well-judged angles are vital in expressing movement and action.

MOVEMENT

This has an intangible quality that is not easy to bring off in a drawing. The effect comes from a multitude of small angles and proportions, and plenty of experience in observing them. A flowing, slightly off-balance feeling is always present.

A few subjects appear to lack horizontal or vertical lines: holding a pencil horizontally or vertically in front of you will reveal the slope of any angle.

The flow of the tiger's walk, the pouring water, the sparrow's alertness, all depend on the careful placing of angles

What to look for (continued)

NUMBERS, COUNTING

This is simple to do, and helps to ensure good proportions and spacing. Counting focuses your concentration, and is the beginning of knowledge wherever forms or shapes are repeated. The act of counting will impress many other features and details onto your mind. Always count if the estimated number is small or in any way critical to the subject. Getting the numbers right will automatically help with proportion and spacing.

TONE

The next section is devoted to tone, the range of darknesses from white to black. Every colour can be converted to an equivalent tone, which varies according to circumstance, so that in extreme cases a white in deep shade can look nearly as dark as a black in brilliant sun.

5 petals, each with 2 lobes. Occasionally there are six petals on flowers that normally have five.

6 outer petals arranged in 2 sets of 3. 6 stamens.

Exact counting is not so necessary if the numbers are between 10 and 20.

Where there are only a few veins, count them. The minor veins and their branches can be ignored.

Count if there are fewer than 10.

Draw in the major stones first, then count how many stones are between them. Count the stones of the arch over the door, and the vertical divisions of the door.

Every colour has an equivalent tone.

Tones of grey from white foam.

The doorway (top) and its shadows readily translate to greys, and the colour of water and foam is already close to tones of grey. The judgement of tonal values is relatively simple with everyday muted colours.

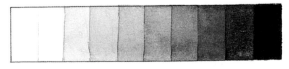

Tones can be conveniently compared to the steps on an imaginary grey scale, as described on p. 18.

COLOUR

Colour can be an elusive and changeable attribute, sometimes appearing differently to different people. Colours seem to change according to the light or time of day, while the colours of shadows are hard to pin down, complicated by the insubstantial darkness. Your eye adapts well to changing light conditions, and much of the way we see and interpret colour is subjective. As an artist you will rarely be asked to match colours exactly, but try to make a habit of being aware of and estimating colours as accurately as you can. They are often influenced by their surroundings, because the eye and brain work to magnify differences of colour and contrast.

Overcast   Good daylight   Electric light

The colour of the light also plays a part. Our eyes adjust to equalise the colouring of almost all lights, but the differences show up in photographs, so make allowances if you use them for reference.

The surrounding colour slightly affects the grey dots.

The effects of surrounding colour and tone on identical dots. ▷
▽

The influence of the surrounding colour on the grey dots is not obvious at first, so look at the circle from about 30cm away, put your eyes out of focus, and stare at it for 30 seconds or more. The grey dots will become notably more colourful.

Stare at a dot for 30 seconds to see colour effect.

The surrounding tone affects the brightness of the reds.

The colour circle shows the effects of different surrounding colours on eight identical grey dots. Each will have a slight tendency towards the complementary colour of its surroundings. The red dots on the grey scale are changed in another way; here their brightness as well as colour is influenced. Compared to the luminous dot on the black background, the dot of identical colour on the white looks relatively dull and brownish, because the surrounding white is much brighter.

Numerous slight variations in colour add to the impression of luminosity and brilliance.

15

What to look for (continued)

PATTERN

Repetition and regularity in some form is universal, and there is a complete range of patterns from the most regular and symmetrical to the completely random. But the brain continually searches for pattern and can usually find it even in apparently random distributions such as the stars, which have long been divided into convenient groupings of recognisable shapes. Many natural objects consist of parts that are similar to each other but not identical, such as the leaf of a cyclamen, where an orderly system may be apparent to an observant person but hidden to another. There is almost always some sort of underlying order, and the ability to find it is one of the most useful skills to develop.

2 sets of spirals

The centres of all daisies are patterns of spirals. The spirals are often distorted but show up clearly on larger flowers. Butterflies and moths share the same layout of veins, varying only in sizes and proportions. The positions of the dots and colours are in turn controlled by the veins.

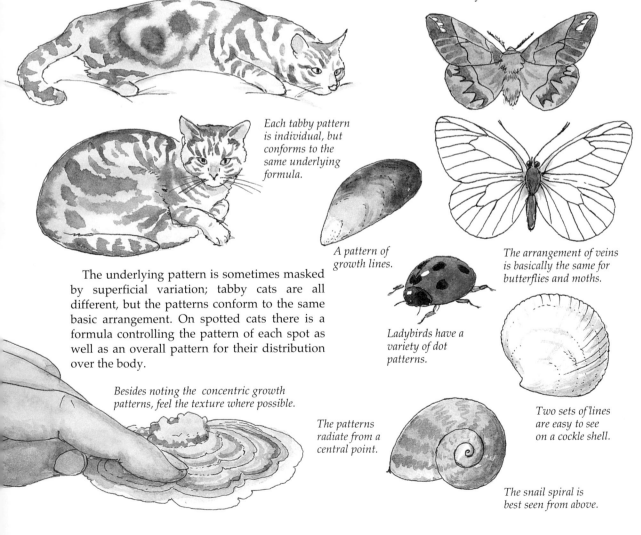

Each tabby pattern is individual, but conforms to the same underlying formula.

A pattern of growth lines.

The arrangement of veins is basically the same for butterflies and moths.

The underlying pattern is sometimes masked by superficial variation; tabby cats are all different, but the patterns conform to the same basic arrangement. On spotted cats there is a formula controlling the pattern of each spot as well as an overall pattern for their distribution over the body.

Ladybirds have a variety of dot patterns.

Besides noting the concentric growth patterns, feel the texture where possible.

The patterns radiate from a central point.

Two sets of lines are easy to see on a cockle shell.

The snail spiral is best seen from above.

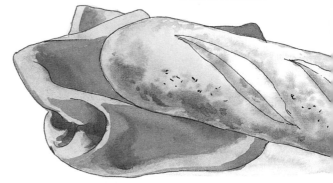

TEXTURE

Felt rather than seen, texture is the very fine detail of the surface itself, independent of any pattern or decoration. Texture seldom plays much part in a painting, but its careful noting will increase your insight into your subject, and its successful rendering contributes an important extra quality.

Two contrasting textures revealed by the way the same light and shade brings out a different progression of tones on the bread and the velvet.

Beyond the blackness, texture is everything in depicting velvety black fur.

DETAIL

Whether you use it or not in your paintings, the more closely you observe fine details, the more your painting will be soundly based on knowledge of your subject. Detail includes everything small, things that have to be searched for – slight shadings of colour and texture, minor differences from the normal.

It is here that the powers of observation have their greatest scope, but also where restraint has to be exercised while painting, to prevent detail from obscuring or distorting the larger forms and tones; selection is everything.

The degree of shine reveals the nature and texture of the surfaces. Small, bright, sharp highlights characterise shiny surfaces, while matt surfaces hardly have them at all. Every intermediate degree of shine is represented on the many surfaces around us.

Texture is often made up from a mass of detail.

SUMMARY

The ability to observe, like drawing easily, only comes with time and practice. Visual development is neglected in many schools, and may need restarting with patience and persistence, but the immediate pleasures of "seeing" more when you look at something will more than compensate for the time it takes to become more proficient.

All styles of realistic painting are ultimately based on the knowledge and feeling for your subject that comes from your observation of it. As you develop your powers of observation, your technique will improve automatically, for much of the technical difficulty people experience is an uncertainty about what they are really painting, stemming from not having looked at it with sufficient attention. Observation also includes noting the things that may seem too obvious, and so be taken for granted; they can therefore be missed just as easily as the subtle detail.

TONE – LIGHT AND DARK

The word "tone" in this book refers to light and dark, expressed in terms of a grey scale going from white to black. Tone is the property which imparts substance and reality; tonal errors are the chief cause of flat-looking pictures, lacking in the third dimension.

The power of tone to convey information is shown by the self-sufficiency of black and white photographs; the same effects can also be achieved by monochrome sketches or paintings in sepia or similar colours. Colour without tone, however attractive, is not by itself enough to produce more than simplistic decorations.

A fully coloured subject can be painted in any neutral colour and look just as convincing. Even the brightest colours have their tonal equivalents.

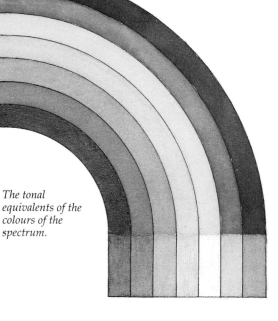

The tonal equivalents of the colours of the spectrum.

THE GREY SCALE
Eleven tones, including black and white, are a convenient number to work with. This allocation of the infinite gradations of the real world into manageable divisions was popularised by the American photographer Ansel Adams, who called it the Zone System. It provides a practical way of assessing tone values. While very few things in a picture are pure white or black, somewhere, however small, a pure white highlight or dense spot of shadow should ideally be present to set the context of all the other tones. As the near-white and near-black tones show little texture, most of the useful tonal range of the average painting lies within the central seven steps.

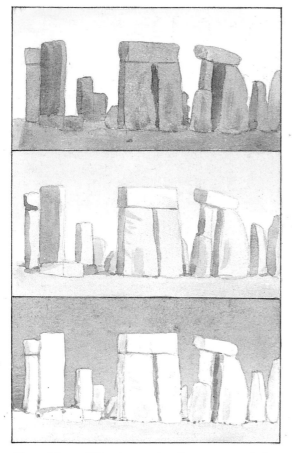

Three pictures of Stonehenge where the arrangement of tones sets the mood. The same scene can offer a number of contrasting moods by using alternative tonal distributions, together with their associated lighting and colour. The central version shows the common daytime view in sunlight.

▷

Shown opposite are four stages of increasing discrimination in the analysis of tones. The idea of visualising a scene in a defined set of tones was developed by the American photographer Ansel Adams, and has since been a valuable aid to artists as well as photographers. The success of your paintings is largely determined by the rendering and placing of the tones within it, and a systematic way of looking at them can help both in composing and executing your paintings. Each picture employs only the tones on its accompanying chart. The effect becomes more subtle with the addition of more tones, but the first examples also show how fewer tones can be more dramatic.

As a general rule, the more tones that can be reproduced, the more subtle the effect and the greater the feeling of quality. Care is always needed to avoid reversing any parts of the tonal range – switching lights and darks without realising it.

CONTRAST AND BRILLIANCE

Contrast is the comparison between opposites, such as the light and dark parts of a subject or picture; it could be full of intermediate tones or completely lacking them. Woodland scenes are often good examples of strong contrasts, with deep shade under the trees and patches of bright sunlight, a difference that usually has to be reduced in a painting.

Brilliance is sometimes mistaken for contrast because a notable degree of contrast usually goes with it. To achieve the effect of brilliance, contrast is combined with an extensive range of close and carefully placed tones, especially at the light end of the scale. While taking note of the important tones close to the light-source, take especial care to avoid hurting your eyes, and in particular, **never look at the sun.**

A Seaport by Claude.
A long range of light tones is needed to reproduce the increasing glare as the sun's disc is approached. Strong shadows are naturally associated with such lighting. This is one of the earliest and most successful attempts to portray the disk of the sun itself, which looks coloured in nature but usually has to be almost white in paintings, to make the most of the limited brightness available to an artist.

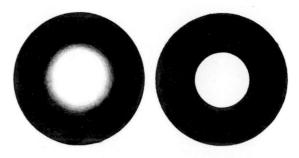

A diagram showing the principle of approaching a bright light gradually. The light on the left has an effect of glare as the brightness overspills its edges. The immediate contrast of the right-hand light is greater, but it fails to correspond to our experience of the way brilliant light spreads and its effect is less powerful.

Many of the Old Master paintings have this quality of brilliance, and close examination will reveal the long and subtle tone ranges. Such paintings have been built up in layers, giving much greater opportunities for numerous and minor variations of tone than paint applied once only and then left. The number of separate tones you can see and reproduce in your own paintings will be a good guide to how well your eye is trained, and your ability to discriminate between tones is one of the most useful attributes to a painter.

A long range of tones show in soft light.

Amanita. (see also p. 48)
The grey scale at the side shows how the mushroom's tones are concentrated at the light end of the scale in a long range of near-whites. A few strong darks show the tone range is complete and set the context for the whites. Because the stem and most of the gills are seen to be naturally white in sunlight, the whole mushroom will be understood to be white, however dark some of the shadows are.In a painting it often requires some courage to put in strong enough shadows on a white object. In general, the darkness or strength of the shadows in any outdoor picture is a measure of the brightness of the light – the stronger the shadow, the brighter the light.

Shadow and fore-shortening cause tones to merge.

Even lighting allows all the minor variations of tone to show clearly. Strong lighting partially masks them in the brilliance of the highlights and the density of the shadows.

Strong light flattens tonal differences.

Tones within the shadow are very close together.

The grey tones converge towards an overall sameness in the large shaded areas, well separated from the tones in the sunlight. The sunlit tones sometimes take on an overall sameness.

The greater the contrast, the nearer the duck. Besides indicating their relative positions in the picture, contrast adds to the impression of being nearer.

THE INTERPRETATION OF TONE

Some artists aim for a complete realism that makes one want to touch the paint surface to feel the texture, one of the greatest compliments a viewer can pay an artist. This tonal mastery allows many minor variations that depart a long way from what is described as "photographic" reality. In some respects such paintings are much more real than any photograph, because a selective interpretation of the subject has been made to correspond to the way our eyes see, which is different from the camera's all-inclusive view.

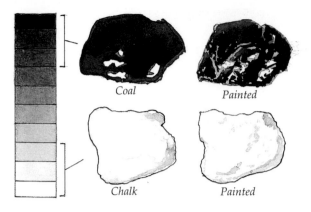

Coal   *Painted*

Chalk   *Painted*

The restricted tonal ranges of the coal and chalk have both been expanded to give truer and more interesting interpretations. The order of tones going from light to dark has been preserved. The eye is not content just to register a piece of coal as black without detail, but will focus in on it, quickly adapt itself to the general darkness, and start to separate out the many tonal variations within the "black".

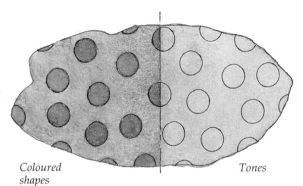

Coloured shapes   *Tones*

The difference between the red and blue is purely in terms of colour, they are equally dark so their tones are the same.

According to the needs of your picture, any parts of its tone range can be expanded or reduced: for instance, the darks could be emphasised and painted both darker and more extensively than they are in the subject itself, or they could be reduced. As long as there is no reversal of tones, (making the lights dark and the darks light), the artist can lighten or darken any part of the tonal or colour range to convey his intentions.

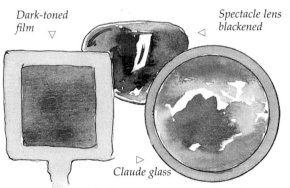

Dark-toned film ▽   *Spectacle lens blackened* ◁

▷ *Claude glass*

The Claude glass was a blackened concave mirror which gave a darkened and reduced image of a scene. The dark surface eliminates most of the colouring, revealing the tones. An old spectacle lens, painted black on the back, will do the same. A darkened film produces a similar effect.

The shadowed areas are several tonal steps darker than the sunlit parts.

Tone plays the main role in the rendition of form. The colour is almost incidental.

THE SPHERE

The sphere is one of the most frequent shapes encountered, often partially hidden within a larger structure. A gradual darkening away from the highlight becomes sudden at the edge of the strong shadow. The illustration at the foot of the page shows the standard tonal progression when the light comes from the artist's left.

The two circular shapes, parts of a spherical surface, can appear either as convex or concave according to where you think the light is coming from.

THE TRANSITION FROM LIGHT TO DARK

The traditional training of art college students used to include the copying of tones across the surfaces of some regular shapes, conventionally lit with a single light to the side and behind the artist, (see Lighting, p. 26). The cube, sphere, cylinder and their related forms underlie many of the more complicated structures or subjects we draw and paint.

Boots by Claude Yvel.
A "trompe l'oeil" painting, the ultimate in painting that corresponds to our way of seeing, rather than the camera's.

Spherical shapes usually appear in part, and their lighting matches the corresponding section of the whole sphere.

TONAL PROGRESSION OVER THE SURFACE OF A SPHERE

■ The highlight faces directly towards the light-source.

■ The natural tone and colour show here. There is a slight gradation from light to dark as we move away from the highlight, darkening more just before the shadow edge.

■ The shadow edge is fairly abrupt.

■ The reflection is tonally part of the shadow.

Light

Highlight

Full light and colour

Reflections

Main shadow zone

The tonal progression over the surface of a sphere.

EGG SHAPES

The egg is a variation of the sphere.

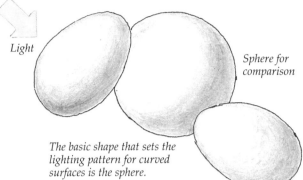

Light

Sphere for comparison

The basic shape that sets the lighting pattern for curved surfaces is the sphere.

The progression of the lighting zones on an egg is the same as the sphere's, but each zone is elongated or shortened according to its aspect. A reference sphere shows the similarities and differences. The tone on any face of an egg shape will match a spot on the sphere's surface facing in the same direction.

Shallow egg forms are particularly frequent on the surface of the body where prominent muscles dominate the form, and the outer surfaces of many flowers follow the egg or sphere contours. The shadows on a concave form are on the same side as the direction of the light, the reverse of the more commonly seen convex forms.

CYLINDERS

The cylinder shows the same gradation across its curved part as a sphere. If you can imagine a sphere being stretched gradually, first into an oval, then into a cylinder, you can see how the lighting zones would be elongated but are otherwise unchanged; the same gradations from light to dark remain, following the new shape. If the cylinder lies at a different angle to the light, the highlight can be reduced in strength or even disappear, and the shadow altered. Look carefully at cylindrical form and lighting.

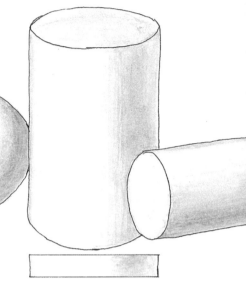

Light

Sphere for comparison

△

Typical cross-sections, showing the same basic progression of light and shade across the surfaces of the curved forms. △

Cylinders, egg shapes and cones are underlying shapes often disguised by surface detail, and frequently merge into each other. They are seen everywhere.

Some egg shapes that can be seen in real life.

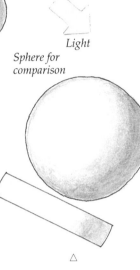

CONES

The cone is related to the cylinder. At the bottom of the cone, where it most resembles a cylinder, an identical spread of tones converges equally to the point at the top. Cones are less easily recognised in real life as the simple form is uncommon, but truncated cones, or half cones like the human nose, can be detected.

Light

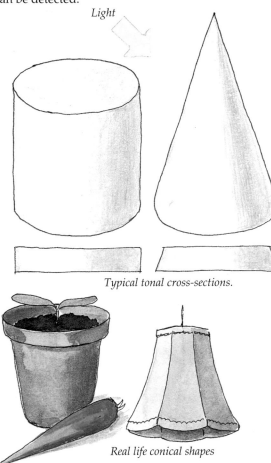

Typical tonal cross-sections.

Real life conical shapes

Light

Cubes at angles

The forms described above underlie, in many and various disguises, most of the forms we see around us. By painting or drawing the tonal progressions across the simple basic forms, artists acquire the ability to visualise and create form with tone, a skill that will repay its learning throughout your artistic career. Look for the simple shapes whenever you draw or paint.

Rectangular shapes and cubes in real life are found everywhere as elements of man-made structures and implements.

CUBES AND RECTANGULAR SHAPES

Much more common than actual cubes are the multitude of rectangular shapes of all sorts. Their lighting is relatively simple for most of the time because a side is either in the light or in the shadow. There are slight variations across both the lighted and shaded faces. The contrast between them appears strongest at the edge adjacent to the brightest face. The brightness of any surface on a cube can be estimated by comparison with a sphere, which will show the tone on the point facing in the same direction.

The majority of man-made forms are rectangular, and in conjunction with the tonal range, perspective reveals their form most clearly, and mistakes in either can undermine the intended effect of a picture.

25

LIGHTING

Lighting reveals form and colour. Photographers, who have the camera to take care of form and perspective for them, take a lot of trouble with their lighting. Artists often give it low priority, concentrating on problems of technique. It takes perseverance to incorporate good lighting into your work as it quickly disappears if tonal errors creep in. Four basic types of lighting will be considered:

LIGHT FROM BEHIND THE ARTIST

This sort of lighting is rarely used – it seems to be simple, but its flatness suppresses many of the usual guides to form and modelling. To be behind the artist, the sun is low in the sky. The light is usually bright and clear but the overall colouration is warm or golden, revealing rich and saturated colouring.

   The gradations of tone that reveal modelling are present but greatly reduced in contrast, except in the few shadows concentrated around the edges; contrast usually has to be increased to compensate. This unusual form of lighting needs tonal accuracy to be rendered convincingly.

Dolphin Lamp-post. Watercolour.
The central highlights on the dolphin's head and body, together with the narrow shadows on the left of the lamp-post, show how the sunlight comes from behind the artist and slightly to his right. The size and the soft edges of the highlights also convey the glistening surface of the metal. Shinier metal would have had brighter, smaller and sharp-edged highlights. The prominent highlight on the head immediately attracts attention to the main subject of the painting.

"Ice Maiden" – Whooper Swan, by Chris Rose. Oil.
The sun is low and just to the left of the artist's head, so the highlights are almost central and the shadows are confined mainly to the edges of the swan. Dark shadows are few, and the strongest darks are the blacks of the bill and legs. This lighting occurs at the beginning and end of the day, and is ideal for the display of rich colour and glowing light.

SIDE LIGHTING

Light from a position above and behind the artist's shoulder is the most usual, as it reveals depth and form in the clearest way. The highlights and shadows are well placed, and there is plenty of scope to show colour as well as form because about three quarters of the subject receives full light, with about one quarter in shadow. The exact angle and height of the light are not critical, neither is its intensity.

The word chiaroscuro, (Chiaro = "light", oscuro = "dark"), suggests the illusion of space and depth given by this lighting, but has come to apply to lighting with a rather exaggerated contrast.

*Strong lighting on
a cactus*

*Softer lighting
on mushrooms*

Female Nude by Dürer. Silverpoint.
*Modified egg, sphere and cylinder forms can be seen,
displaying the same gradations as in the standard shapes on
p. 24. The reflections are brighter than usual.*

The Sisters. Watercolour.
*This painting, by the contemporary artist Jan Kunz,
shows clear-cut side-lighting.*

27

THE SUBJECT AGAINST THE LIGHT

This is typically the lighting of a low sun or sunset, also called "contre-jour" lighting. The light can be anywhere on the far side of the subject, giving brilliantly lit edges, casting much of the subject into shadow, and suppressing detail. Very spectacular effects can be produced when you are looking towards a light source which implies strong contrast and dazzling light. With paint there is a limit to the brightness that can be achieved around the back-lit edges, but with careful balancing of the light and shade this form of lighting is very effective, though not often seen.

The Breaking Wave by John Spence. Photograph.

The tulips above are lit up against a dark background; the brightness of the flowers is conveyed through their transparency. The tulips become shapes, almost without a third dimension in this example.

Grand Cat, oil.
The rim of light around the cat imparts a strong three-dimensional quality to the picture. Because the lighting is soft, plenty of detail and colour is still visible in the shaded areas.

DIFFUSED LIGHTING

This could be described as no lighting at all; in some paintings this is a true description. Three-dimensional form is visible, but not emphasised, so the accent is on shape and colour. In practice there is almost always some general direction to the light, however diffuse, and we assume that as the brightness of the sky is "above", so the strongest light is from above, and the shadows are beneath.

Apples in a Bowl by Courbet. Oil.
Where the lighting is indefinite strong colours are possible. No natural lighting would combine such dense shadow and brilliant colour, but the artist has used his imagination to over-ride the literal facts.

The intense blue of the flowers shows to best effect in soft light.

Diffused lighting is useful in pictures full of detail and incident where numerous highlights and shadows would distract from the intention of the artist. Although completely flat lighting also comes into this category, it is best reserved for special decorative or atmospheric effects, for pictures where colour in some form is predominant.

The Blue Skirt. Oil.
In a complex picture, full of detail and small but important forms, the lighting is sufficient to bring them out without adding its own shadows. The additional shapes of shadows would begin to obscure the picture's design and clarity. The colour scheme is restrained for the same reason.

SUNLIGHT

Sunlight gives an impression of a clear-cut distinction between light and shade. The small size of the sun's disk in the sky means that the shadows it casts are relatively sharp-edged. Two distinguishing features that will put sunlight into your pictures, if consistently observed, are:

1 – the sharpness of the shadow edges.

2 – sufficient contrast in brightness between light and shade.

It is surprisingly difficult to be consistent and to maintain the strength of the shadows throughout a picture. Subconsciously one doesn't want to spoil good parts or colours by drowning them in dark tones, so they are often overlooked and the resulting light tones nullify the shadows. In the sunlit parts of the picture the lights have to be kept clean and bright, avoiding the strengthening of colours or detail, or overworking half-tones. If they become too dark, and bridge the tonal separation between light and shade, the sunlit effect disappears.

Sunlight is of course not always so clear-cut, and there is an infinite variety of effects brought about by differing thicknesses of cloud, the angle of the sun, the time of day and location. But the effect of sunlight in a painting is always dependent on the ratio of sunlit tone to shadow. In general the sunlit areas of an object need to be about four times as bright as the shadows.

The grey scales shown in the section on Tone, p. 18, can be used as a guide. The tonal difference between strongly sunlit and shaded areas is conveniently represented by about four steps on the scale. The ratio need not be exact to be effective, and soft sunlight naturally requires less contrast. While over-heavy shadows diminish the illusion of light, more often they are not painted strongly enough.

Number 13 Portofino, by Judy Morris. Watercolour. *The strength of the sunlight is conveyed by the two strong tonal areas; no individual parts are allowed to override their general tone. As strong light and colour normally work to neutralise each other, it is an achievement to combine such bright light and intense colour so successfully. The powerful effects possible with watercolour are well shown by this painting.*

Minor shadows within the main light areas

Clear whites facing the sun

Normal shadows

Cast shadows

Partially illuminated shadows

Reflected light

Cast shadow from the petal above it

Within the lighted areas there is a whole range of close tones, depending on the angles of the minor folds and other changes of direction. The shadows contain varying reflections and places where the petals are translucent, leading to a series of tones that are related but more diverse than those of the lights.

The strong contrast and the sharpness of the chimney's shadow cast on the white wall is characteristic of sunlight. Further away in the distant landscape the same effect is muted by the aerial perspective which softens both contrast and colour. The ratio of light to shadow on the sunlit and shaded walls is approximately four to one, as recommended opposite. The well separated sunlit and shaded tones can both contain their own range of internal tones, enabling the artist to insert whatever amount of detail is thought necessary.

Strong, clear cut shadows on a Spanish villa

ARTIFICIAL LIGHT

This can also look bright because our eyes adapt to it, although it is never as bright as the sun. As artificial light is never far from the subject, the shadows show strong perspective effects as they fan out from the light-source.

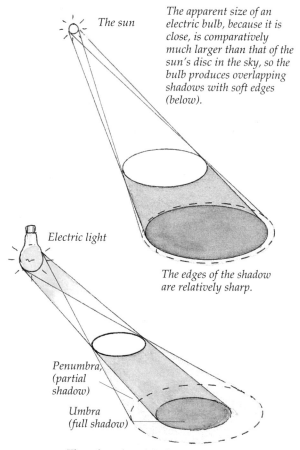

The sun

The apparent size of an electric bulb, because it is close, is comparatively much larger than that of the sun's disc in the sky, so the bulb produces overlapping shadows with soft edges (below).

Electric light

The edges of the shadow are relatively sharp.

Penumbra (partial shadow)

Umbra (full shadow)

The softer edge of shadows cast by artificial light.

The light-source itself is usually relatively large in close up subjects, with the result that shadows are more diffuse at the edges than in sunlight. The section on perspective (see p. 82), shows how to construct the appropriate shadows.

Maximum light intensity is at the source, and there is a noticeable diminution of brightness with distance. Most artificial light is coloured compared to daylight, but the eye adapts to it and filters out the colour, so it appears white, the same as daylight.

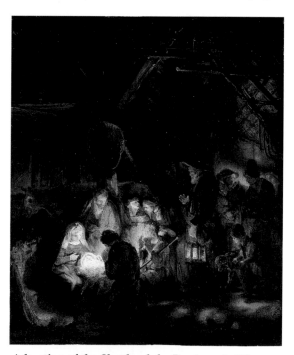

Adoration of the Shepherds by Rembrandt. Oil.
A single artificial light source, fading quickly into the surrounding shadows. Few painters would risk such a small area of light in so much darkness.

31

THE NATURE OF COLOUR

The choice of colour is one aspect of painting where the artist has considerable freedom. Colour has the power to heighten or lessen the impact of your paintings, although it is worth remembering that form and tone are always the foundations, to which the delights of colour are an addition: colour is the icing on the cake rather than the cake itself. Its importance lies more in its emotional effect than as an addition to realism.

People seem to see colours differently, and although colours can be scientifically analysed and quantified just as light and tone can be measured, there is no advantage in this for the artist. Colour preferences lie more within the field of psychology than of physical science, and it can be very difficult to explain why a colour combination or colour scheme may be satisfying or not.

The word *hue* is often used to describe the colour itself, independently of tone, intensity or any other attribute. *Chroma* refers to brilliance of hue – where a bright yellow has a high chroma, browns have lower values.

LOCAL COLOUR

The colour of an object in normal daylight is called its local colour. Local colour is the starting point, but need not be a fixed entity in a picture, it can be altered within reason, as an object's form and tone-range will be sufficiently descriptive and convincing by themselves. Exact colour-matching is rarely needed, usually only in flower-painting and some still-lifes, but in every painting the artist will make the most of the colours that strengthen the effect he is aiming at. Colours in a painting may often appear to be natural even when they are not.

One of these roses is painted in its true colours

All the roses are equally "real"

Any of these colours could be the real one – the colour doesn't affect the picture's credibility.

A typical everyday view of a seascape. The natural colours are muted and almost incidental.

WARM AND COLD COLOURS

Colours are frequently described as being "warm" or "cold", and this is a fundamental division based on real associations.

The sun is classified as a yellow star, and in spite of its blinding glare, accidental glimpses of it leave an impression of golden warmth. Yellow, orange and red, the colours of the sun and fire are colours implying warmth.

Blues and blue-greens are the cold colours, associated with ice and the blues of Antarctica and its icebergs. The more the blues tend towards the green, the more they represent archetypal cold colours.

White and black both behave mainly as cold colours, and cool the mixtures in which they are used.

The mood is completely changed by different colours, which have become the main feature of the picture.

The warm colours match the subject. It is almost impossible to visualise such a scene of warmth without the colours that go with it.

The cold is evident in every part, even the sunlight seems chilly. Associations play a part in our reactions to scenes like this.

LIGHT AND COLOUR

Light is made up of many colours, as a prism held in its path demonstrates, but to an artist the word light generally denotes colourless, or white, light.

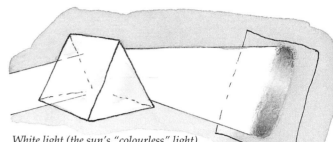

White light (the sun's "colourless" light) can be split up into its constituent parts.

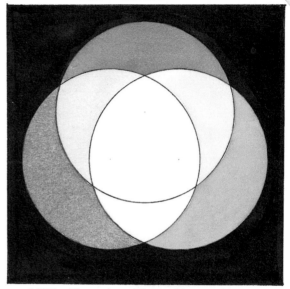

Additive. Three coloured lights add up to white.

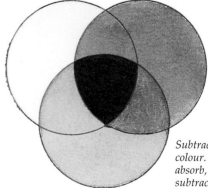

Subtractive colour. Pigments absorb, or subtract, colour.

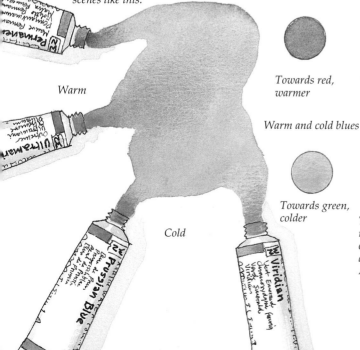

Warm

Towards red, warmer

Warm and cold blues

Towards green, colder

Cold

*The middle diagram above shows three coloured lights mixing together and **adding** up to white where they all overlap. The lower diagram shows pigmented colours absorbing or **subtracting** from the light falling on them. An artist deals in colours, which are subtractive.*

33

THE EFFECTS OF LIGHT ON COLOUR

Pictures full of sunlight seldom include the strongest and most intense colours, for strong colour and strong lighting compete with each other; the effect of bright sunlight is to bleach colours out, so in a painting depicting brilliant light, brightness of colour is suggested rather than painted in at its natural strength. The impression of strong colour is achieved, however, because the brain unconsciously recognises the lighting and its effect on colours, and will automatically "know" what the real colours are.

Something you can try out for yourself. The shadows on a white cloth from the candle flame and the window are distinctly coloured. The shadow made by the flame only receives the blue window-light, while the cloth shaded from the window-light is illuminated just by the yellow candle flame. If either light-source were to be cut off, the colouring in the remaining shadow would disappear.

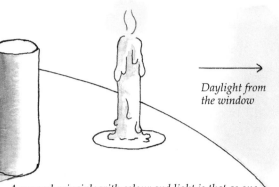

Daylight from the window

A general principle with colour and light is that as one becomes stronger the other becomes weaker (not infallible because artists are always trying to get round it, sometimes fairly successfully). In conditions of soft flat light, colours are able to register at their full intensities.

The evening sky. The diagram, (right), shows a natural progression of colour and tone at sunset. The gradation of the sky is determined by the thinning of the upper atmosphere, which allows the bluer light rays to pass through easily. Lower down, the thicker and dustier air scatters the blue light but allows the yellow and red to penetrate.

The degree of warmth in the lower sky depends very much on the weather conditions and changes quickly as the sun disappears. Our eyes adjust automatically to neutralise the increasing blueness of the late evening light.

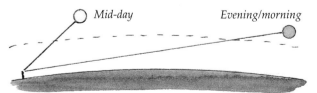

Mid-day *Evening/morning*

The warm yellow, orange and red rays of sunlight (above) are able to penetrate the many miles of atmosphere that the light travels through when the sun is low, while the blue light is scattered and lost to us in its passage through the intervening air.
The blue of the upper sky changes gradually to the warm colouring near the horizon with just a hint of green.

CONTRAST AND VARIATION

The effect of contrasting colours is to intensify each other, so that red beside green is more intensely red than the same colour next to pink or brown. To achieve the full effect simply, the colours need to be equal in tone, so that colour is the only difference. Where possible, artists subtly emphasise contrasts of both colour and tone in their pictures, to increase the feeling of liveliness.

The perception of any colour is influenced by the surrounding colours. The greater the contrast between the colours, the more they intensify each other, and the quicker they neutralise each other when mixed. See also the colour contrasts shown on p. 15.

The different greens enhance the liveliness of the colour, and are more satisfying than shades of a single green.

CONTROLLING THE COLOUR SCHEME

There need be no limit to your choice of paints as long as they are mixed with care to harmonise with an intended colour scheme. The control of a colour scheme requires experience and relies on control over your colour mixing, rather than limiting the number of paints you use. Limiting your palette without a corresponding knowledge of colour can also limit your artistic growth. Colour harmony derives from the mind, not from a shortage of colours.

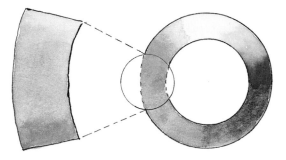

The picture below develops the blue and green colours with the aid of a wide range of neutral greys, making the few warm colours all the more effective.

Mei Ki by George W. Delaney. Watercolour.
Harmonious shades of blue permeate the whole area of the picture.

AERIAL PERSPECTIVE

Colours are filtered by the intervening air carrying dust and water vapour, softening both contrast and colour increasingly with distance: bright colours are gradually muted with distance, (see the red vans, right), and the contrast between lights and darks is reduced towards a middle tone. This is sometimes accompanied by an alteration of colour, and occasionally a distinct blueness is characteristic of some mountainous areas.

The close-up red geranium and the line of red vans illustrate how a bright colour steadily loses its intensity with increasing distance. Tonal contrast also diminishes at the same rate; both blacks and whites move towards a medium grey.

A Herdsman with Cows by a River by Albert Cuyp. Oil.
Like Claude, (see p. 20), Cuyp was a master of the enveloping light and air that imparts an ethereal quality to the distant parts of his landscapes.
The light on the nearest sail is magical, and the whole painting is suffused with a glow to which every tone and colour is subject. The sparkle of the water in the foreground, and the light and shade on the cows and figures provide the contrast to the softness of the distance.

The reduction of both tone and colour contrast is usually very marked, and contributes strongly to the impression of distance in a painting.

Even in still-life and other close-up subjects, aerial perspective is an effective way of suggesting distance. Although close-up subjects possess insufficient depth for true aerial perspective to be useful, its principles can still be applied by emphasising the contrast assumed to be possessed by objects closest to the front of the scene, reinforcing their larger size and their overlapping of more distant objects: the greater the degree of contrast, the closer an object will seem to be.

The morning mists or fogs show aerial perspective in an extreme but instructive way. In particular the early morning mist seen against the sun concentrates its effect in close-up scenes. Every particle of mist seems to catch the light. The perspective of the sun's rays is also illustrated. This is described more fully on p. 74.

COLOUR MATCHING

The colour circles are convenient ways of showing relationships between the brighter colours. The three colours picked out as Primaries are spaced equally from each other. In a more exact circle the primaries would only be represented by very narrow bands, because the colour change around the circle is continuous and any one shade merges quickly into its neighbours. Many theorists have hoped that all colours could be mixed from the three primaries, and although this isn't possible the idea is valuable as a basis for understanding colour mixing.

THE STANDARD PRIMARY COLOURS

A primary colour is one which cannot be made by any mixture of different colours: no two colours can be mixed to make a red, except by using other reds, whereas orange can be made with a mixture of yellow and red. By using three selected "primary" colours, a clear YELLOW, a cold RED called "Magenta" and a greenish BLUE called "Cyan", all the intermediate colours can be approximated. These, plus black, are the colours used in printing this book.

Lemon Yellow

Where conditions limit the choice, colours such as these three can match the widest range of hues.

Permanent Rose

Cerulean Blue (Horadam)

Primary Yellow

Cadmium Yellow

Cadmium Lemon

Orange

Green

Cerulean

Prussian Blue

Phthalo

Cobalt Blue

Ultramarine

Cadmium Red

Primary Red

THE PRIMARIES EXPANDED

A more flexible system for experienced painters who like to limit their palettes is to double the number of "primaries", to have two yellows, two reds and two blues. This recognises that no one colour can perform two opposing functions at once. Each one of the pair is inclined in colour towards its neighbour on the colour circle, so the yellow on the side of the circle towards the blue will show a slight tendency towards blue, while the other, warmer, yellow on the red side has a tendency towards red.

Primary Blue

Violet

Permanent Rose

Five mixtures showing the relative proportions of primary colours in their make-up.

COLOUR MIXING WITH SIX PRIMARIES

Most of the common colours around us can be mixed from the six primaries used here. The ideas, rather than the practice, are valuable because they will guide you towards the colours you need for mixing a colour. Think of the brighter colours in terms of their proportions of yellows, reds and blues, and the ideas will become second nature, making colour mixing surprisingly easy. Some colours that can be used as primaries are listed below:

Cadmium Lemon, Scheveningen Yellow Lemon, Permanent Yellow Light.

Cadmium Yellow (Medium), Permanent Yellow, Gamboge Hue

Cadmium Red, Cadmium Scarlet, Scheveningen Red Scarlet

Permanent Rose, Permanent Red Deep

Ultramarine, Cobalt Blue

Cerulean Blue, Prussian Blue, Zurich Blue

BRIGHT AND MUTED VIOLETS

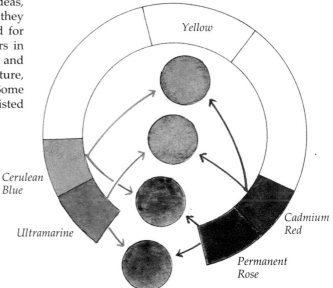

Bright violets are hard to make from mixtures as most red and blue mixtures are on the muted side.

BRIGHT AND MUTED ORANGES

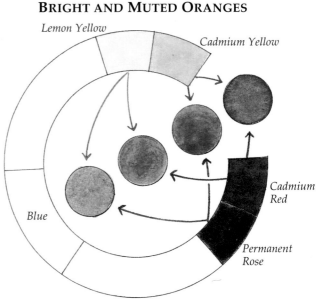

The brighter mixtures are a clear orange, but others have more than a hint of brownness. Bright oranges are almost as difficult as bright violets to mix, but are fortunately rarely necessary.

In mixing colours with the theoretical help of the 3-colour system, paint is seen in terms of its proportions of yellow, red and blue. The colour you are matching can also be seen in the same terms. Differences seen as a need for more "blueness" or "yellowness" or "redness" will guide you to the colour. It can take time to absorb this way of seeing colour, but this is the secret of colour mixing.

BRIGHT AND MUTED GREENS

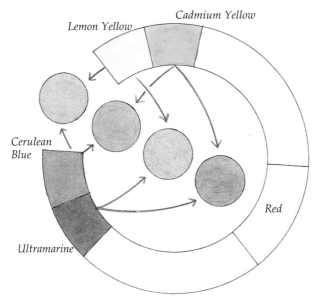

A green blue like Cerulean, mixed with a slightly green yellow such as Lemon Yellow makes clear bright green. The blue and yellow tending towards the red combine to make a richer green in oil and a very dull one in watercolour. Cadmium Yellow is a colour that varies from one maker to the next, some are paler and others more golden. Check with your own yellows and blues to see the range you can achieve.

SECONDARY COLOURS IN MIXTURES

The secondary colours, violet, green and orange, are each mixtures of two primary colours.

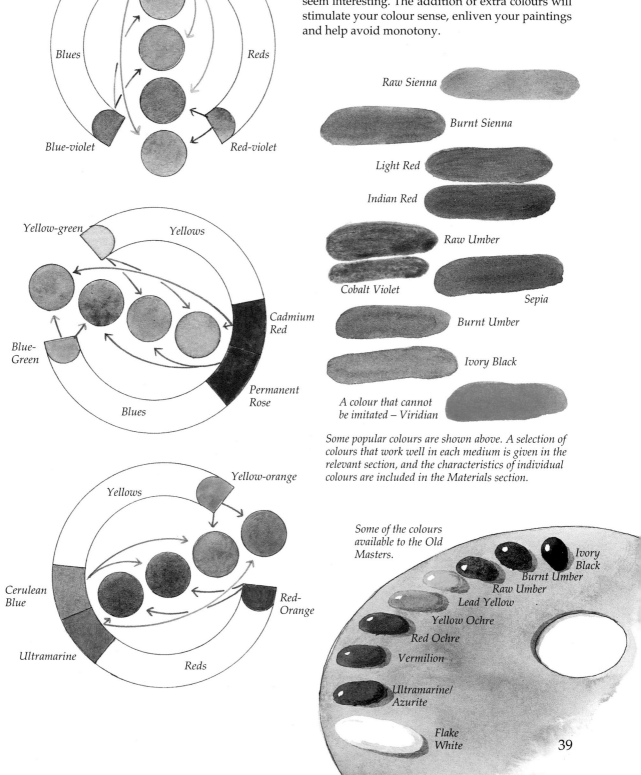

Lemon Yellow   *Cadmium Yellow*

Blues

Reds

Blue-violet

Red-violet

Yellow-green

Yellows

Blue-Green

Cadmium Red

Permanent Rose

Blues

Yellows

Yellow-orange

Cerulean Blue

Red-Orange

Ultramarine

Reds

ADDITIONS TO THE PALETTE

When experimenting with the six primaries you may have found that a lot of time was spent making the browns and greys. Ready-made browns, golds, black, and other colours have been found invaluable by artists throughout the history of painting, and possess qualities that are not easily matched. Once you understand the basics of colour mixing, don't hesitate to try out other paints that seem interesting. The addition of extra colours will stimulate your colour sense, enliven your paintings and help avoid monotony.

Raw Sienna

Burnt Sienna

Light Red

Indian Red

Raw Umber

Cobalt Violet

Sepia

Burnt Umber

Ivory Black

A colour that cannot be imitated – Viridian

Some popular colours are shown above. A selection of colours that work well in each medium is given in the relevant section, and the characteristics of individual colours are included in the Materials section.

Some of the colours available to the Old Masters.

Ivory Black

Burnt Umber

Raw Umber

Lead Yellow

Yellow Ochre

Red Ochre

Vermilion

Ultramarine/ Azurite

Flake White

39

THE COLOURS OF SHADOWS

Unlike local colours, which are usually real enough to touch and to lay your sample alongside for comparison, shadows are curiously insubstantial and difficult to pin down for colour. Use the following formula which works well in most instances:

To any colour you wish to shade (e.g. green), add a) more green, and b) a little of its complementary colour (red); the complementary will initially both darken the main colour and reduce its brightness, two of the main characteristics of shadows. Too much of the complementary colour will neutralise the original completely, and lose the effect of a

MAKING SHADOWS WITH COMPLEMENTARY COLOURS

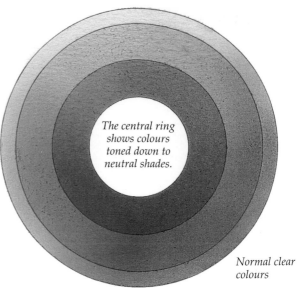

The central ring shows colours toned down to neutral shades.

Normal clear colours

The diagram above shows an outer ring with the usual colours, and two inner circles showing related browns and greys. The regular brown paints you use can be seen as toned down yellows, oranges and reds: they therefore need very little extra in the way of complementary colours to darken them.

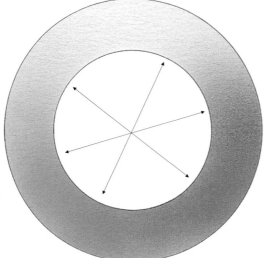

Complementary colours are those opposite each other on the circle. Arrows point out three pairs.

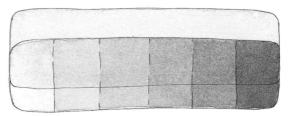

The strength of the complementary colour needs to be matched to the colour it is shading. There is too much green at the light end and not enough at the dark end.

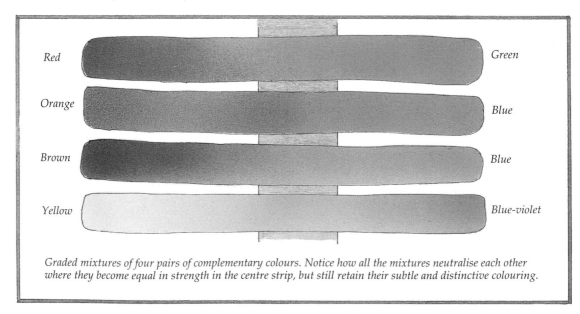

Red — Green

Orange — Blue

Brown — Blue

Yellow — Blue-violet

Graded mixtures of four pairs of complementary colours. Notice how all the mixtures neutralise each other where they become equal in strength in the centre strip, but still retain their subtle and distinctive colouring.

SHADOWS WITH BROWN AND GREY

Sepia behaves as a warm black and is good for shading certain colours, especially the bright yellows. By referring to the shaded colour circle on the opposite page you can see that a colour like sepia is found in the most shaded ring of the yellow and orange section.

MAKING SHADOWS WITH BLACK

Black is the theoretical result of a mixture of the three primary colours: in adding black you are adding equal parts of yellow, red and blue. There is prejudice against black, but the frequent claim that there is no black in nature overlooks the presence of black birds and cats.

Do not reject black, but use it lightly and sparingly. In small amounts, or well diluted, it works well for lightweight shadows on pale colours; and like any other colour, it needs using with discretion. Where it has been carefully used, it is almost impossible to tell whether shadows were made with complementary colours or with black. Its use in no way rules out the addition of other colours to modify it or to introduce reflections.

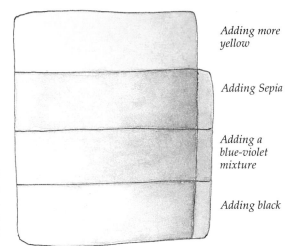

Adding more yellow

Adding Sepia

Adding a blue-violet mixture

Adding black

Alternative ways of making shadows on yellow.

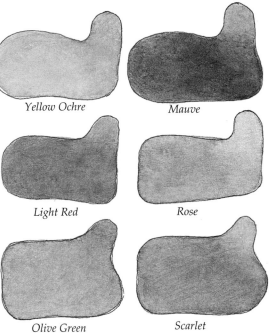

Yellow Ochre *Mauve*

Light Red *Rose*

Olive Green *Scarlet*

Small amounts of black added to some standard colours.

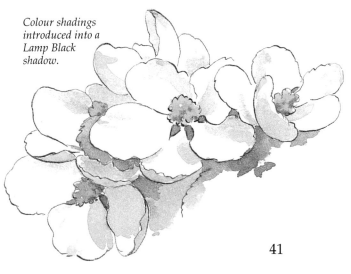

A mixture of the 3 primary colours will produce a near black which dilutes to grey with water.

NATURAL AND ELECTRIC LIGHT

Good daylight is the best for judging colour. Electric light is much yellower, but if it is bright enough to see clearly, your eyes will adapt and get most colours right. The most difficult colours are pale violets and flesh colours; for violets, mix up a stock of your matching colour in daylight, and when you apply it in the evening ignore the apparent differences. If you know your colour is accurate in daylight it will look perfectly natural when the picture is finished. The alternative is to paint with the aid of "daylight" bulbs in your table-lamp, which may solve most of your problems.

Colour shadings introduced into a Lamp Black shadow.

41

COPYING & CREATIVITY

The roles of copying and creativity have suffered from misunderstanding in our time, so that instead of being seen as partners they have been looked upon as enemies.

In many schools, creativity and originality have been made into prime objectives of art, but thought of as so fragile that the discipline of learning about technique would destroy them. The reduction in formal instruction has left many artists having to find their own way, leaving them to "re-invent the wheel" rather than building on the traditions of craftsmanship that enabled the painters of the past to produce so much work of high quality. Isaac Newton said that if he could see a little further than others it was because he had been able to stand on the shoulders of giants, his scientific predecessors.

Almost everyone who has achieved success in any field has at some time had a model or teacher to guide them by example. In learning a complex skill, good practice is to watch, listen to and copy the best teachers and examples one can find.

This can still be done by copying paintings you admire as closely as possible, using the same medium and working as near to the original size as is practical; this will probably depend on the size and quality of the reproduction. The copyright laws allow copying for private study in this way.

In the early days of painting, the apprenticeship system instilled the studio's style into the student, as well as imparting a sound technique; a part of learning this technique was copying, a way of acquiring the highest skills, as acknowledged by Delacroix's statement – "Copies and copying. That has been the education of almost all the great masters". It was a widespread practice until the early years of this century, with Rubens one of the most assiduous, in copying, among others, twenty-one pictures by Titian and nine by Raphael.

Creativity grows out of a rich diet based on practical knowledge of what has gone before, which is most effectively gained by imitation. When you copy a work by a favourite painter, you learn to see his way and do things his way for a time, after which you will retain some of the skills that are useful to you. The proficiency and knowledge gained through copying will fuel and develop your own vision more strongly and quickly than any other method.

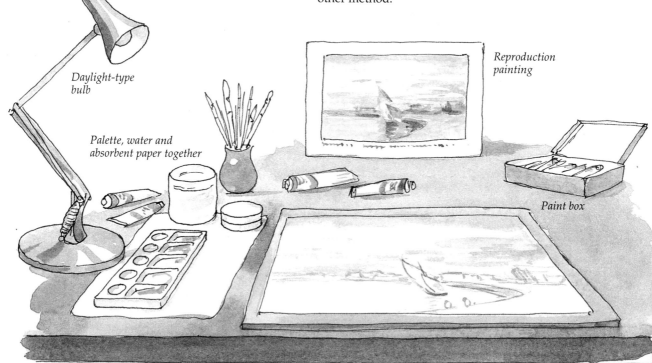

Daylight-type bulb

Palette, water and absorbent paper together

Reproduction painting

Paint box

A typical working set-up for watercolour, with the painting to be copied where it can most easily be seen.

SOME AIDS TO DEVELOPING CREATIVITY

What is often vaguely called creativity is a widespread attribute which can either be cultivated or left to become dormant, but it never disappears. Develop it steadily, wherever you start from. The characteristics of people in many fields, who are considered to be creative, have now been widely studied, especially in the USA, and some consistent traits emerge:

■ Some artists, composers and inventors have a great store of knowledge about their subject and learn everything possible concerning it. Study, practice and copying build their resources.

■ They are highly motivated. Strength of desire is the driving force opening minds to the solutions of problems; working only to satisfy or please others is not sufficient. Determination to succeed is essential – even more important than "talent".

■ Their aims are clearly defined, so their efforts are accurately directed towards the desired results.

■ Imagination is encouraged and nurtured through practice, day-dreaming and visualisation.

ELECTRIC LIGHT

Many artists must paint in artificial light, or opportunities to learn would be few and far between. The chief consideration in artificial light is the degree of illumination rather than its colour; although our eyes readily adapt, electric light gives out only a fraction of the brightness of daylight, so close-up extra light in the form of a desk lamp, (shown opposite), is almost essential for comfortable work and the avoidance of eye-strain.

Yellowness of the light mainly affects pale violets, yellows and flesh colours. Match violets and flesh colours in daylight and mix enough paint to last for the whole evening. Pale yellows should be kept extra pale and checked and adjusted in the daylight.

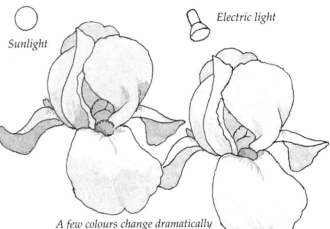

Sunlight

Electric light

A few colours change dramatically under electric light.

TIME SAVERS AND PHOTOGRAPHIC AIDS

If you use photographs their quality is important, as you depend on them to transport you back to the scene. Photographs can provide detail impractical to draw in on the spot.

35mm slide projector

Projectors are noisy but versatile and will project a 35mm transparency to any size. Transparencies are more adaptable than prints, but a projected image is harder to focus on than the printed image.

Table top slide projector

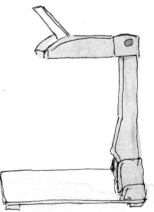

Overhead projector for prints

Table-top viewers are silent, having no fan, and enable you to work directly from slides rather than prints. Larger ones are the most useful. The overhead viewer will project larger work.

TRACING AND ENLARGING

There are two methods of tracing, with tracing paper or with Transtrace, a paper like carbon paper but which uses graphite. Making your own tracing materials is possible but messy.

TRACING WITH TRACING PAPER

■ Lay the tracing paper over the drawing. In an emergency, grease-proof paper will do.

■ With a hard, H or 2H pencil, trace over the main outlines.

■ Turn over the tracing paper and trace over your first line as exactly as you can, using a slightly softer pencil, an HB.

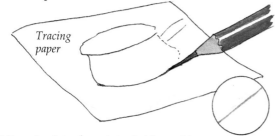

Tracing paper

■ Turn back to the original side and lay in position on the watercolour paper. Tack one edge down.

The back will look just like the front

■ Press back and forward over the lines with your finger-nail or any smooth rounded object, pressing the pencil line onto the paper.

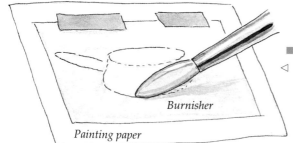

Burnisher

Painting paper

■ Tidy up the transferred drawing. The tracing is rarely as accurate as the original, so go over it carefully improving curves and equalising the strength of line.

TRACING WITH TRANSTRACE

The picture you are tracing from needs to be on thin paper as you will be pressing through it.

■ Attach the picture you wish to trace in position over your clean paper, holding it in position along one edge with masking tape.

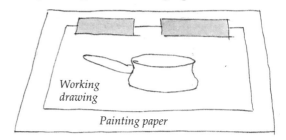

Working drawing

Painting paper

■ Slide the Transtrace between the papers, coloured side face-down onto your white paper.

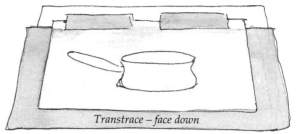

Transtrace – face down

■ Press along the outlines of the picture you are copying with the point of a knitting needle or biro. The point must be rounded so it doesn't tear the paper.

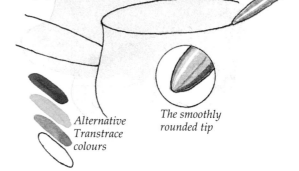

Alternative Transtrace colours

The smoothly rounded tip

■ Tidy up the drawing after removing the tracing materials. Neither of these methods requires any messy scribbling over the picture areas on the back of the tracing paper, and there are no extra steps. If you do a lot of tracing then an agate burnisher, shown opposite, is ideal for pressing the lead from the tracing onto the paper. Complicated flower pictures are often drawn in separate parts and traced into position.

ENLARGING

There are two ways of doing this: the traditional method of squaring up, and the modern method of photocopying. To square up:

ENLARGING WITH A GRID

■ Make a squared grid over the picture you wish to enlarge. To avoid marking it, lay tracing paper over it and make the grid on that.

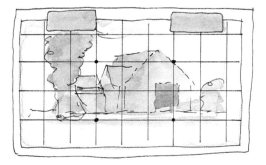

> ■ Decide on the magnification, and draw out a larger but similar grid on your paper.
> ■ Copy the drawing square by square.
> ■ Rub out the grid. To avoid marking or damaging the paper, make the enlarged grid on tracing paper.

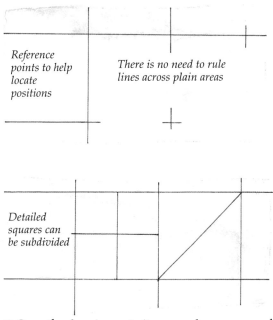

Reference points to help locate positions

There is no need to rule lines across plain areas

Detailed squares can be subdivided

■ Copy the drawing onto it, square by square, and trace it by one of the methods shown opposite.

ENLARGING WITH A PHOTOCOPIER

Photocopying can be more convenient and labour-saving. Make a tracing onto tracing paper and have it enlarged.

■ Make a strong tracing of the picture on tracing paper. Weak pencil can get lost on photocopies.

Tracing paper

■ Measure, (say, 200mm), and decide how much bigger it needs to be (say, 250mm).

> ■ With a calculator, work out the percentage magnification as follows:
>
> Press keys for large number, (250)
> Press ÷ (divide)
> Press keys for small number, (200)
> Press =

The screen will show the answer (125), which is the magnification. Have your tracing enlarged to 125% at your local photocopying shop. Trace from the photocopy as above.

TRANSFERRING LARGE DRAWINGS

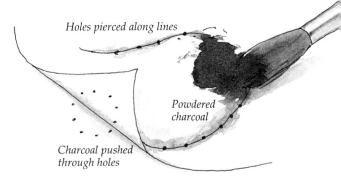

Holes pierced along lines

Powdered charcoal

Charcoal pushed through holes

Pouncing – prick holes along the outlines, then rub charcoal through the holes. Join up the dots.

COMPOSITION

Composition is the part of painting where personal opinion, as opposed to rules, plays a part; there are not many books on such a controversial subject. By studying paintings you like, you will gradually absorb the type of composition you prefer; design your own pictures along the same lines until your own style develops. The following principles are to help you during the design stage, when composition should be worked out.

An Extensive Landscape with a Ruined Castle and a Village Church, after Jacob van Ruysdael. Oil.

THE CENTRE

The eye naturally homes in on the central area of the canvas or paper, so the first attention should be directed towards the centre rather than the edges. The imaginary centre-line from top to bottom also plays a vital part in the picture's balance.

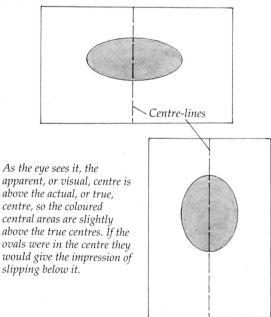

Centre-lines

As the eye sees it, the apparent, or visual, centre is above the actual, or true, centre, so the coloured central areas are slightly above the true centres. If the ovals were in the centre they would give the impression of slipping below it.

OFF-CENTRE

Pictures usually have their main interest slightly to one side of the centre. This allows a more complex design with room for more important secondary centres of interest. The diagrams below show the balancing of pictorial weight on either side of the centre-line. Composition revolves around the centre, it is not essential for it to be occupied. The left-to-right balance around the centre line is a fundamental requirement of composition.

Subject importance

The hidden balance within every picture. The weight of tone and interest should balance on either side of the centre-line.

Centre-line of picture

The distant centre of interest (above), balances the larger central one (right). The further it is from the centre, the greater its pulling power.

***The hollow centre,** ringed above, occurs if too much empty space has been left. Such a picture can easily lack focus or impact.*

BALANCE – SIDE TO SIDE

The all-important imaginary centre line divides the picture into two halves which should balance each other, by whatever means. The difficulty in composition is in the asymmetrical balancing of the two sides so that the effect is satisfying but hidden. The diagrams on the previous page show this aspect of composition.

BALANCE – TOP TO BOTTOM

There is less requirement to balance from top to bottom, beyond the need for some stability in the design. In most pictures the top and bottom are entirely dissimilar, imitating the real world. Because the dictates of gravity apply here rather than those of balance, important parts should not be allowed to slip down to the bottom.

Compare the balance from side to side with the vertical progression of tone, or weight. The dark blue sea could easily be higher or lower, but not on one side only without an effective counter-attraction. The low placing of the main weight of tone gives stability.

The eye-catching cat's head on the left is balanced by the larger area of whiter fur on the right. The legs going into the top corner pull the eye away to the edge, also helping to balance the head.

THREE DIMENSIONS – NEAR AND FAR

This is composition based on depth, the contrast between "near" at the bottom and "distance" at the top. The sides are asymmetrical but balanced, not competing with the compelling vertical dispositions. There is still plenty of space at the bottom of the picture below the large nearby rock.

The slightly greater size and brightness of the right-hand flower is compensated for by adding the coloured bud at the top left, leading to a satisfying balance.

STABILITY

For a picture to be satisfying, a certain stability is an advantage, without letting it become static because of too much symmetry. In the same way that the centre makes a useful starting point for your design, so the position of the tonal weight of the picture affects its apparent stability. A lower positioning of the darker tonal weight is generally more comfortable. Raphael and Leonardo regularly used the stable triangular design for their easel pictures. Even the most dynamic designs need a fundamental steadiness to balance the movement.

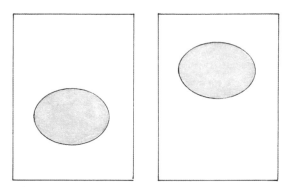

The positioning of the main tonal weight, represented symbolically by an oval. The lower position is the basis of many satisfying designs; the reverse can lead to more dynamism where required. Neither should be too close to the edges without good reason.

Lighter and more open areas of tone

A more solid block of tone and colour

Saintpaulia

Rose "Albertine". Less stable, more dynamic

RHYTHM, FLOW

Once a balance has been achieved, the eye is guided around the picture by more subtle means, such as the directions and strength of line, tone and colour. Repetition of line creates rhythms that attract attention, while the eye is drawn along lines, whether curved or straight, and which may be interrupted.

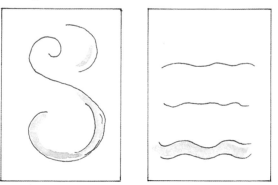

Long lines usually underlie designs and are seldom readily visible. Careful emphasis here and there strengthens their effects.

A picture made of flowing lines, mainly radiating from a nearly central point. See also p. 21.

Repetition usually helps to hold designs together and is nearly always present in some form.

Flower paintings can be stabilised by the weight of darker leaves below the flower heads. The balance of the rose is light and airy. The flow counts for more than the tonal balance.

TONE AND COLOUR

Both have potent eye-catching capacities which can be used to draw attention to certain parts of the picture. Strong tonal contrast is usually more powerful than colour.

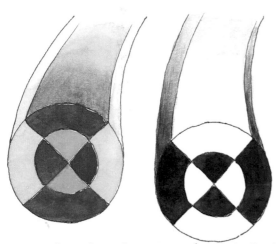

Warm colours advance, but strong tonal contrasts attract attention first. Cool colours recede.

Mooncat. Oil.
An example of this use of tone and colour: an intense tonal contrast at the main centre of interest, and a colour contrast in which the warm colours of the bricks and leaves advance, while the cool blue of the sky recedes.

EXCEPTIONS

The principles of design set out in these pages are only a brief guide. Many great pictures have been painted which appear to contradict the normal guidelines, but further study can usually discover the means by which they achieve their balance. "Rules" are most successfully broken by artists who fully understand them and override them for clear reasons.

THE GOLDEN SECTION

The Golden Section is the division of a line in a particular harmonious proportion of 1:1.62. These proportions are used for the sides of the Golden Section Rectangle, used in the design of the facade and ground plan of the Acropolis and also in many paintings.

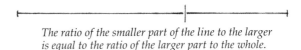

The ratio of the smaller part of the line to the larger is equal to the ratio of the larger part to the whole.

The rectangle can be sub-divided into a square and a further Golden Section Rectangle any number of times until they become too small to be practical.

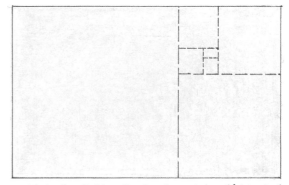

While the Golden Section is mainly of historical interest, it can be a very successful and satisfying design element if you have the opportunity to make use of its proportions.

The Birth of Venus by Botticelli. Egg Tempera.
The proportions of the canvas – its height and width – match those of the Golden Section.

SUMMARY

Three things to remember:

- Design from the centre outwards.
- Make everything contribute to the overall effect.
- Composition is the strongest way of seeing (Edward Weston).

PRESENTATION

To see your picture through to a satisfactory conclusion, one final effort has to be made – to present it in its best light. Mounting and framing are often treated as an afterthought, but they can improve your picture out of all recognition and provide a fitting setting for it. Both mounting and framing are skilled operations requiring expensive machinery, best done by professionals. Without modern equipment home framing cannot match it for quality.

MOUNTS

Pictures should be mounted on the basis of the visual centre, not the true centre. If the picture was in the true centre of the mount it would look as if it had slipped down slightly towards the bottom. Raising it to the visual centre makes it look central to the eye. The diagram shows how this works. Look for the deeper bottom border in well-mounted pictures in good galleries.

Because modern mount-cutters are quick, efficient and mechanical, many framers regularly make all the sides equal.

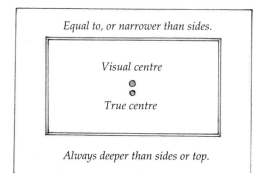

Until you are certain they remember, you may have to remind the framers to make the bottom border deeper.

QUALITY

Most mounts are made of card which eventually stains the paper. To avoid this, use Museum or Conservation grade mounts, or have acid-free paper inserted between the mount and the painting.

Stained edge of paper, caused by the mount.

CHOOSING MOUNTS

Framers have corner pieces in many colours; try them against your picture, as the colours are not easy to visualise in advance – what you had in mind may not exist. If in doubt, cream is safer than a darker colour. Grey and dark green can look "safe", but can deaden the picture.

Try the samples on more than one corner. Most mounts need further decoration to avoid looking too plain.

DECORATIVE LINES

The framer will advise and add lines for you, which will considerably improve a plain mount. You can add your own with a felt-tip or a ruling-pen.

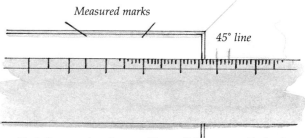

Mark the mount as shown with pencil first as a guide for the pen. The 45° line will show you where to stop at the corners.

Felt-tip lining-pen for a gold line.

Mix up a colour of your choice to use as an "ink" for the ruling-pen. Try it out first on a piece of spare paper or card.

WASH LINES

In combination with lines, these look very fine. The framer will do them for a price, but if you wish to try, keep to pale colours, then:

- Rule the edges in position in pencil.
- With as large a brush as will fit, and a straight-edge guide, (wooden ruler, p. 144), wash in one side with almost all water and a touch of colour.
- Before it dries, quickly do the other 3 sides.
- Repeat with the actual colour while the mount is still damp or wet.

DOUBLE MOUNTS

A double mount gives an extra dimension of depth to your pictures and allows the use of a harmonious colour for the inner mount. The inner mount can be a colour featuring in the painting, which might be over-powering if used over the whole mount.

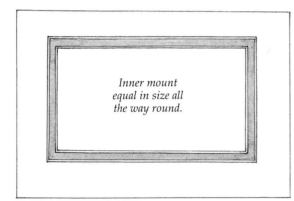

Inner mount equal in size all the way round.

Like wash and decorative lines, this sort of mount makes your picture look more valuable. The width can be constant all round, but remember to check that the proportions of the outer mount are retained. The cost of the extra mount is nominal compared to the cost of framing, and once you have tried it you are unlikely to go back to single mounts.

GLASS

Like watercolours and drawings, Acrylic paint needs the protection of glass. Some framers offer "non-reflective" glass instead of normal glass. Reflections are reduced rather than eliminated, but owing to the fine granular texture that breaks up the reflections, the glass looks grey and dull, and kills the sparkle of anything seen through it. Normal glass is by far the best, so:

Don't use non-reflective glass

FRAMES

Frames, like mounts, have to be chosen with the corner samples at hand. Frames with some gold go well with almost everything, otherwise choose to suit the room where the picture will hang. Brightly coloured frames, including bright gold, can compete too successfully with the picture within. Made-up frames tend to look slightly thicker than the sample pieces.

This type of moulding looks good with any picture. It gives depth, accentuating that of the painting itself, and separates the picture well from its surroundings. Choose this sort if in doubt about the type of frame.

Flatter mouldings rely on width for their effect, but do not increase the three-dimensional appearance of the painting. Moulding intermediate between this and the first is worth trying as well. Useful for larger pictures to avoid bulk.

This type pushes the picture forward towards you. It unexpectedly suits some pictures, especially if their colouring and texture are good.

Try the wider frames on small pictures. They can make the picture seem more impressive and concentrate its effect. Moulded and ornate frames suit detailed pictures.

PERSPECTIVE

WHY IT IS USEFUL TO YOU

Perspective is regarded with deep suspicion as being too geometrical and mathematical, something gladly left behind at school, but it plays a part in almost every picture. A basic knowledge of perspective is essential, and useful to apply as a check to a drawing once it is underway. It will help:

■ To make your drawing convincing – all the lines in it must slope in the right directions.

■ To achieve the effect of distance – a proportional diminution of size according to distance.

■ To measure and position windows, doors, etc. correctly.

■ To work out directions and positions for cast shadows.

Perspective can be very simple once the ideas of the eye-level line and the vanishing points have been understood, and to help achieve this they are repeated regularly throughout this section. Some parts can be difficult to follow at first, but can be made easier to understand by drawing the diagrams yourself. There are times when it may be more profitable to go first through the motions according to the instructions, trusting that understanding will follow later.

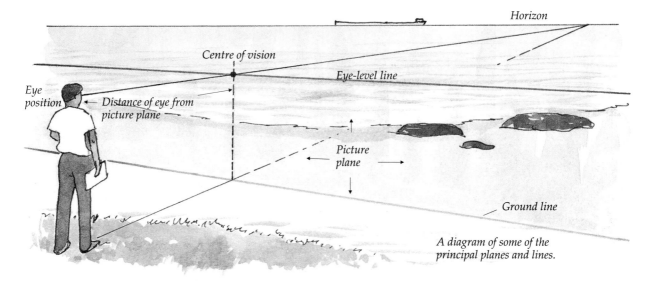

A diagram of some of the principal planes and lines.

WHAT THE WORDS MEAN

■ **Eye-level**: when the artist looks straight ahead, the eye-level line is level with the artist's eyes. Sometimes called the horizon line, which is exactly at eye-level also, but usually obscured by intervening landscape. The diagram above shows the difference between the two lines, but from the artist's point of view in practice they coincide with each other.

■ **Horizon**: see Eye-level, above.

■ **Ground plane**: the ground, starting from your feet and going away to the horizon.

■ **Picture plane**: an imaginary upright plane, often likened to a sheet of glass between you and the scene. It can be close to you, or at some distance away, as you wish. For more detail see p. 55.

■ **Ground line**: a line on the ground directly below the eye-level line, where the picture plane touches the ground.

■ **Height line**: if units of measurement are marked on the ground line, the same units can be marked on a vertical line to determine heights. A height line can be constructed at either end of the ground line.

■ **Centre of vision**: keeping your head level, look straight ahead, and the centre of vision is directly in front of you (on the level of the eye-level line). If you turn your head, the centre of vision turns with it.

■ **Vanishing point**: a point to which a set of parallel lines appear to vanish in the distance, on the horizon or eye-level line.

WHERE TO START – EYE-LEVEL

Eye-level in perspective is **your** eye-level. Look straight ahead, neither up nor down, and that is your eye-level, a line right across the picture, level with your eyes. The artist's eye-level determines the layout of the picture. The perspective of every picture is founded upon this horizontal line and all perspective starts with it.

The Avenue, Middleharnis by Hobbema. Oil.
A clear example of simple perspective, where the artist was looking straight ahead towards the lower centre, where the eye-level line coincides with the horizon. All the lines of the avenue converge towards a "centre of vision".

HOW TO LOCATE EYE-LEVEL

To locate the eye-level on a scene already drawn or photographed, choose a wall sloping away at an *angle* to you, then find a horizontal line on it, of brick or stonework perhaps, and this will be at eye-level. Other lines above or below will slope upwards or downwards towards the vanishing points on the eye-level line.

The wooden wall on the left slopes away at an angle from the artist's position. The lines of the planks on it slope towards their vanishing point, (not shown), on the eye-level line. Where the planks slope neither up nor down, but are level, that is the eye-level line.

Sloping

Eye-level

Sloping

Board or bricks facing the artist appear horizontal.

53

EYE-LEVEL AND THE HORIZON

The horizon (the line where the sea, or land, meets the sky) coincides with eye-level, when you are looking straight ahead, because the horizon line is at the same height, directly behind the eye-level line. If the true horizon was always visible it would be more convenient to use it and only have to refer to one line, but in practice it is almost always obscured. However, the two lines are effectively the same, and some people prefer the term horizon line, rather than eye-level line.

Horizon and eye-level

Where the sea meets the sky is where the horizon and eye-level lines coincide.

Eye-level

Where the land is flat enough, the two lines may also coincide. The vanishing point for the railway lines is on this combined line.

HIGH AND LOW VIEWPOINTS

Eye-level line

The distant horizon will match your eye-level. If you are on a cliff-top, your eye-level is likely to be near the top of the picture, and the horizon will thus be high up as well.

Eye-level line

If you are standing at sea-level, your eye-level and the horizon will be nearer the centre of the view, giving a more equal relationship of sea and sky.

Eye-level line

If you are sitting on the beach, your eye-level will be close to the ground, the horizon will be low and the sky will fill much of the picture.

EYE-LEVEL – LOOKING UPWARDS OR DOWNWARDS

There are times when instead of looking out levelly, you see a potential picture by looking either up or down. The horizon line is unchanged, and lines on the ground, like the railway lines shown above, will still have their vanishing points on it.

If you look downwards, then the imaginary line that is level with your eyes moves downwards also. The plane of the picture, (see opposite page), becomes tilted as it has to be always at right-angles to your line of sight.

The effect is that lines previously vertical will converge to a vanishing point below them. This leads to three-point perspective, discussed on p. 87.

As paintings are hung vertically on walls, their picture-plane should be vertical to look comfortable on the wall; this implies a horizontal eye-level. Pictures where the eye-level is angled noticeably up or down can look out of place when hung. A painting needs to be viewed at the same angle at which its subject was viewed.

THE PICTURE PLANE

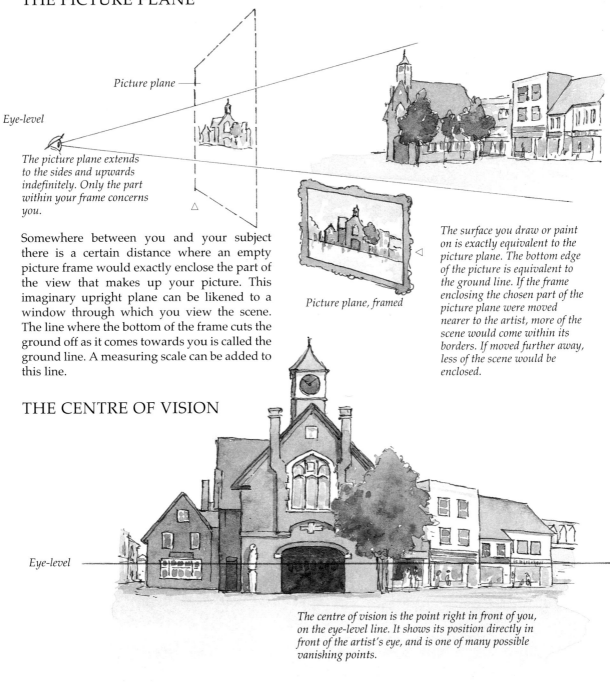

Picture plane

Eye-level

The picture plane extends to the sides and upwards indefinitely. Only the part within your frame concerns you.

Somewhere between you and your subject there is a certain distance where an empty picture frame would exactly enclose the part of the view that makes up your picture. This imaginary upright plane can be likened to a window through which you view the scene. The line where the bottom of the frame cuts the ground off as it comes towards you is called the ground line. A measuring scale can be added to this line.

Picture plane, framed

The surface you draw or paint on is exactly equivalent to the picture plane. The bottom edge of the picture is equivalent to the ground line. If the frame enclosing the chosen part of the picture plane were moved nearer to the artist, more of the scene would come within its borders. If moved further away, less of the scene would be enclosed.

THE CENTRE OF VISION

Eye-level

The centre of vision is the point right in front of you, on the eye-level line. It shows its position directly in front of the artist's eye, and is one of many possible vanishing points.

Ground line

The ground line can be used for measuring by adding a scale along it.

This diagram shows the simple arrangement of two lines, the eye-level line and the ground line, with the centre of vision coinciding with the central dark door. The height of the eye-level line above the ground line is usually taken to represent about 1.7m, so a standing figure drawn on the picture plane would be standing on the ground line with his eyes at the height of the eye-level line.

VANISHING POINTS

Parallel lines on level ground, receding from you, will move steadily closer and closer to each other until they appear to meet and vanish at a point on the horizon called a vanishing point. In these diagrams the eye-level line coincides with the line of the horizon.

If you follow the two parallel rails, (diagram, right), along into the far distance you will see they converge and finally vanish at a point on the eye-level line. If they are truly horizontal, any set of parallel lines will converge towards a vanishing point on the eye-level line.

Vanishing points, together with the eye-level line, shape your drawing. With their aid you can line up all the windows, doors, roofs and other details in your buildings. The eye-level line may accomodate further vanishing points for other sets of lines moving in different directions away from the artist or viewer.

By looking straight along the track, the rails appear to meet and merge directly ahead on the combined eye-level and horizon line.

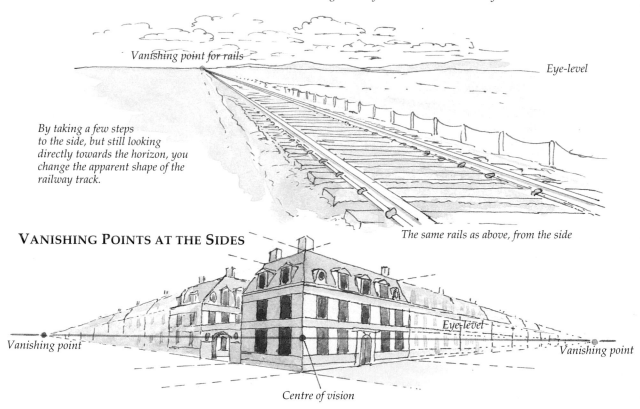

By taking a few steps to the side, but still looking directly towards the horizon, you change the apparent shape of the railway track.

The same rails as above, from the side

VANISHING POINTS AT THE SIDES

Each set of parallel lines has its own vanishing point and there can be any number of them according to the needs of the subject being drawn. One or both are often outside the picture area, but can be located and made use of (see p. 62). Most pictures, like the diagram above, use two vanishing points, both of which normally lie on the eye-level line.

Lines may recede from the artist at any angle rather than conveniently moving to a vanishing point straight ahead, and in the following pages an angle of 45° for the receding lines is used as an example.

VANISHING POINTS OF LINES AT AN ANGLE TO THE ARTIST

When a line moves away at an angle from the picture plane, its direction can be found by making a scale diagram to show the artist's position, and using a protractor to measure the angle from that point.

The woman's figure shows how the height of the eye-level line is related to the ground line, and to a scale of measurement. The height line at the left is marked in the same dimensions as the ground line. The height of anyone or anything standing on the ground line can be measured directly from it.

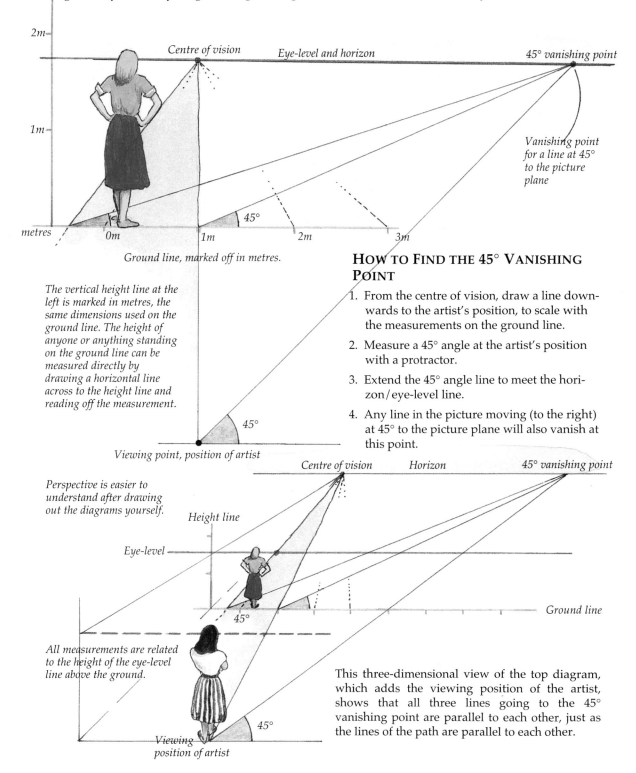

Ground line, marked off in metres.

The vertical height line at the left is marked in metres, the same dimensions used on the ground line. The height of anyone or anything standing on the ground line can be measured directly by drawing a horizontal line across to the height line and reading off the measurement.

Viewing point, position of artist

Perspective is easier to understand after drawing out the diagrams yourself.

All measurements are related to the height of the eye-level line above the ground.

HOW TO FIND THE 45° VANISHING POINT

1. From the centre of vision, draw a line downwards to the artist's position, to scale with the measurements on the ground line.

2. Measure a 45° angle at the artist's position with a protractor.

3. Extend the 45° angle line to meet the horizon/eye-level line.

4. Any line in the picture moving (to the right) at 45° to the picture plane will also vanish at this point.

This three-dimensional view of the top diagram, which adds the viewing position of the artist, shows that all three lines going to the 45° vanishing point are parallel to each other, just as the lines of the path are parallel to each other.

57

MEASURING DEPTH

Once there is a scale on the ground line, the depth of a square or any other regular shape can be found. In the case of a square, its diagonal crosses at an angle of 45°. After locating the 45° vanishing point, draw in the diagonal; where it cuts the line on the other side marks the square's far corner; draw a line from this corner across the top to complete the square. Any number of squares can be drawn in by this method.

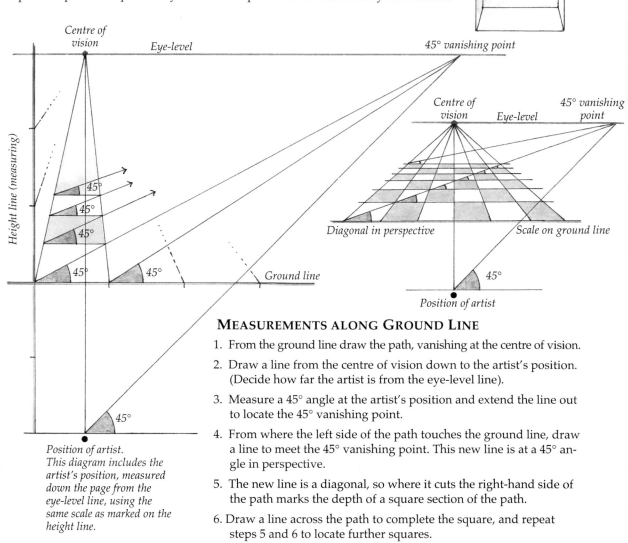

MEASUREMENTS ALONG GROUND LINE

1. From the ground line draw the path, vanishing at the centre of vision.

2. Draw a line from the centre of vision down to the artist's position. (Decide how far the artist is from the eye-level line).

3. Measure a 45° angle at the artist's position and extend the line out to locate the 45° vanishing point.

4. From where the left side of the path touches the ground line, draw a line to meet the 45° vanishing point. This new line is at a 45° angle in perspective.

5. The new line is a diagonal, so where it cuts the right-hand side of the path marks the depth of a square section of the path.

6. Draw a line across the path to complete the square, and repeat steps 5 and 6 to locate further squares.

Position of artist. This diagram includes the artist's position, measured down the page from the eye-level line, using the same scale as marked on the height line.

A SIMPLER METHOD

A working knowledge of perspective becomes more and more useful as your drawing improves, but for many drawings it may be sufficient to estimate the sizes and distances of important nearby objects by eye and extrapolate from there; this was done in the example opposite.

After drawing the path up to the eye-level line, you can estimate the depth of the first square, draw a diagonal across it, and extend it to locate the 45° vanishing point. Further squares can then be added as in steps 5 and 6 above.

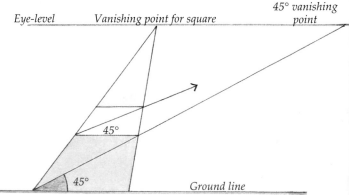

Any appropriate scale of measurements can be used along the ground line.

REGULAR SPACING IN PERSPECTIVE

The need to space out regular dimensions arises frequently. Draw in the first panel and the eye-level line. Draw both diagonals to find the centre of the panel, then draw the centre line (1) to the vanishing point. Draw a new diagonal (2), which will locate the top corner of the second panel. Draw in the new vertical division (3), and repeat the process down the line.

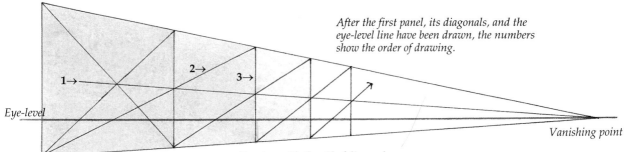

After the first panel, its diagonals, and the eye-level line have been drawn, the numbers show the order of drawing.

1→

2→

3→

Eye-level

Vanishing point

Spacing with the aid of diagonals

TRANSFERRING UNEQUAL SPACINGS

A special measuring line is used. It can be below or above. Start the measuring line from the near corner of the steepest slope, which in the bridge diagram is the bottom left corner where the line of pillars slopes upwards towards their vanishing point.

BRIDGE DIAGRAM

■ Draw the bridge lightly and include the eye-level line.

■ From the near corner of the bridge draw a ground line marked with the spacings of the arches and pillars. Any convenient scale will do, as long as a) the line touches the bottom of the nearest pillar at one end of the scale, and b) from the other end, a line can be drawn to cut the eye-level line at a freely chosen special vanishing point conveniently close to the near end.

■ Draw a line from each point on the scale towards the special vanishing point.

(continued below)

Eye-level

Special vanishing point for scale

Pillar   *Pillar*   *Pillar*   *Pillar*

Ground line marked with scale measurements

Wall   Window   Wall   Doorway   Wall   Window   Wall

■ Where the lines cut the bottom line of the bridge (where the pillars touch the water), will mark the spacings of the pillars. Draw the verticals of the pillars and then complete the arches.

Eye-level

Special vanishing point for the measuring scale

WALL DIAGRAM

The same system works from a measuring line at the top.

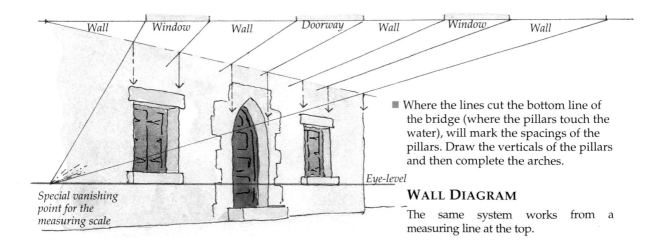

SPACING WITH A VERTICAL SCALE

In a drawing where the shallowness of the sloping lines makes the previous methods difficult or inaccurate, horizontal spacings can still be found by marking them onto a vertical scale, which, in conjunction with a diagonal, converts the spacings back to horizontal ones in correct perspective. Draw the building lightly, put in the scaled spacings and extend them to their vanishing point on the eye-level line.

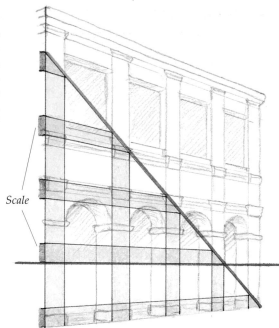

Scale

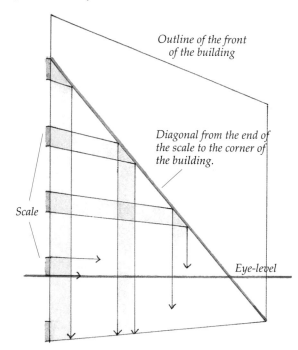

Outline of the front of the building

Diagonal from the end of the scale to the corner of the building.

Scale

Eye-level

The way the lines are drawn is shown by the simplified diagram above. The measured vertical scale shows the spacings of the pillars rising from the ground. The eye-level line assists in locating the vanishing point of all the lines.

- Draw a convenient scale, showing the ground-level spacings, on the near corner of the building. If the scale is drawn further out, for convenience of scaling, draw lines from the scale towards the vanishing point passing through the near corner.

- Draw a diagonal from the top of the scale on the near corner, to the farther bottom corner of the building.

- From each point on the scale, draw a line towards the vanishing point until it reaches the diagonal.

- Wherever a line touches the diagonal, draw the verticals down to ground-level from that point. The pillars will be exactly placed and positioned.

PICTURE SIZE, VIEWING DISTANCE AND SCALE

The diagram shows how image size is related to distance; the nearer the picture plane is to the subject being drawn, the larger the size of the image. Conversely, the closer the picture plane is to you, the smaller the image. Visualise the picture plane moving towards the artist to see how this happens.

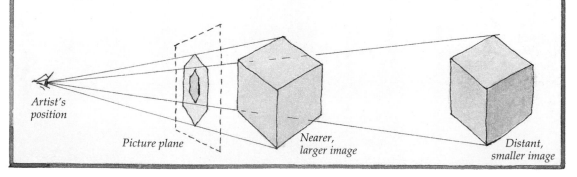

Artist's position

Picture plane

Nearer, larger image

Distant, smaller image

SCENES WITH A SINGLE VANISHING POINT

In some scenes, like the pictures below, there is only one important vanishing point. In a full-face view of a building, or any box shape, all the lines across the front remain parallel, without noticeable convergence. Other lines that are naturally level with the ground will go to a central vanishing point, which coincides with the centre of vision. Tilted lines, delineating the bridge's nearby girders, move to separate "downhill" or "uphill" vanishing points, examined on pp. 62-3.

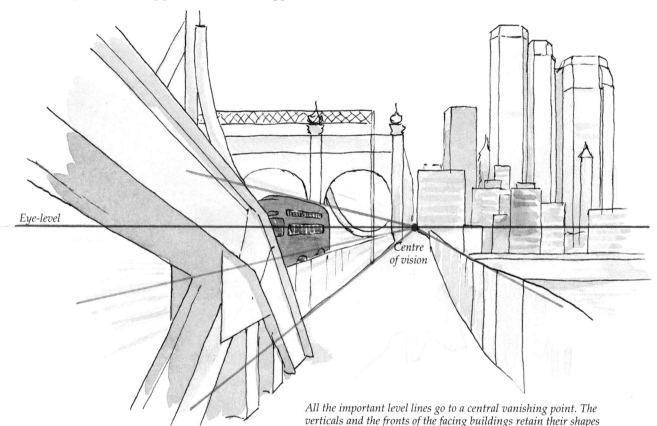

All the important level lines go to a central vanishing point. The verticals and the fronts of the facing buildings retain their shapes and aspects unchanged.

INTERIORS

Interior views are conveniently depicted with a vanishing point near the centre. The facing wall, right, is perfectly rectangular and the sides, floor and ceiling converge towards the central point. By moving your position far enough to one side or another, the symmetry goes, as the end wall is no longer seen from square on, and it will acquire its own distant vanishing point far outside the picture area.

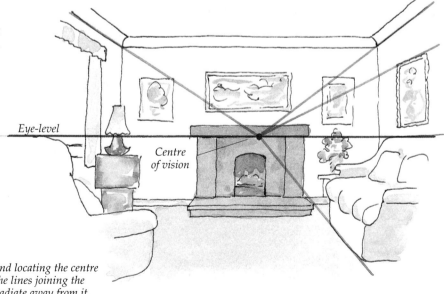

After drawing the end wall and locating the centre of vision straight ahead, all the lines joining the walls with floor and ceiling radiate away from it.

61

HOW TO DEAL WITH A VANISHING POINT OFF THE PAPER

One of the usual two vanishing points is frequently well outside the picture. The procedure is: 1) find the eye-level line, 2) make any vertical scale of your choice across the large end of the building, 3) follow the roof-line or some other line, and extend it to the paper edge, 4) make a smaller scale there with the same number of divisions, and 5) use the two scales as a grid.

The two scales have the same number of divisions and the lines show the grid that guides the directions.

THE PERSPECTIVE OF SLOPING SURFACES

Imagine a book on a table, with its sides lining up with the vanishing point at the centre of vision. As you gradually raise the cover, its vanishing point will move vertically upwards, directly above its original vanishing point. Try this out.

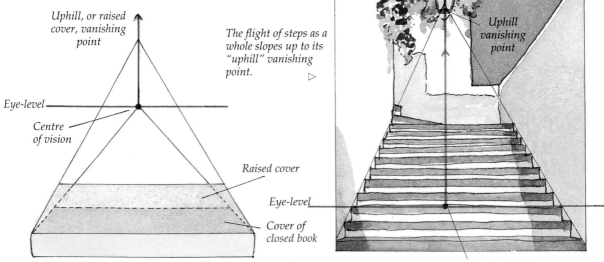

Uphill, or raised cover, vanishing point

The flight of steps as a whole slopes up to its "uphill" vanishing point. ▷

Eye-level ——

Centre of vision

Raised cover

Eye-level

Cover of closed book

Uphill vanishing point

Eye-level

Centre of vision

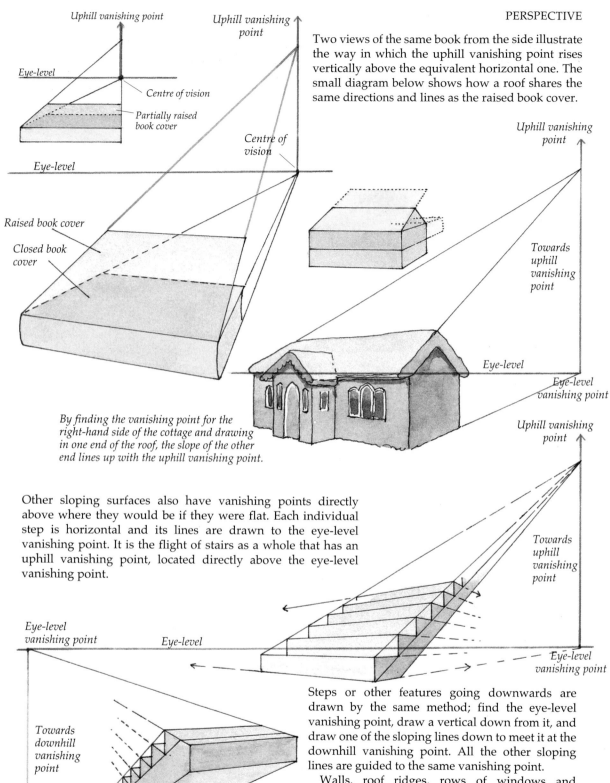

Uphill vanishing point

Uphill vanishing point

Eye-level

Centre of vision

Partially raised book cover

Eye-level

Two views of the same book from the side illustrate the way in which the uphill vanishing point rises vertically above the equivalent horizontal one. The small diagram below shows how a roof shares the same directions and lines as the raised book cover.

Centre of vision

Uphill vanishing point

Raised book cover

Closed book cover

Towards uphill vanishing point

Eye-level

Eye-level vanishing point

By finding the vanishing point for the right-hand side of the cottage and drawing in one end of the roof, the slope of the other end lines up with the uphill vanishing point.

Uphill vanishing point

Other sloping surfaces also have vanishing points directly above where they would be if they were flat. Each individual step is horizontal and its lines are drawn to the eye-level vanishing point. It is the flight of stairs as a whole that has an uphill vanishing point, located directly above the eye-level vanishing point.

Towards uphill vanishing point

Eye-level vanishing point

Eye-level

Eye-level vanishing point

Steps or other features going downwards are drawn by the same method; find the eye-level vanishing point, draw a vertical down from it, and draw one of the sloping lines down to meet it at the downhill vanishing point. All the other sloping lines are guided to the same vanishing point.

Towards downhill vanishing point

Walls, roof ridges, rows of windows and doorways are exactly level in real life, even if the ground below slopes, so their vanishing points are always at eye-level. Roads and the vehicles on them, fences, roof gables and staircases are examples that can have their vanishing points above or below the eye-level vanishing points.

Downhill vanishing point

63

LOOKING UPHILL

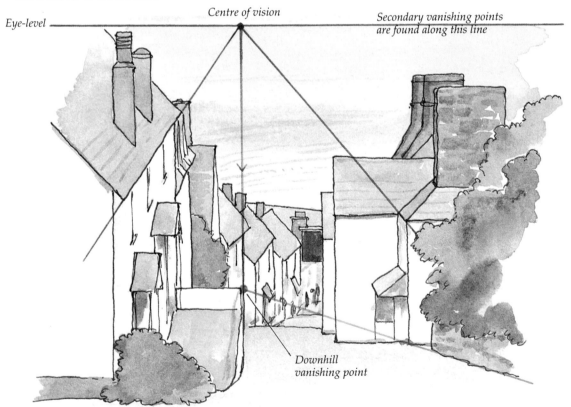

Uphill vanishing point

Eye-level

Principal vanishing point

The level features of the houses on the left are used to discover the eye-level line and the horizontal vanishing point. The uphill slope of the road comes to a point directly above it.

LOOKING DOWNHILL

Eye-level

Centre of vision

Secondary vanishing points are found along this line

Downhill vanishing point

The vanishing point of the road is a long way below the centre of vision, an indication of steepness. As the road curves down to the right, so the houses turn with it; the vanishing points of their roofs are accordingly displaced to the right, also on the eye-level line as the roofs' edges are level, under the words 'secondary vanishing points'.

PERSPECTIVE EXAMPLES – GABLE ENDS

All of these constructions depend on locating the centre-line of the roof, whether it is set back or brought forward from the main part of the roof. The numbers indicate a logical order of drawing the lines, but not the only one. These constructions occur very frequently in paintings of buildings, and although they arise naturally out of the principles of perspective already described, they are useful as quick references and examples.

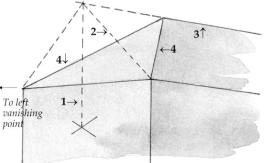

Once the centre-line of the roof has been found, the sloping end can be set back anywhere along the ridge, 3, and the edges 4 joined to it.

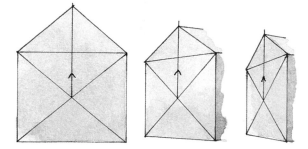

To find the centre-line of the roof, locate the corners of the rectangular part of the end of the building; draw in the diagonals from corner to corner. From the cross-over, draw a vertical line upwards, and the centre of the roof will be on that line. This works for any angle of view.

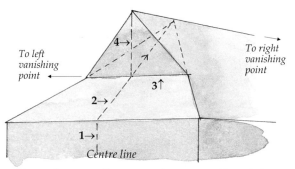

From the preceding example, a centre-line, 2, is drawn in to locate the vertical line, 4, which begins at the change of direction, 3.

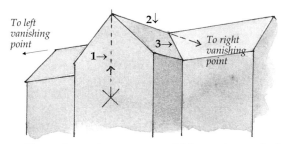

The main roof goes to a vanishing point on the left, while the roof of the bay has its vanishing point on the right. The roofs are both the same height, so line 2 meets the ridge of the main roof.

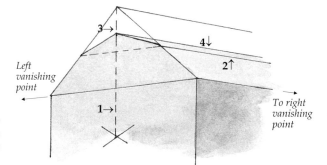

Starting from the main roof construction, the line 4 marks the beginning of a shallower top section, using the same vertical, 3.

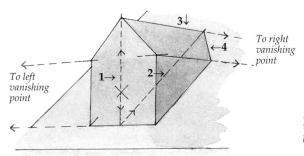

To find the angle of the join, (line 4), find the centre-line of the bottom of the dormer window. From it, draw a line, 2, up the slope of the roof. The ridge line, 3, will cross it, marking the top end of line 4.

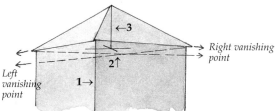

Two diagonals across the top of the tower locate its centre. The ridges can then be joined to the vertical line, 3. From many angles of view, the shallowness of the diagonals makes the crossover difficult to locate.

PILLARS, TOWERS AND STEEPLES

A few construction lines can correct architectural drawings. The two principal guides are a) the eye-level line and the two vanishing points, left and right, set on it; these will ensure the soundness of the main shapes, and b) the location by diagonals of the centre points, which are often invisible.

Draw the larger forms first, then add on the smaller parts. These smaller parts follow the same rules, and are most easily located by finding their centres; their square or rectangular shapes can then be projected outwards from these, towards their respective vanishing points

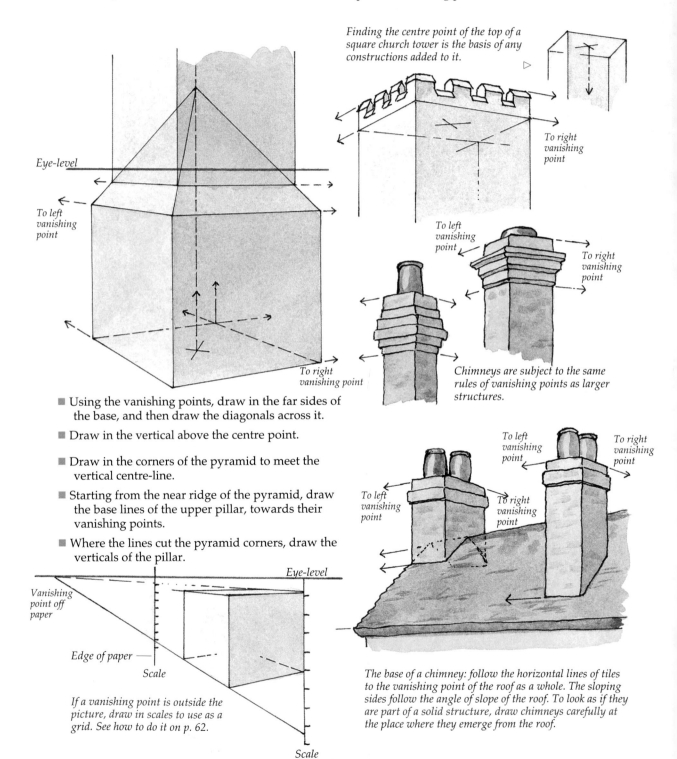

Finding the centre point of the top of a square church tower is the basis of any constructions added to it.

To right vanishing point

Eye-level

To left vanishing point

To right vanishing point

To left vanishing point

To right vanishing point

Chimneys are subject to the same rules of vanishing points as larger structures.

- Using the vanishing points, draw in the far sides of the base, and then draw the diagonals across it.

- Draw in the vertical above the centre point.

- Draw in the corners of the pyramid to meet the vertical centre-line.

- Starting from the near ridge of the pyramid, draw the base lines of the upper pillar, towards their vanishing points.

- Where the lines cut the pyramid corners, draw the verticals of the pillar.

To left vanishing point   *To right vanishing point*

To left vanishing point   *To right vanishing point*

Eye-level

Vanishing point off paper

Edge of paper

Scale

If a vanishing point is outside the picture, draw in scales to use as a grid. See how to do it on p. 62.

Scale

The base of a chimney: follow the horizontal lines of tiles to the vanishing point of the roof as a whole. The sloping sides follow the angle of slope of the roof. To look as if they are part of a solid structure, draw chimneys carefully at the place where they emerge from the roof.

To construct a two-part steeple on a square tower, the tower is drawn first, including the unseen part behind, which is lightly pencilled in. The position of the octagonal tower is accurately marked off around the edges and the height of the steeple marked in lightly.

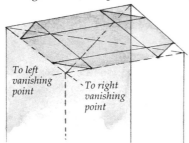

Further squares can be drawn inside the first with the aid of the diagonals.

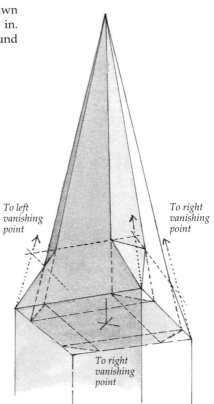

1. Locate the centre of the tower using diagonals, and draw a line up to the tip of the steeple directly above it.

2. From the marks showing the octagon on the top edge of the tower, draw lines up to the steeple's tip.

3. Draw faint guide-lines from the tower's four outer corners towards the tip. Then join them across in perspective to show where the triangular corner shapes begin.

4. Join up the top edges of the corner shapes on the steeple, then connect them to the outer corners of the tower.

The Stonemason's Yard, by Canaletto. Oil.
Perspective is the artist's servant, seldom obvious, but everywhere present.

67

A SYSTEM FOR MEASURING

Occasionally in a drawing there is a need to know how far back the side of a building goes, or how far into the picture to place a pillar, window or door. If the viewing distance and the true proportions of the subject are known, a scale can be made on a ground line.

Lightly draw the general aspect of the subject first, to establish the intended proportions, because purely perspectival constructions have a way of distorting the shapes if the initial angles are incorrectly estimated.

The section on measuring depth, p. 58, shows how to find the depth of a square that is square-on to the artist; the first diagram below recapitulates how to find the depth of such a square with sides of 4m. A second method, shown in the bottom diagram, becomes the basis for measuring the depth of a square at any angle to the artist's position.

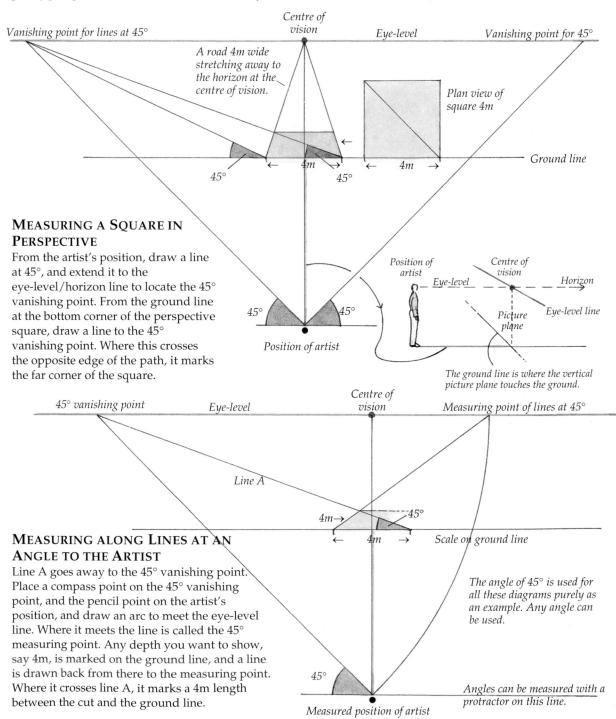

MEASURING A SQUARE IN PERSPECTIVE

From the artist's position, draw a line at 45°, and extend it to the eye-level/horizon line to locate the 45° vanishing point. From the ground line at the bottom corner of the perspective square, draw a line to the 45° vanishing point. Where this crosses the opposite edge of the path, it marks the far corner of the square.

MEASURING ALONG LINES AT AN ANGLE TO THE ARTIST

Line A goes away to the 45° vanishing point. Place a compass point on the 45° vanishing point, and the pencil point on the artist's position, and draw an arc to meet the eye-level line. Where it meets the line is called the 45° measuring point. Any depth you want to show, say 4m, is marked on the ground line, and a line is drawn back from there to the measuring point. Where it crosses line A, it marks a 4m length between the cut and the ground line.

68

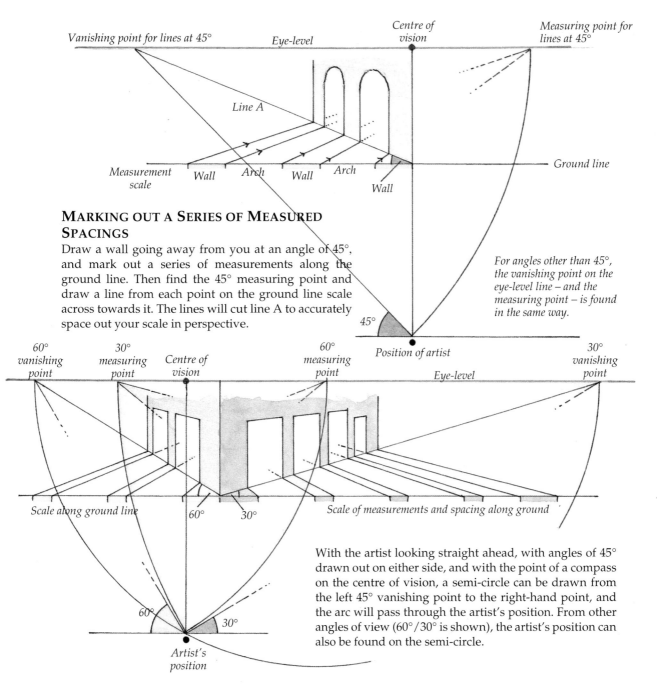

Vanishing point for lines at 45° Eye-level Centre of vision Measuring point for lines at 45°

Line A

Measurement scale Wall Arch Wall Arch Wall Ground line

MARKING OUT A SERIES OF MEASURED SPACINGS

Draw a wall going away from you at an angle of 45°, and mark out a series of measurements along the ground line. Then find the 45° measuring point and draw a line from each point on the ground line scale across towards it. The lines will cut line A to accurately space out your scale in perspective.

For angles other than 45°, the vanishing point on the eye-level line – and the measuring point – is found in the same way.

45°

Position of artist

60° vanishing point 30° measuring point Centre of vision 60° measuring point Eye-level 30° vanishing point

Scale along ground line 60° 30° Scale of measurements and spacing along ground

60° 30°

Artist's position

With the artist looking straight ahead, with angles of 45° drawn out on either side, and with the point of a compass on the centre of vision, a semi-circle can be drawn from the left 45° vanishing point to the right-hand point, and the arc will pass through the artist's position. From other angles of view (60°/30° is shown), the artist's position can also be found on the semi-circle.

In the diagram above, the artist's position is shown further along the arc to the left; so instead of seeing each wall equally, the right-hand wall is seen at an angle of 30° to the artist's position, and the other wall at 60°. Remember that the two angles, one on either side of the artist's position, add up to 90°.

Place the compass-point on the 30° vanishing point, and with the pencil point on the artist's position, draw an arc up to the eye-level line to find the 30° measuring point.

From the scale drawn out along the ground line below the right-hand wall, draw lines towards the 30° measuring point. Where these lines reach the base of the wall, the correct spacings can be marked off. Mark off the spacings for the other wall in the same way and connect to the 60° measuring point.

REFLECTIONS IN WATER

Still water acts like a mirror, and in the simplest case of distant mountains reflected in an unruffled lake the reflection is a simple upside-down version of the real landscape. Sometimes reflections are distorted by other factors, but the mirror-like surface is the basis of all calculations.

HOW TO DRAW REFLECTIONS

■ A reflection is vertically below the object being reflected.

■ The vertical depth of a reflection is measured from the point where the water-level theoretically passes beneath the object, not from where the object touches the ground.

■ By looking down into the water you are seeing an image projected from water-level; therefore you see the underside, never the top.

The diagrams below all illustrate the three points above. The farther away from the water the reflected image is, the closer it matches the object; the nearer to the water, the more you see it from a different and lower angle.

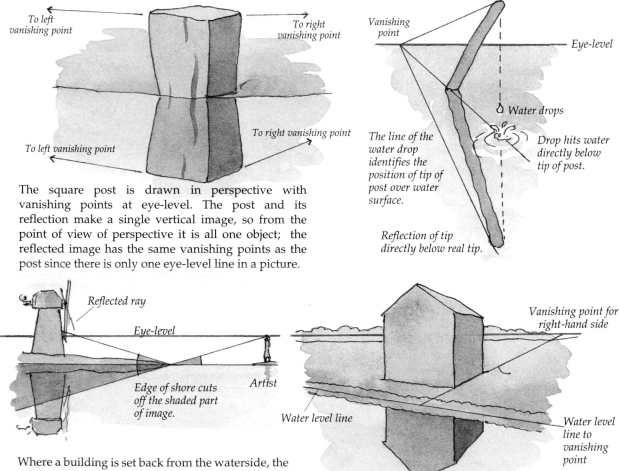

The square post is drawn in perspective with vanishing points at eye-level. The post and its reflection make a single vertical image, so from the point of view of perspective it is all one object; the reflected image has the same vanishing points as the post since there is only one eye-level line in a picture.

Where a building is set back from the waterside, the intervening land cuts off the lower part of the reflected image. The windmill diagram shows how the bank cuts off part of the reflected image, so part of the image is lost. See the second proposition in the box above.

Besides the cutting off of the lower part of the house's reflection, by the bank, the house is seen as if from water-level.

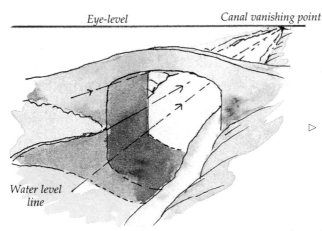

Eye-level *Canal vanishing point*

Water level line

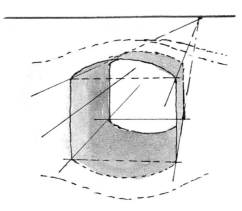

From high up, a reflection can look very different from the object causing it. From this viewpoint the underside of the bridge is invisible, but makes up the main part of the reflected image.

The right-hand diagram shows the perspective of the bridge more clearly. Note that the reflection shares the same vanishing points as the bridge itself.

Smooth

Wind

Smooth

Sky and tree reflections here

Underwater stones begin to show

When the surface becomes disturbed the single mirror becomes many, breaking up the reflected image into many parts and introducing sky reflections among them. With enough wind, the reflection disappears altogether as the surface is no longer smooth enough to act as a mirror.

At angles steeper than 41° light is no longer reflected, but goes on down into the water. The effect is that when you look down into the water, the reflections disappear, and you see the stones at the bottom instead.

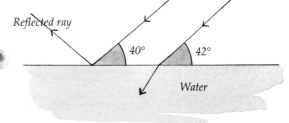

Reflected ray

40°   42°

Water

The swan's reflected image is so distorted by the uneven surface that close observation has to replace reliance on rules. The most important guideline is to remember that you are still looking at an underside view.

THE PERSPECTIVE OF SHADOWS

An understanding of perspective allows you to plot the positions of shadows. The subject has to be drawn in normal perspective first because the construction of shadows makes use of the eye-level line and vanishing points. The examples below will describe how to find the shapes of the shadows. Drawing shadows yourself is the only way to learn how, starting with simple ones. It is easy to overlook that the cast shadow itself always starts on the ground directly below the point or edge touched by the light ray.

HOW TO CONSTRUCT SHADOWS

- Make an accurate perspective drawing and decide where the sunlight is coming from.
- Draw light-rays to touch all corners where light and shade meet. The sun's rays are parallel; they are sometimes drawn in perspective, sometimes not, depending on the sun's position compared to the artist's.
- Work out where the sun rays hit the ground, by plotting an extension of the ground plan outwards in the direction of the rays.
- A shadow on the ground follows normal perspective like any other shape.

SUNLIGHT COMING FROM THE SIDE

The sun's rays are always drawn parallel to each other in side lighting. Sun rays from the side will reach the ground on a line level with the base of the cube, post or building. Draw this horizontal line level with the base. The sun rays touch the corners where light and shade meet, and continue down to meet the horizontal line on the ground.

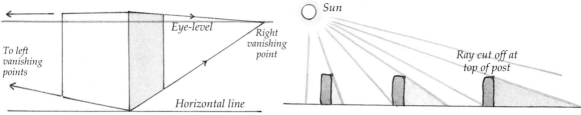

The above diagram of the cube shows the horizontal line drawn level with the bottom corner. In the right-hand diagram the row of posts shows differing angles of sunlight making shadows of differing length.

The diagram below shows the sloping rays passing each corner and reaching the ground at points found by:
a) locating the spot on the ground directly below the corner
b) drawing a line, horizontally from each corner on the ground, to meet the rays.

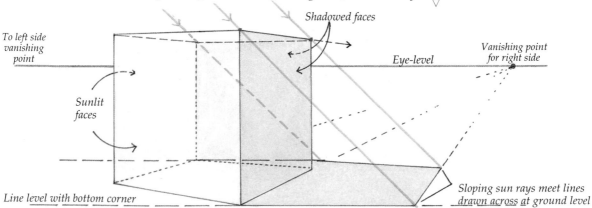

Level lines on the ground, drawn from each corner, show the direction on the ground of sun's rays going straight across from left to right

SOME EXAMPLES

The house can be seen as a number of block-like shapes side by side. Carefully mark each corner or edge where there is any change in direction of roof or wall. Draw the parallel sun rays. Directly below each marked point, draw a horizontal line on the ground, going towards the right. Join all the cut-off points.

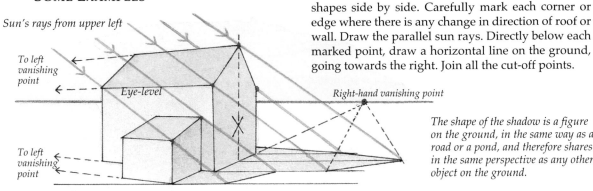

Sun's rays from upper left

To left vanishing point

Eye-level

Right-hand vanishing point

To left vanishing point

The shape of the shadow is a figure on the ground, in the same way as a road or a pond, and therefore shares in the same perspective as any other object on the ground.

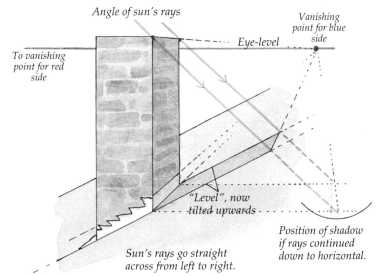

Angle of sun's rays

Vanishing point for blue side

Eye-level

To vanishing point for red side

"Level", now tilted upwards

Position of shadow if rays continued down to horizontal.

Sun's rays go straight across from left to right.

When the "ground" is not horizontal, such as a hillside or roof, the lines that were previously drawn horizontally are drawn to follow the angle of the slope, either up or down.

As the sun is square on to the chimney, just two top corners are marked, and the rays touching them are drawn in. The slope of the roof is drawn, starting from the two points directly below the corners touched by the rays. The shadow ends where the rays and the roof lines meet each other. The diagram also shows where the shadow would have reached if the roof was flat. If the slope was going down to the right instead of up, the shadow would have become very long.

Shadows sometimes have to follow more complex shapes on the ground, and where they are interrupted you have to re-locate the path of the horizontal line as it goes up and down the obstacles.

The horizontal lines bounding the shadow on the ground were started from directly below the two top corners where light changes into shadow. Before the lines on the ground can meet the sun rays they meet a vertical wall. They travel vertically up the wall to resume their horizontal progess. On reaching the next wall they again follow it up vertically until cut off by the sloping rays. The diagram also shows where the shadow would have reached if the ground had been flat.

Angle of sun's rays

Ground level of far side

Shadow stopped by wall, continues up wall till it reaches sun's rays.

Level, raised up

Levels, sunlight from side

Shadow on level ground is stopped by the wall, and continues up it, before continuing horizontally again.

SHADOWS – AGAINST THE LIGHT

The sun, when it is in front of you, is a small object in the sky, so the rays streaming from it fan outwards, as if from a point, according to the rules of perspective. The two things that guide the construction of shadows against the light are:

1. The sun rays vanish back at the sun's disk, (but don't look at the sun to try and check this).
2. The shadows on the ground vanish at a point on the horizon / eye-level line directly below the sun.

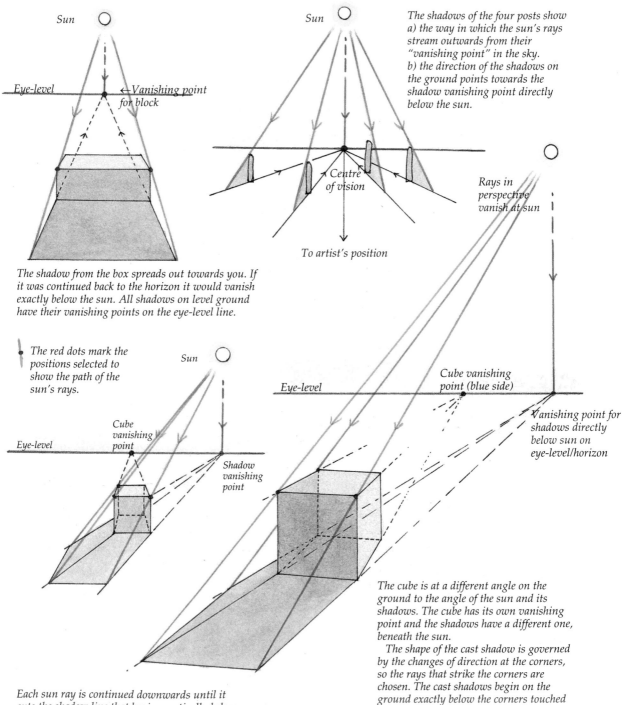

The shadows of the four posts show a) the way in which the sun's rays stream outwards from their "vanishing point" in the sky. b) the direction of the shadows on the ground points towards the shadow vanishing point directly below the sun.

The shadow from the box spreads out towards you. If it was continued back to the horizon it would vanish exactly below the sun. All shadows on level ground have their vanishing points on the eye-level line.

The red dots mark the positions selected to show the path of the sun's rays.

Each sun ray is continued downwards until it cuts the shadow line that begins vertically below its corner on the cube.

The cube is at a different angle on the ground to the angle of the sun and its shadows. The cube has its own vanishing point and the shadows have a different one, beneath the sun.

The shape of the cast shadow is governed by the changes of direction at the corners, so the rays that strike the corners are chosen. The cast shadows begin on the ground exactly below the corners touched by the sun rays.

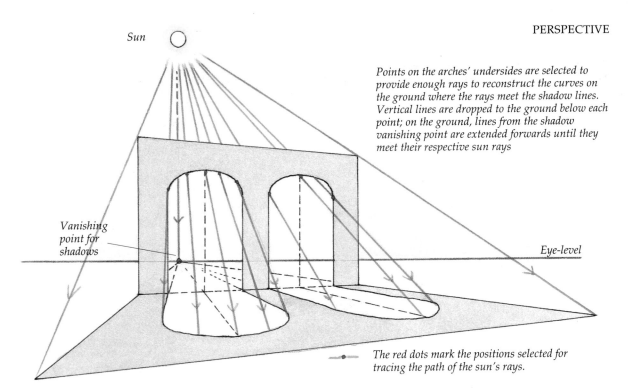

Points on the arches' undersides are selected to provide enough rays to reconstruct the curves on the ground where the rays meet the shadow lines. Vertical lines are dropped to the ground below each point; on the ground, lines from the shadow vanishing point are extended forwards until they meet their respective sun rays

Sun

Vanishing point for shadows

Eye-level

The red dots mark the positions selected for tracing the path of the sun's rays.

SHADOWS ON WALLS

An extra vanishing point needed for wall shadows can create problems in visualising how they work. By turning the page sideways you see the diagram from the same orientation as the cube shadows opposite, so the similarities become more apparent: while viewing in this way, ignore the main eye-level line; a secondary horizon line at right-angles to it is more useful.

■ Draw the ledge and the vanishing point on the same side as the sun in the normal way, then put in the sun's position.

■ From the wall vanishing point, draw a vertical line up to the height of the sun's position.

■ Draw a horizontal line from the sun to meet the vertical line. Where the lines meet is the vanishing point for the shadows on the wall. Note that this lines up with the wall's <u>vanishing</u> point on the the eye-level line.

■ Draw in the sun rays and the shadow direction lines on the wall.

■ The cast shadows are on a vertical surface, so their vanishing point must be on a vertical line.

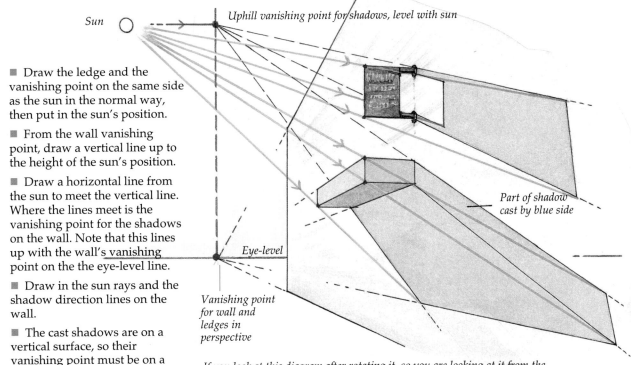

Sun

Uphill vanishing point for shadows, level with sun

Eye-level

Part of shadow cast by blue side

Vanishing point for wall and ledges in perspective

If you look at this diagram after rotating it, so you are looking at it from the outside edge of the page, some similarities between these wall shadows and the ground shadows on the opposite page (bottom right) become apparent. The wall shadows require the extra vertical dashed line (step 2) to make the wall and shadow vanishing points line up with each other.

SHADOWS – THE SUN BEHIND THE ARTIST

When the sun is behind you, you cannot locate its position on the paper, but the vanishing point of its rays is in front of you, and therefore can be drawn in.

As the sun itself is above the horizon, so its rays vanish to a point below the horizon. The sun ray vanishing point is in every respect the opposite of the sun's position, and all the sun ray lines are drawn from it.

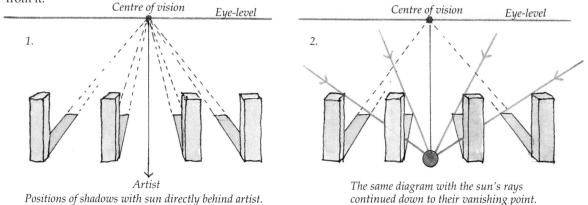

Positions of shadows with sun directly behind artist.

The same diagram with the sun's rays continued down to their vanishing point.

Start by drawing the cube and put in its vanishing point on the right hand side. Draw a ray from the sun touching one of the corners, at whatever angle you wish, and continue it downwards to a chosen sun ray vanishing point. The angle of your ray, and the position you decide on for the sun ray vanishing point, will fix the position of the shadows.

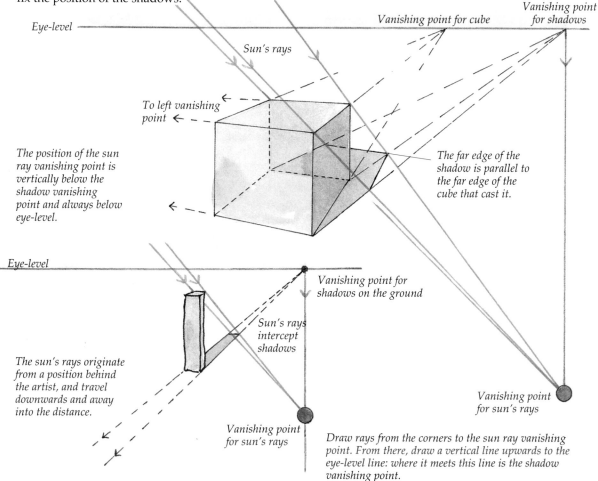

The position of the sun ray vanishing point is vertically below the shadow vanishing point and always below eye-level.

The far edge of the shadow is parallel to the far edge of the cube that cast it.

The sun's rays originate from a position behind the artist, and travel downwards and away into the distance.

Draw rays from the corners to the sun ray vanishing point. From there, draw a vertical line upwards to the eye-level line: where it meets this line is the shadow vanishing point.

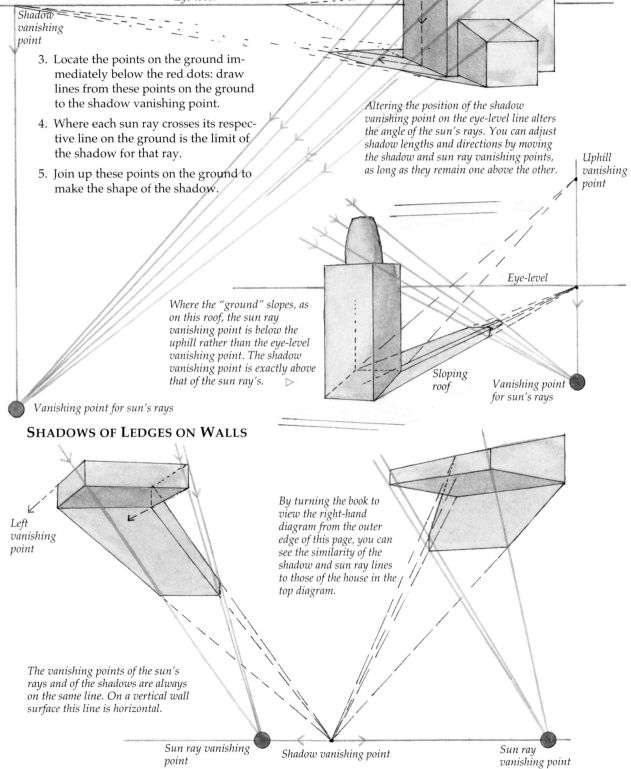

1. Draw the rays to the sun ray vanishing point.
2. Draw a vertical line up to the eye-level line to locate the shadow vanishing point.

Eye-level

Shadow vanishing point

3. Locate the points on the ground immediately below the red dots: draw lines from these points on the ground to the shadow vanishing point.

4. Where each sun ray crosses its respective line on the ground is the limit of the shadow for that ray.

5. Join up these points on the ground to make the shape of the shadow.

Altering the position of the shadow vanishing point on the eye-level line alters the angle of the sun's rays. You can adjust shadow lengths and directions by moving the shadow and sun ray vanishing points, as long as they remain one above the other.

Uphill vanishing point

Where the "ground" slopes, as on this roof, the sun ray vanishing point is below the uphill rather than the eye-level vanishing point. The shadow vanishing point is exactly above that of the sun ray's. ▷

Eye-level

Sloping roof

Vanishing point for sun's rays

Vanishing point for sun's rays

SHADOWS OF LEDGES ON WALLS

Left vanishing point

By turning the book to view the right-hand diagram from the outer edge of this page, you can see the similarity of the shadow and sun ray lines to those of the house in the top diagram.

The vanishing points of the sun's rays and of the shadows are always on the same line. On a vertical wall surface this line is horizontal.

Sun ray vanishing point

Shadow vanishing point

Sun ray vanishing point

EXAMPLES OF THE PERSPECTIVE OF SHADOWS

The eye-level line goes right across both pages to show the relationships and positions of all the vanishing points below the eye-level line.

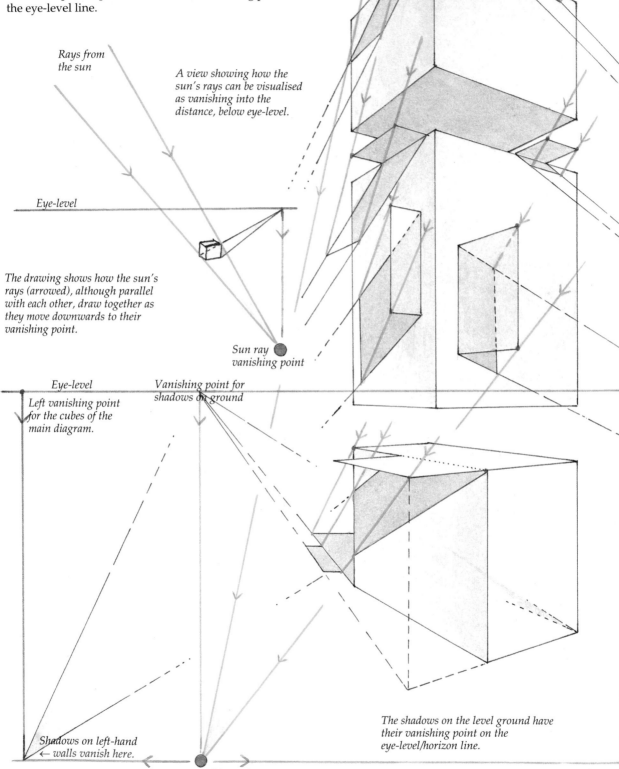

Rays from the sun

A view showing how the sun's rays can be visualised as vanishing into the distance, below eye-level.

Eye-level

The drawing shows how the sun's rays (arrowed), although parallel with each other, draw together as they move downwards to their vanishing point.

Sun ray vanishing point

Eye-level

Left vanishing point for the cubes of the main diagram.

Vanishing point for shadows on ground

Shadows on left-hand ← walls vanish here.

Sun ray vanishing point

The shadows on the level ground have their vanishing point on the eye-level/horizon line.

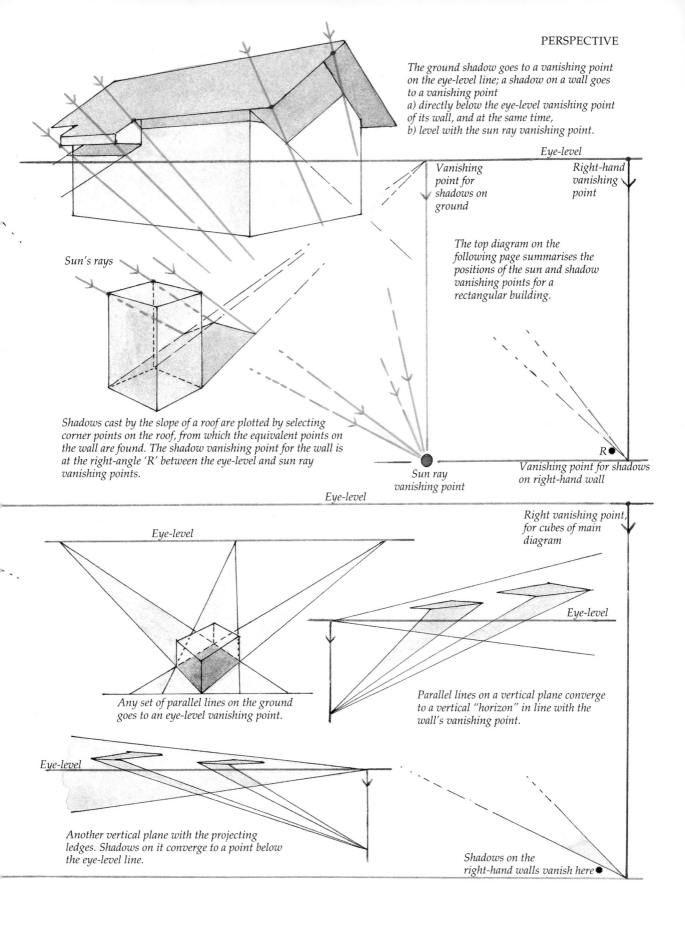

The ground shadow goes to a vanishing point on the eye-level line; a shadow on a wall goes to a vanishing point
a) directly below the eye-level vanishing point of its wall, and at the same time,
b) level with the sun ray vanishing point.

Eye-level

Vanishing point for shadows on ground

Right-hand vanishing point

The top diagram on the following page summarises the positions of the sun and shadow vanishing points for a rectangular building.

Sun's rays

Shadows cast by the slope of a roof are plotted by selecting corner points on the roof, from which the equivalent points on the wall are found. The shadow vanishing point for the wall is at the right-angle 'R' between the eye-level and sun ray vanishing points.

R

Sun ray vanishing point

Vanishing point for shadows on right-hand wall

Eye-level

Eye-level

Right vanishing point, for cubes of main diagram

Eye-level

Eye-level

Any set of parallel lines on the ground goes to an eye-level vanishing point.

Parallel lines on a vertical plane converge to a vertical "horizon" in line with the wall's vanishing point.

Eye-level

Another vertical plane with the projecting ledges. Shadows on it converge to a point below the eye-level line.

Shadows on the right-hand walls vanish here

79

SHADOWS UNDER EAVES, WINDOWS, ARCHES

The diagram to the right is a reminder of the relative positions of the several vanishing points when the sun is behind the artist. There is rarely room on any drawing paper for all of them.

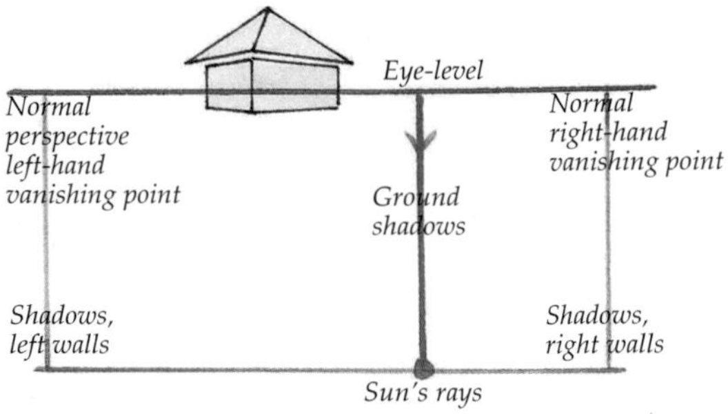

Eye-level

Normal perspective left-hand vanishing point

Normal right-hand vanishing point

Ground shadows

Shadows, left walls

Shadows, right walls

Sun's rays

The location of vanishing points for shadows.

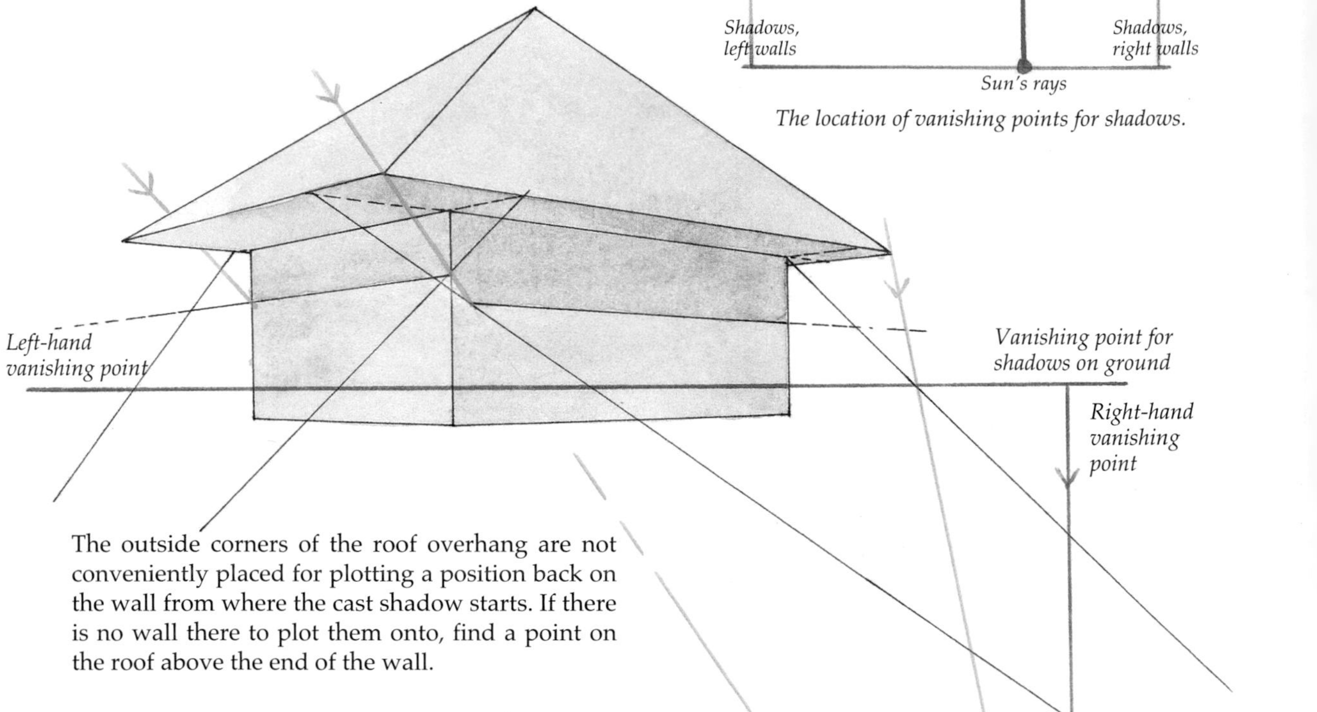

Left-hand vanishing point

Vanishing point for shadows on ground

Right-hand vanishing point

The outside corners of the roof overhang are not conveniently placed for plotting a position back on the wall from where the cast shadow starts. If there is no wall there to plot them onto, find a point on the roof above the end of the wall.

SHADOWS IN NICHES

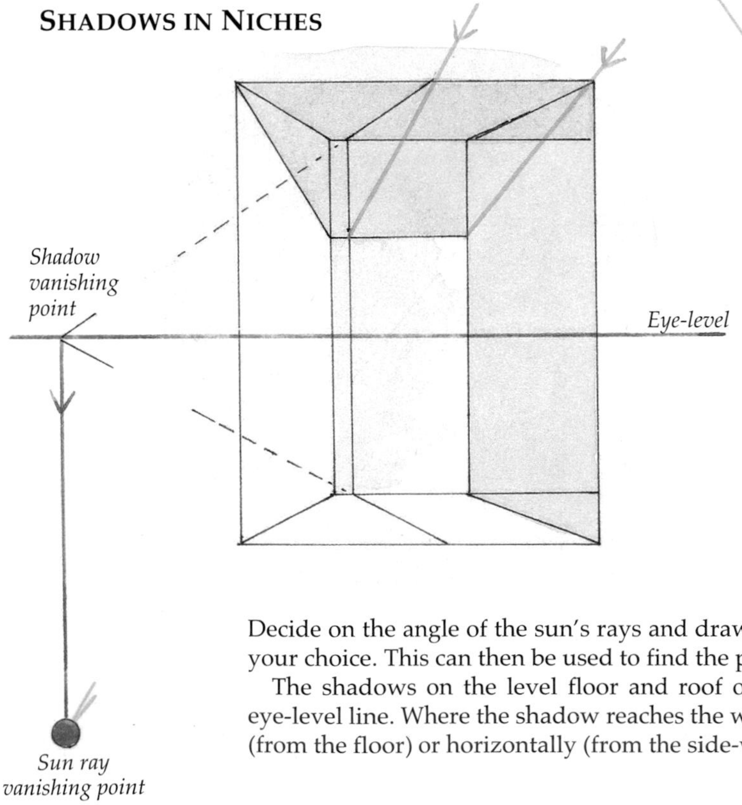

Shadow vanishing point

Eye-level

To left-hand shadow vanishing point

To right-hand shadow vanishing point

Vanishing point for sun's rays

Sun ray vanishing point

Decide on the angle of the sun's rays and draw a ray down to a sun ray vanishing point of your choice. This can then be used to find the position of the shadow vanishing point.

The shadows on the level floor and roof of the niche go to a vanishing point on the eye-level line. Where the shadow reaches the wall it changes direction to continue upwards (from the floor) or horizontally (from the side-walls).

80

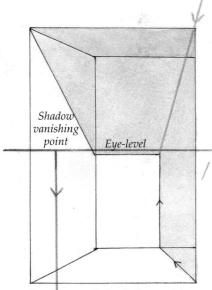

Shadow vanishing point

Eye-level

Sun rays

One ray reveals the shadow position.

Extra corners need extra sun rays to follow the shapes.

Select enough points to be able to construct the shadow curve.

Sun ray vanishing point

Three niches. The first shows the simplest case. The light-rays strike the front edges, at points selected by the artist. Dotted construction lines are drawn vertically down from the points where sun rays strike. When a construction line touches the bottom edge, it is drawn across the flat sill towards the shadow vanishing point, which is on the eye-level line directly above the sun ray vanishing point.

When the construction line meets the rear wall, and can go no further towards its vanishing point, it continues vertically upwards until it cuts the line of its originating sun ray. The meeting point marks the edge of the shadow.

Sun rays striking the top corners are generally sufficient to find the shadow shapes. Once the points where the shadows of the corners are have been located, they are joined up by lines drawn parallel to their respective edges.

SHADOWS FROM CURVES

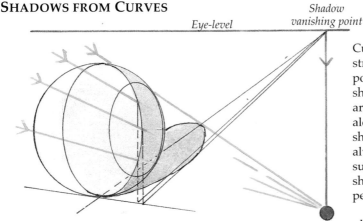

Eye-level

Shadow vanishing point

Sun ray vanishing point

Although it is useful to be able to plot curved shadows, it is seldom necessary to do so except as a general guide to their positions.

Curved edges act in the same way as straight edges, except that a number of points where the light-rays touch the shadow edge have to be plotted; these are then projected, downwards or along, onto the surface on which the shadows lie. Shadow vanishing points always lie on the same plane (or surface) as the cast shadows, and the shadows follow the normal rules of perspective that apply to that surface.

On the level ground, lines from the plotted points (going towards the shadow vanishing point) are crossed by the light-rays. The points are then joined up as smoothly as possible.

SHADOWS IN ARTIFICIAL LIGHT

Shadows in artificial light fan out appreciably more than outdoor shadows because the light is close to the subject. There is rarely any occasion to treat the light-rays as parallel to each other.

The main difference in constructing the shadows is the location of the shadow vanishing point, which for the floor is directly below the light. For walls, the geometry is the same: the light travels the same path, directly onto the surface at right-angles to it, and shadows on that surface vanish at that point.

Besides the shadow perspective difference, artificial light itself fades as it becomes more distant from the source, an effect seen frequently in the paintings of Rembrandt, such as 'The Adoration of the Shepherds', p. 31.

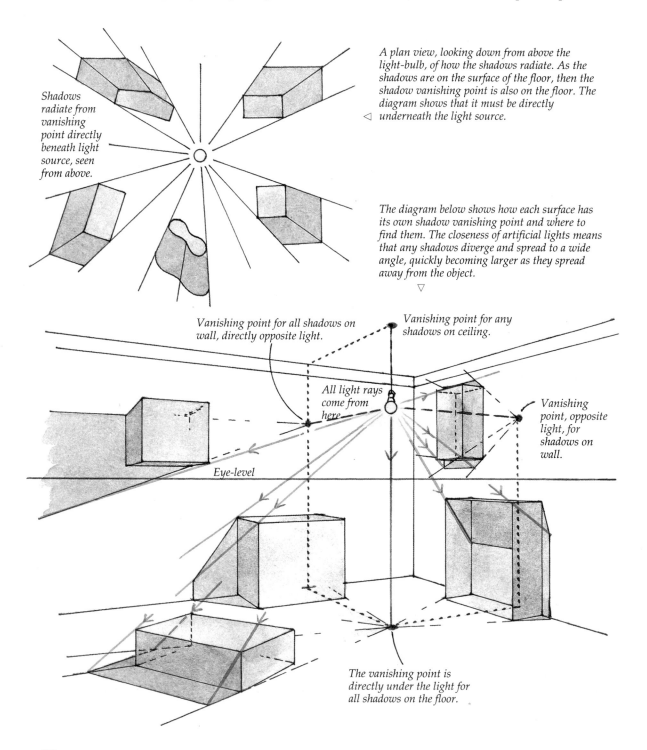

A plan view, looking down from above the light-bulb, of how the shadows radiate. As the shadows are on the surface of the floor, then the shadow vanishing point is also on the floor. The diagram shows that it must be directly
◁ *underneath the light source.*

Shadows radiate from vanishing point directly beneath light source, seen from above.

The diagram below shows how each surface has its own shadow vanishing point and where to find them. The closeness of artificial lights means that any shadows diverge and spread to a wide angle, quickly becoming larger as they spread away from the object.
▽

Vanishing point for all shadows on wall, directly opposite light.

Vanishing point for any shadows on ceiling.

All light rays come from here

Vanishing point, opposite light, for shadows on wall.

Eye-level

The vanishing point is directly under the light for all shadows on the floor.

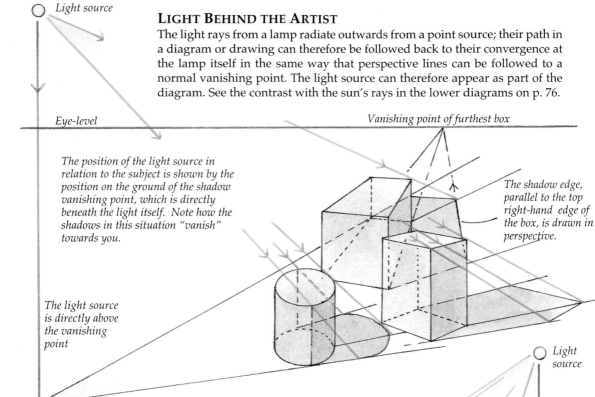

LIGHT BEHIND THE ARTIST

The light rays from a lamp radiate outwards from a point source; their path in a diagram or drawing can therefore be followed back to their convergence at the lamp itself in the same way that perspective lines can be followed to a normal vanishing point. The light source can therefore appear as part of the diagram. See the contrast with the sun's rays in the lower diagrams on p. 76.

Light source

Eye-level

Vanishing point of furthest box

The position of the light source in relation to the subject is shown by the position on the ground of the shadow vanishing point, which is directly beneath the light itself. Note how the shadows in this situation "vanish" towards you.

The shadow edge, parallel to the top right-hand edge of the box, is drawn in perspective.

The light source is directly above the vanishing point

Vanishing point for shadows

LIGHT IN FRONT OF THE ARTIST

In front of the artist, artificial light perspective resembles the perspective characteristics of sunlight, and the construction of the shadows is the same except that the shadow vanishing point is directly below the light on the ground, and therefore not on the eye-level line. The light is much closer than the horizon.

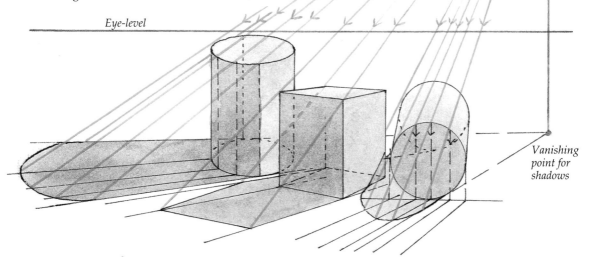

Light source

Eye-level

Vanishing point for shadows

Selected points on the illuminated edge are projected onto the ground directly below them, from where lines radiating away from the shadow vanishing point are drawn to meet their respective light-rays. The shadow vanishing point is on the ground just beyond the objects and below the light, not nearly far enough away to be on the eye-level/horizon line.

HOW TO DRAW CIRCLES IN PERSPECTIVE

Circles appear in pictures as bowls, pots, wheels and flowers, sometimes in parts, sometimes overlapping, as with car wheels. The easily made divisions of a square can be used to help make a guide to inscribing a circle. In practice, such constructions are more often used for ellipses, which are circles in perspective. By drawing the enclosing square and its divisions in true perspective, the ellipse can be constructed to its correct angle and size. Note that the widest part of an ellipse does not coincide with the centre of the circle.

- Draw a square the size of the intended circle.
- Find the centre with two diagonals, then use the centre to draw horizontal and vertical lines to find the centres of the sides.
- Join up the centre points on the sides of the square to make a diamond shape.
- In each corner triangle make a mark halfway from the diamond edge to the corner of the square.
- Draw the circumference of the circle through the eight points.

The circle touches the square at the centre of each side. In the corner triangles the circumference passes just inside the halfway marks. Circles are not normally drawn this way, but the divisions as constructed are useful in understanding how the different sections of a circle vary when seen at an angle.

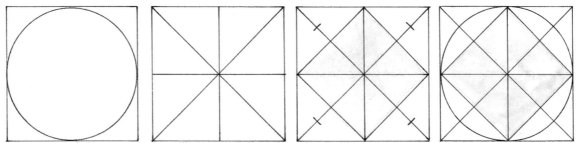

A circle in perspective is an ellipse; as a circle can be enclosed within a square, so its appearance as an ellipse can be shown inside a square in perspective.

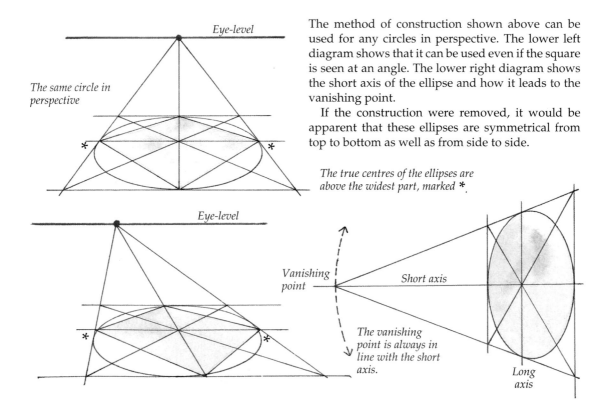

The method of construction shown above can be used for any circles in perspective. The lower left diagram shows that it can be used even if the square is seen at an angle. The lower right diagram shows the short axis of the ellipse and how it leads to the vanishing point.

If the construction were removed, it would be apparent that these ellipses are symmetrical from top to bottom as well as from side to side.

*The true centres of the ellipses are above the widest part, marked *.*

Eye-level

The same circle in perspective

Eye-level

Vanishing point

Short axis

The vanishing point is always in line with the short axis.

Long axis

CIRCLES IN THREE DIMENSIONS

To give an impression of three dimensions the true centres of ellipses have to be positioned in perspective along a common short axis.

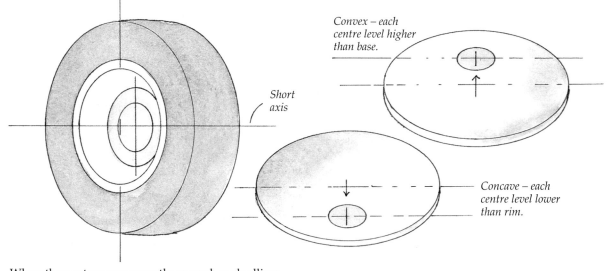

Short
axis

Convex – each centre level higher than base.

Concave – each centre level lower than rim.

When the centres are correctly spaced, each ellipse can be drawn in position. The convex and concave discs show how the positions of the centres affect appearances. The daisy has three levels, with a concave bowl in the very centre of the raised yellow disc. The stem attachment is below the flower and the white petals radiate from the centre of the bottom of the flower, not from the yellow disk.

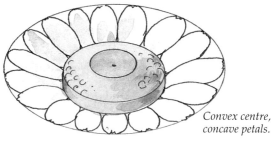

Convex centre, concave petals.

ELLIPSES AT VARIOUS ANGLES

A wheel is not always upright, so draw the two axes first to fix the angle. Whatever angles an ellipse may be, the long and short axes are always at right-angles to each other.

The angle of view determines how much the ellipse departs from the circular.

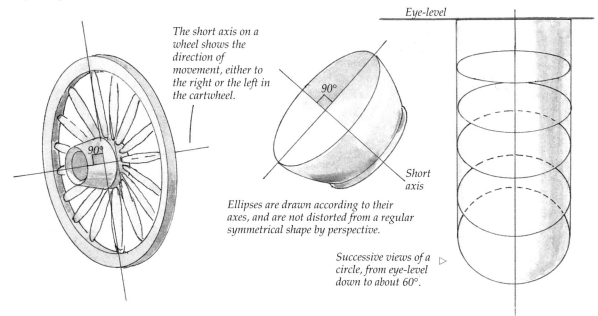

The short axis on a wheel shows the direction of movement, either to the right or the left in the cartwheel.

Eye-level

90°

90°

Short axis

Ellipses are drawn according to their axes, and are not distorted from a regular symmetrical shape by perspective.

Successive views of a circle, from eye-level down to about 60°.

BOXING IN FORMS

Complex shapes with sinuous curves need containing within simple regular shapes to make them accessible to perspective. The boxes should be drawn to touch somewhere useful on each side, but all other points have to be projected or estimated. A little time spent on boxing in difficult shapes will prevent elementary errors being made, and will especially assist in foreshortening. When a foreshortened box has been drawn, carefully mark some positions of important points along the sides, perhaps halfway or a third of the way along, for example; then draw in your subject, compressing the curves to fit within the marked spaces.

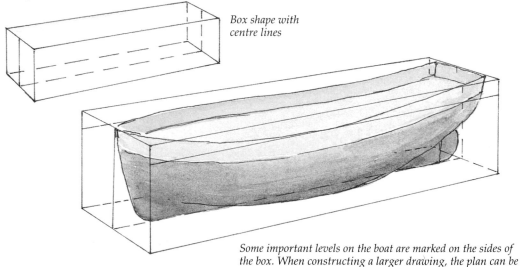

Box shape with centre lines

Some important levels on the boat are marked on the sides of the box. When constructing a larger drawing, the plan can be transferred to the top of the box and the elevation to the side, and lines from them projected inwards.

A car has few points of useful contact, but the proportions are more easily maintained in a box than in a freehand drawing. Until you have enough experience to feel confident with freehand drawing, draw some sort of box first to contain the shape, then place the vehicle carefully within it.

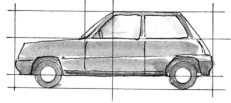

The more box-like cars can be subdivided. Town pictures increasingly need cars to make them look lived-in.

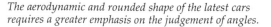

The aerodynamic and rounded shape of the latest cars requires a greater emphasis on the judgement of angles.

THREE-POINT PERSPECTIVE

A true perspective view has a third vanishing point for the third dimension, height. In most pictures it can be conveniently ignored because its effects at eye-level are very small and are corrected by the brain. An added degree of realism can be achieved by making allowances for it whenever height or depth play a significant part in the design.

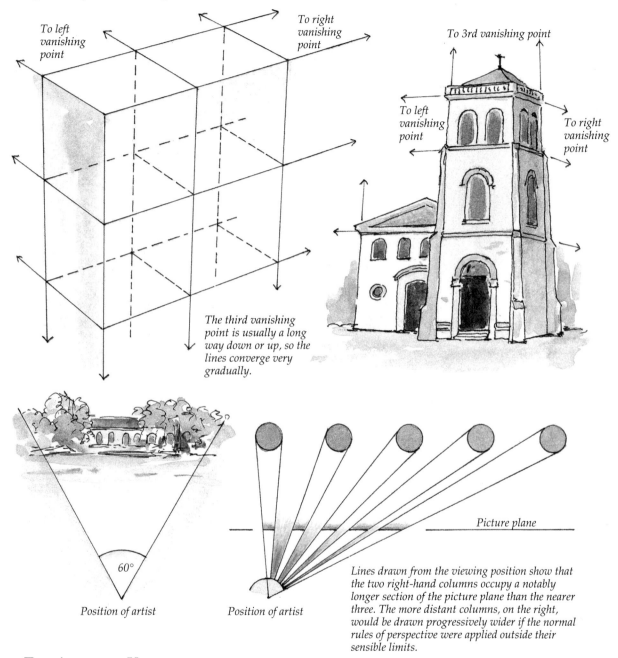

To left vanishing point

To right vanishing point

To 3rd vanishing point

To left vanishing point

To right vanishing point

The third vanishing point is usually a long way down or up, so the lines converge very gradually.

60°

Position of artist

Position of artist

Picture plane

Lines drawn from the viewing position show that the two right-hand columns occupy a notably longer section of the picture plane than the nearer three. The more distant columns, on the right, would be drawn progressively wider if the normal rules of perspective were applied outside their sensible limits.

THE ANGLE OF VISION

Many interesting effects require a wider angle of vision than 60°, so steps have to be taken to avoid distortion, for example by having two or three centres of vision, so each part of the view is faced in turn and drawn face on. If you are drawing from life, check the true shapes of objects towards the edges and adjust your perspective construction in that part of the picture to suit them.

The intervening parts can be blended in with each other as long as the centres are not too far apart, but it is unwise to try and construct such a view theoretically until you have drawn some wide-angled scenes from life.

THE COLOURS

INTRODUCTION

In early paintings and drawings, the materials were mainly natural products, coloured earths such as yellow or red ochres or naturally occurring red minerals like cinnabar; a few pigments, like White Lead, were manufactured by chemical processes even in Roman times. The rise of chemistry before and during the industrial revolution began the modern explosion of bright new colours that has accelerated during the last sixty years.

The craftsman's familiarity with his materials, part of the background of artists such as Veronese, Titian and Rubens, has been largely lost in the past century, when the idea took root that artists should paint as the mood took them, unrestrained by practical cares that might inhibit creativity. During this time knowledge of materials and technique declined to a low level, but the modern awakening of interest in painting as a hobby and the re-emergence of realistic and figurative painting have brought a renewed interest in materials and how to use them.

Painting is a craft as well as an art, and an understanding of your materials' properties can often make a difference to your apparent skill – a change to another brush, a new oil-painting medium, a different paper or paint, can transform your work.

This section is essentially practical, describing or recommending quality, permanence and convenience rather than delving into chemistry or physics; most amateur painters have neither the time nor means to pursue technical matters.

Modern technology has provided us with materials of the finest quality and dependability, and in astonishing variety, but the use of natural ingredients is not always a guarantee of reliability, as a number of natural pigments like Carmine, Sap Green and Sepia fade badly, while their synthetic replacements can be faultless. Manufacturers may substitute ingredients from time to time in such colours to improve light-fastness, and improved labelling is making it easier to assess permanence for ourselves.

The concentration in this section is on pigments; their great number and the confusion of names make them a subject of mystery to artists. Other materials, such as binders, brushes, paper and canvas, will be considered in more detail in the section on each medium. The enormous range of pigments includes many that are currently impermanent and for reason of space, most of these I have omitted.

Cornelissen's shop in London is one of many suppliers who will post materials to you.

PIGMENTS AND PAINT

An artist's pigment takes the form of a powder that retains its colour and character when made into a paint and used under normal conditions. The powdered grains of differing pigments may vary greatly in size and those of some minerals, or earths like the ochres, are much larger than the tiny grains of colours like Prussian Blue and Phthalocyanine Blue.

Pigments must be able to resist alteration by reasonable heat, light or chemical action, such as dissolution in a solvent used in painting.

Some pigments are prone to separate from their binders in the tube, and wax or other additional ingredients are sometimes added to stabilise the mixture. Extenders are colourless fillers added by some makers to economise on the quantity and cost of expensive or over-powerful pigments. Preservatives are occasionally used to prevent mould. Before the invention of tubes in 1850, oil paint was stored in pigs' bladders, and extracted by piercing with a pin which was afterwards used to seal the hole.

Cadmium Red

Yellow Ochre

Raw Sienna

Cobalt Blue

Muller for grinding paint

Typical pigments and a hand grinding tool.

Cross-section of a paint film, showing each grain surrounded by the binder.

Before the invention of tubes, paint was stored in pig's bladders.

Watercolour half pan

Whole pan

Air pollution is a long-term risk to a few pigments, such as Flake White and Chrome Yellow, and the use of these is confined to oil paints where the pigment grains are protected by a coating of oil. Other pigmented materials that dissolve in a liquid while retaining their colouring are called dyes, but this is not the same as being thinned or diluted, when the paint grains are spread thinly but are still intact.

Pigments are in the form of particles and are insoluble.

A dye can be dissolved in liquid.

Pigment sources used to range from plant extracts, earths and naturally occurring minerals, but except for the earths, they are now mostly manufactured by the chemical industries. A paint is a simple mixture in which the pigment is held in suspension by a binder that dries after application.

Some trays of pigments used by Old Holland for their paints. Careful grinding using stone rollers produces the highest quality paints and brings out the most intense colour. Most pigments are commercially available in dry powder form if you wish to make up your own paints or if you paint in egg tempera.

BINDERS, MEDIUMS AND SOLVENTS

Each medium has its own binder; gum arabic for watercolour, plastic emulsion for acrylic and egg-yolk for tempera. There are two main types, the oily and the watery media; the watery media, gum arabic and egg, stick most strongly, and can therefore be diluted safely to a greater degree than the oils. Resins are also employed with oils, which have their own solvents, chiefly spirits of turpentine and white spirit. Media are discussed in detail in their appropriate sections.

Dammar varnish

Mastic pieces

Amber

Beeswax

Cold pressed linseed oil

THE NAMING OF PAINTS

The names of colours reflect the history of paintmaking from the early Middle Ages to the more recent developments of new pigments. A consequence of this history is a confusion of colour names, for in the process of improving paints, familiar names have sometimes been retained while the pigments themselves have often changed completely. An example is the modern Scarlet Lake from Winsor & Newton, a brilliant and useful scarlet that bears little resemblance to the original dull red Scarlet Lake, although some manufacturers still match their versions to the old colour. All the Lake colours, which had a dubious reputation, have been improved, and the word Extra is sometimes added to the name to emphasize the change.

New and inconvenient chemical names are often avoided by makers who invent their own simpler ones. To avoid using the word phthalocyanine, the blues made with it are sold under the names of: Phthalo Blue, Thalo Blue, Winsor Blue, Blockx Blue, Brilliant Blue 2, Cyanin Blue, Helio Blue, Hoggar Blue, Hortensia Blue, Mineral Blue, Monestial Blue, Old Holland Blue, Scheveningen Blue, Blue Lake and Rembrandt Blue. Many colours are also mixtures, varying in composition according to the maker. The impermanent mixtures are currently being replaced by dependable substitutes, and ingredients listed on the labels.

Some useful names to remember are: Permanent White in gouache or watercolour is Titanium White; Chinese White in watercolour is Zinc White; Cremnitz White is a variety of Flake White. Among the greens, Cadmium, Emerald, Hooker's and Permanent Greens are mixtures regularly containing Phthalocyanine Green (also know as Winsor Green etc.) and are strongly influenced by it. The technical books listed under Further Reading, p. 252, give lists of the considerable number of synonyms and alternative names that reflect the continuing history of pigments.

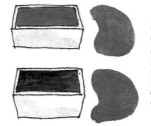

Mixtures of cobalt and aluminium oxides are always COBALT BLUE but Phthalocyanine Blue, made of copper phthalocyanine, PB15, has many names.

New and sometimes inconvenient chemical names are often avoided by makers who invent their own simpler ones.

PERMANENCE TO LIGHT

The ability of a pigment to stand up to light is crucial to its usefulness, and every maker has a system of stars or letters printed on the tubes or wrappings to show permanence. A safer guide is the new ASTM system, detailed below, which some manufacturers already use. The examples give an idea of the dangers to your picture of using colours that fade. Such colours are steadily being replaced as a result of ASTM testing and increasing public awareness, but some still contain unstable pigments.

Traditional Alizarin Crimson, before and after exposure.

The unchanging Permanent Mauve.

The dramatic fading of a fugitive pigment.

A LIST OF INGREDIENTS

The recent testing of pigments by the American Standards of Testing and Materials, (ASTM), is the most thorough and co-ordinated effort to bring order into a confusing field where names live on but ingredients alter.

ASTM tests grade pigments in one of five Categories of light-fastness, or permanence: Category 1 is completely light-proof, 2 is permanent under all normal conditions, 3 is the borderline group where colour should be used with caution, and the use of colours in 4 and 5 should be avoided.

The chart below lists many of the permanent ingredients in use, their colour index names, and their ASTM grading. Many colours have a higher grading in oils and acrylics than in watercolour.

A GUIDE TO COMPOSITION AND PERMANENCE

Paintmakers' colour charts and the paints themselves now supply more information on ingredients, and the ingredients are the best guide to permanence, especially in colours that were fugitive. The guide only works where the Colour Index is given, as the name Arylide covers both safe and unsafe colours and is sometimes labelled as Azo instead. The list concentrates on permanent pigments in common use.

No.	Name	Permanence	No.	Name	Permanence
PY1	Arylide Yellow G	5	PV14	Cobalt phosphate	1
PY1:1	Arylide Yellow G	3	PV15	Ultramarine Violet	1
PY3	Arylide Yellow 10G	2	PV16	Manganese Violet	1
PY31	Barium chromate	1	PV19	Quinacridone Violet	2
PY35	Cadmium zinc sulphide	1	PV23	Dioxazine Purple	4
PY37	Cadmium sulphide	1	PV23:1	Dioxazine Purple special	2
PY40	Cobalt potassium nitrate	2	PV49	Cobalt ammonium phosphate	2
PY42	Synth. iron oxide (Mars Yellow)	1			
PY43	Yellow Ochre	1	PB15	Phthalocyanine Blue	2
PY53	Nickel titanate	2	PB27	Ferri-ammonium ferrocyanide	2
PY53	Diarylide Yellow HR70	1	PB28	Cobalt and aluminium oxides	1
PY97	Arylide Yellow FGL	2	PB29	Ultramarine	1
PY119	Zinc iron oxide	2	PB33	Barium manganate and sulphate	1
PY120	Stable monoazo	2	PB35	Cobalt and tin oxides	1
PY129	Azomethine Yellow	2	PB36	Cobalt, chromium, aluminium oxides	1
PY151	Stable monoazo	2	PB60	Anthraquinone	2
PY153	Nickel dioxine Yellow	1			
PY154	Benzimidazalone Yellow H3G	1	PG7	Phthalocyanine Green	1
PY177	Irgazin Yellow	2	PG17	Chromium sesquioxide	1
			PG18	Hydrated chromium sesquioxide	1
PO20	Cadmium sulpho-selenide	1	PG19	Cobalt and zinc oxides	1
PO36	Benzimidazalone Orange	1	PG23	Green earth	1
PO43	Perinone Orange	1	PG36	Phthalocyanine Green	1
PO49	Quinacridone Deep Gold	1	PG50	Nickel, cobalt, titanium oxides	1
PO62	Benzimidazalone Orange H5G	1			
PO65	Methin Nickel Orange	2	PBr7	Natural iron oxide (Raw Sienna)	1
PO69	Isoindolin	2	PBr7	Iron oxide & manganese (Raw Umber)	1
			PBr7	Burnt Sienna	1
PR83	Dihydroxyanthraquinone (alizarin)	4	PBr7	Burnt Umber	1
PR88	Thioindigoid Violet MRS	1			
PR101	Synth. iron oxide	1			
PR102	Calcined natural iron oxide	1	PW1	Basic lead carbonate	1
PR108	Cadmium seleno-sulphide	1	PW4	Zinc oxide	1
PR122	Quinacridone Magenta	3	PW6	Titanium dioxide	1
PR170	Naphthol Red FR3K-70	2			
PR178	Perylene Red	2	PBk6	Carbon (Lamp Black)	1
PR188	Naphthol AS	1	PBk7	Carbon (carbon black)	1
PR192	Quinacridone Red	1	PBk8	Charcoal	1
PR207	Quinacridone Scarlet	1	PBk9	Carbon (Ivory Black)	1
PR209	Quinacridone Red Y	1	PBk11	Black iron oxide	1

1 is the highest rating for permanence, 5 is the lowest. Oils and acrylics usually rate higher than watercolour

YELLOWS

The bright yellows are dominated by the opaque Cadmium Yellows, which perform satisfactorily in every way. A good variety of semi-transparent yellows is now available. A medium bright yellow is essential in every palette, while a lemon and a deep yellow are both useful additions.

CADMIUM YELLOW

A range of powerful, opaque, and very permanent colours, sold as Cadmium Yellow Light, or (Pale), Medium, and Deep. The Lemon and Orange shades are discussed separately. Each maker has their own idea of the depth of colour that constitutes a particular shade, so there is a slight overlap in the naming. The pigment is cadmium sulphide, in which varying shades correspond to different particle sizes; the lemon shades are the smallest while the particles of the deep shades are up to 50 times bigger. The Cadmium Yellows first became available around 1830, and are among the most satisfactory of all yellows in any medium. Their opacity is seldom a problem in watercolour as they are brushed out so thinly.

Cadmium Yellow Lemon can effectively replace all the Lemon Yellows for strength and brilliance. It is slightly richer in colour and more expensive than the other Lemon Yellows.

Cadmium Yellow Pale

Cadmium Yellow shades vary a little according to who makes them.

If you get paint "everywhere" when working, try to avoid using Cadmium colours as cadmium is poisonous. Health warnings are becoming more widespread on labels.

LEMON YELLOW

An umbrella name for a shade of clear pale yellow tending towards green rather than orange. The original colour, made of barium or strontium nitrate, was weak and opaque with little to recommend it except its permanence, and the usual modern alternative made of Arylide Yellow 10G is superior. Some versions contain the weak pigment nickel titanate, which is a weaker and chalkier colour, more like the original Lemon Yellow. Modern Lemon Yellows combined with Yellow Ochre make a passable medium yellow for those using a very limited palette.

When mixing, the lack of any red or warm-coloured element in the make-up of Lemon Yellow can cause mixtures to appear chalky.

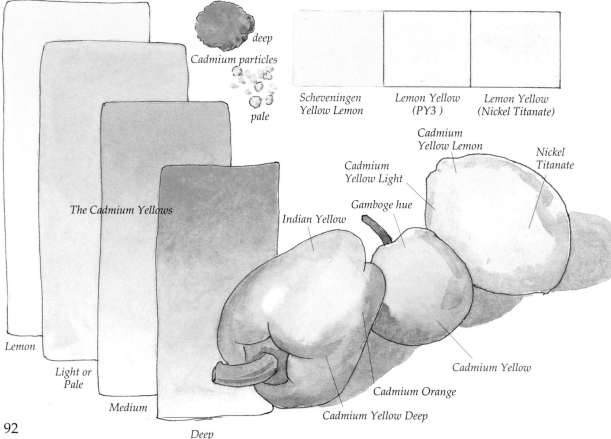

deep

Cadmium particles

pale

The Cadmium Yellows

Lemon

Light or Pale

Medium

Deep

Scheveningen Yellow Lemon

Lemon Yellow (PY3)

Lemon Yellow (Nickel Titanate)

Cadmium Yellow Lemon

Cadmium Yellow Light

Gamboge hue

Indian Yellow

Nickel Titanate

Cadmium Yellow

Cadmium Orange

Cadmium Yellow Deep

Colours that look the same and perform in the same way as Lemon Yellow are Winsor Yellow, Permanent Yellow Light, Chrome Yellow Lemon and Brilliant Yellow I, from Schmincke. Old Holland supply the oil colours Nickel Titanium Yellow and the strongly pigmented Scheveningen Yellow Lemon, which has a slightly greenish cast compared to Cadmium Lemon, which is always an alternative to any of the above, although more expensive.

GAMBOGE

Gamboge is an old colour that was made from lumps of resin collected from species of oriental trees. Genuine Gamboge fades badly, and is usually replaced by substitutes that are often but not always more dependable. The yellow is similar to the medium cadmiums, not quite so bright or strong, but attractive and more transparent. Gamboge by Talens and Gamboge Hue from Rowney in watercolours and Gamboge Lake Extra, an oil from Old Holland, are reliable.

Natural gamboge resin

Gamboge Hue (Rowney) a reliable substitute

INDIAN YELLOW

All available artist's pigments are substitutes for the original colour, whose essential characteristic was a very long range from deep golden yellow right through to a clear pale tone. Derived from the urine of Indian cows fed on mango leaves; the bright yellow urine was concentrated within the cows by depriving them of water, a practice banned since the 1920s. Excellent replacements with a similar range include Indian Yellow by Lukas and the Old Holland oil colours which give a choice of three shades. Old Holland Red Gold Lake is orange at full strength, thinning to a brilliant transparent yellow.

Indian Yellow (Lukas)

Old Holland Red Gold Lake

PERMANENT YELLOW

A number of yellows are sold under this name, which doesn't always mean what it says. Reliable versions are Permanent Yellow Deep (Holbein), and the Lemon and Deep yellows from Maimeri.

Permanent Yellow Lemon (Maimeri)

Permanent Yellow Deep (Holbein)

CHROME YELLOW

The Chrome Yellows equal the Cadmiums in possessing an attractive and pleasing range of colours, from lemon to orange, but are not always reliably permanent except where reliable ingredients have been substituted. True Chrome Yellows are made of basic lead chromates, so especially in watercolour, where the pigment is less protected, hydrogen sulphide in the air reacts with the lead to blacken it, progressively changing the yellow to green. Chromes are more permanent in oils where the pigment grains are protected by the coating of oil. Chrome Yellows were introduced around 1815.

Only one watercolour, Chrome Yellow Lemon, from Schmincke is currently reliable because there is no genuine Chrome Yellow in it.

Light   Middle   Deep

Chrome Yellows are bright but mostly unsafe.

Indian Yellow

AUREOLIN

At full strength Aureolin looks rather like mustard, but on dilution reveals itself as a clear bright transparent yellow, somewhat on the sharp side. Also known as Cobalt Yellow, it is permanent, and was introduced around 1850. It is more often made up as a watercolour than an oil.

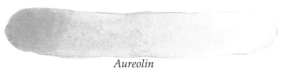

Aureolin

MISCELLANEOUS YELLOWS

Many yellows are given special brand names by their manufacturers; the colours sometimes duplicate the range of the Cadmiums as an economical alternative, and some are different from all other yellows. In each case their permanence should be checked from the maker's own grading system or by looking up the ingredients.

The four Scheveningen Yellows, oils from Old Holland, parallel the cadmiums in range. Yellow Medium Azo is a brilliant transparent yellow from Liquitex; Greenish Yellow from Holbein is like a strong greenish ochre at full strength, brightening considerably on dilution in a similar way to the more luminous Aureolin. Their Yellow Grey, (see also under Mars Yellow), is a softer colour. Stil de Grain (Maimeri) is another greenish yellow.

Aureolin (Holbein)	*Yellow Medium Azo (Liquitex, acrylic PY74)*	*Greenish Yellow (Holbein)*

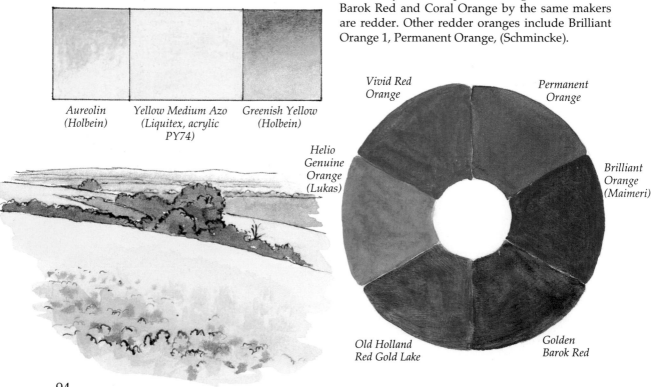

ORANGE

Orange is an infrequent colour in paintings; there is little call for it as a ready-made colour, but a number of reliable oranges are offered, shading from almost yellow to almost scarlet. Bright orange is a difficult colour to mix from the average red and yellow, so a tube could be useful.

CADMIUM ORANGE

Cadmium Orange, in a variety of shades, is sold by all makers. It has the sound qualities of the other Cadmiums including their opacity. Cadmium Orange Light and Cadmium Yellow Orange are the yellowest, Cadmium Red Orange is almost as red as Cadmium Red Light.

Cadmium Orange

MISCELLANEOUS ORANGES

The oranges mentioned below are among the permanent examples.

Chrome Orange (Schmincke) is a true medium orange, contains no chrome and is completely dependable. Helio Genuine Orange from Lukas uses the same pigment. Brilliant Orange from Maimeri employs a transparent pigment perinone, PO 43. Vivid Orange Red is a brilliant medium orange acrylic from Liquitex. Old Holland Red Gold Lake is a bright yellowish orange that becomes yellower upon thinning while Golden Barok Red and Coral Orange by the same makers are redder. Other redder oranges include Brilliant Orange 1, Permanent Orange, (Schmincke).

Vivid Red Orange

Permanent Orange

Helio Genuine Orange (Lukas)

Brilliant Orange (Maimeri)

Old Holland Red Gold Lake

Golden Barok Red

NAPLES YELLOW AND THE EARTH YELLOWS

Naples Yellow is a soft creamy yellow often listed in colour charts separately from the bright yellows, and with a different usefulness to an artist. The colour range grades naturally into the Yellow Ochre and its related ochres (there are a considerable number, which will be considered as a group), which in turn grades through intermediate colours into the Earth Reds.

The paler creamy yellows are valuable in mixtures for softening the brashness of other colours. They make interesting mixtures with browns and violets, and are also useful as ingredients for flesh colours. The simple mixture of White and Yellow Ochre gives a yellower colour than Naples.

NAPLES YELLOW

The name represents a range of warm creamy colours, valuable in all mediums, and supplied by some makers in alternative shades. This ancient colour, originally manufactured in Naples, was poisonous in its original form of lead antimoniate, so modern versions, strictly Naples Yellow Hues, are mixtures of great variety often containing cadmium yellow and white with a synthetic (Mars) earth colour. They dilute well to give a hint of warmth for sunny white surfaces. Old Holland Yellows in three shades are similar, also Unbleached Titanium, (Liquitex).

JAUNE BRILLANT

Jaune Brillant, (occasionally called Brilliant Yellow), is usually a slightly pinker variety of Naples Yellow and is variable, according to the maker.

Jaune Brillant (Schmincke)

FLESH TINT

Flesh Tint is another mixture varying a great deal. Try comparing the colour from a maker's colour chart with your own skin if in doubt over its usefulness. Liquitex call their colour Light Portrait Pink.

Flesh Tint (Winsor & Newton)

YELLOW OCHRE

Ochre is a sort of gritty clay, coloured naturally with hydrated iron oxide. The brightest sorts come from the south of France, and the pigment can be obtained in a number of colour varieties, in spite of which some "Yellow Ochres" contain Mars Yellow instead. A valuable semi-transparent colour in all mediums, but especially in tempera where it can serve as the principle yellow.

Gold and Golden Ochres are usually deeper and redder varieties of Yellow Ochre, sometimes combined with other pigments. A darker form of Yellow Ochre is used by itself in the Gold Ochres from Blockx, Talens and Yellow Ochre Half Burnt, (Old Holland). Sennelier's Stone Gall is a deep Yellow Ochre. All are permanent.

Naples Yellow

Naples Yellow, Reddish

Yellow Ochre (Schmincke)

Yellow

Naples Yellow

Jaune Brillant

Gold Ochre

Naples Yellow, Reddish

95

MARS YELLOW

The pure iron oxides that pigment the earth colours were synthesised in the 1950s, and are frequently used as alternatives to the natural colours; they are just as permanent. Mars Yellow is a powerful, usually glowing colour, brighter than Yellow Ochre, and its colour varies according to manufacturer. A number of watercolour Yellow Ochres are made from Mars Yellow, and the only watercolour named as Mars Yellow, from Sennelier, consists chiefly of Yellow Ochre. Mars Yellow is sold under its own name in oils, but seldom in watercolour. Transparent Yellow Oxides are usually varieties of Mars Yellow, while Yellow Grey, (Holbein), is Mars Yellow mixed with Black and White.

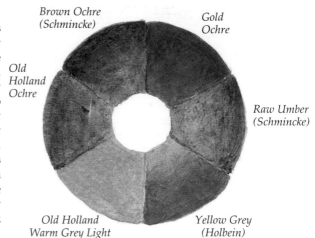

Brown Ochre (Schmincke)

Gold Ochre

Old Holland Ochre

Raw Umber (Schmincke)

Old Holland Warm Grey Light

Yellow Grey (Holbein)

Mars Yellow

Italian Earth (Old Holland)

Raw Sienna

Raw Sienna (Winsor & Newton)

RAW SIENNA

A natural earth consisting of hydrated iron oxide and silica, taking its name from Sienna in Italy, the source of some of the best colour. It is browner, darker and more transparent than Yellow Ochre, and not a strong colour in mixtures. It is absolutely permanent. Surprisingly few makers employ the genuine pigment in watercolour, only Maimeri, Liquitex, Schmincke and Old Holland, all the others currently using a darker variety of Yellow Ochre instead.

OTHER YELLOWS AND BROWNS

A number of light to medium brown colours are based on varieties of Ochre, Sienna or similar pigments, such as Italian Earth (Old Holland), yellower and brighter, Old Holland Ochre, which is dark enough at full strength to count as a brown, and Brown Ochre Light (Old Holland), which is redder.

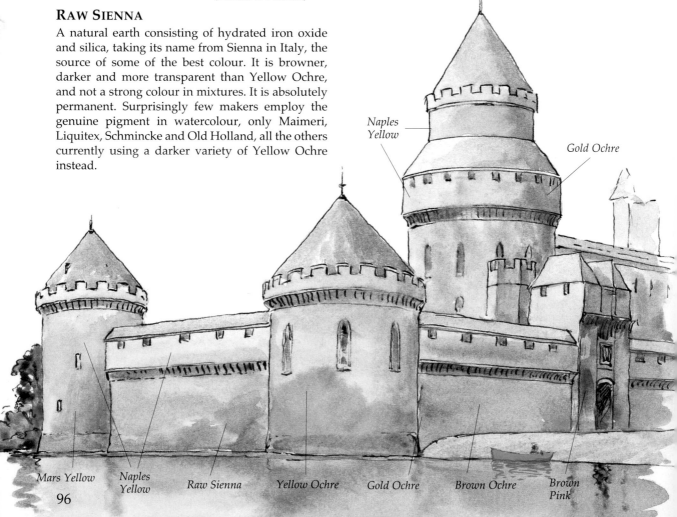

Naples Yellow

Gold Ochre

Mars Yellow   *Naples Yellow*   *Raw Sienna*   *Yellow Ochre*   *Gold Ochre*   *Brown Ochre*   *Brown Pink*

BROWNS

There is no clear-cut boundary between the Yellows and the Browns because there is a continuous range of colours between them; the dividing lines between yellows, browns and earth-reds are matters of individual preference and convenience. Browns are traditionally earth colours, and few in number, although Old Holland supply a comprehensive range in oils.

RAW UMBER

A natural earth containing manganese in addition to iron oxides, silica and clay. Widely found in Europe and America, it is one of the most variable of all colours, ranging from greenish-brown shades to those of a warmer brown. The manganese in Umbers makes them into very quick driers, which in addition to the suitability of the colour, has made them important for underpainting in oils. It is a very strong dark colour in oils, but unbelievably different in watercolour, often gummy and weak. The manganese makes Umbers toxic. Similar browns include Old Holland's Brown Ochre Deep.

Raw Umber – oil (Winsor & Newton)

Raw Umber – watercolour (Winsor & Newton)

BURNT UMBER

A distinctly reddish brown made by strongly heating Raw Umber until the desired colour is attained. A fast dryer in all mediums, especially in watercolour where pans are prone to harden, and makes good darks mixed with Ultramarine. Burnt Green Earth from Schmincke is a selected shade of Burnt Umber.

Similar browns include Deep Ochre, and Red Umber, (Old Holland), which is much redder.

Burnt Umber

Red Umber

Transparent Brown (Blockx)

VANDYKE BROWN

The original colour was a rich deep transparent brown derived from a bituminous soft coal containing unstable organic ingredients that later faded to a greyer shade. Reliable replacements are made by Talens, Liquitex, Old Holland, Schmincke. Transparent Brown, Blockx, is similar.

Vandyke Brown (Schmincke)

SEPIA

The original Sepia was the ink of the cuttlefish, *Sepia officinalis*, said to be capable of blackening 100 gallons of sea-water within seconds. The brown-black ink fades in the light to the well-known gingery colour sometimes described as sepia. The modern versions are nearly always mixtures of permanent colours such as Burnt Sienna with Lamp Black.

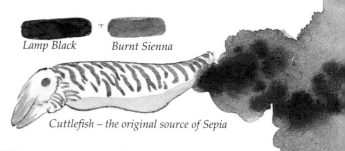

Lamp Black   +   *Burnt Sienna*

Cuttlefish – the original source of Sepia

MISCELLANEOUS BROWNS

Mars Brown is a strong red-brown, redder than Burnt Umber, and available in oils only. Old Holland Ochre is a medium brown, similar to Brown Ochre Light from Blockx. Lukas's Burnt Green Earth is a warmer and stronger mixed brown, more like Burnt Umber in appearance, and Burnt Umber is the pigment used in Schmincke's Burnt Green Earth.

Bitume (Asphalte) from Sennelier is another permanent yellow-brown, unfortunately named after a notorious non-drying pigment.

Deep Ochre (Old Holland)   *Mars Brown*

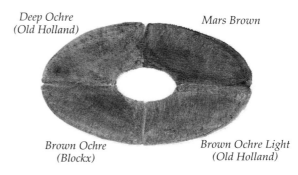

Brown Ochre (Blockx)   *Brown Ochre Light (Old Holland)*

EARTH REDS

Great confusion surrounds the naming of this group because most of the colours are very similar but the names are many and various.

The names of the places where the colours originated have become labels for particular shades, which may be made up either from natural earths or from synthetic iron oxides. The synthetic colours are just as good as the natural ones, and any colours within the group may be bought with complete confidence, so you can choose which you like according to your preference.

The main colouring agents of the earth reds are the range of ferric (iron) oxides, Fe_2O_3. The hydrous iron oxides, familiar as rust, include water molecules in their structure, and these provide the yellower and warm red colours. Anhydrous oxide, without water, is a dark purple brown, and is the basis of the dark reds. Pure iron oxides of excellent quality are easy to manufacture, so most of these pigments are now produced synthetically, and sometimes include calcium sulphate as an extender with little loss of colouring power. They are all very strong, opaque and completely permanent.

Each maker produces a range which is a selection of the colours they think most useful. They may differ slightly in their ideas of what any particular colour looks like, and sometimes use different ingredients for the oil and watercolour versions of the same colour.

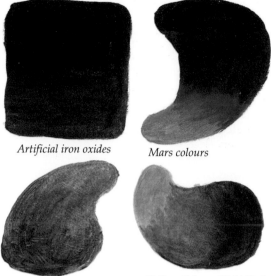

Artificial iron oxides *Mars colours*

Sienna *Yellow Ochre – Light Red*

The effect of strongly heating yellow earth colours.

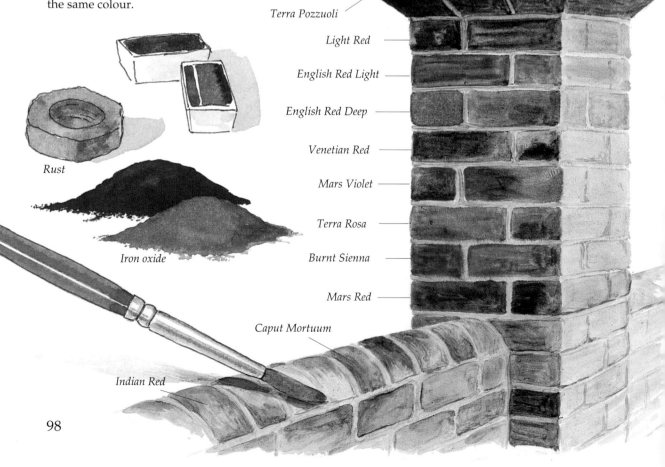

Terra Pozzuoli

Light Red

English Red Light

English Red Deep

Venetian Red

Mars Violet

Terra Rosa

Burnt Sienna

Mars Red

Caput Mortuum

Indian Red

Rust

Iron oxide

IRON OXIDE REDS

ENGLISH RED

A bright brick red, with middle and light tones tending towards the pink, sometimes available in Light or Deep shades. This is the most frequent red on the continent, but English manufacturers supply the slightly yellower Light Red. Red Oxide is very close to English Red, and is an acrylic colour from Liquitex. Light Red Oxide, an Alkyd oil colour, is also very close.

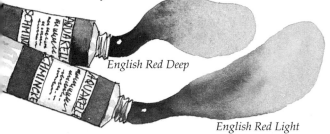

English Red Deep

English Red Light

VENETIAN RED

One step darker than the preceding colours, but otherwise very similar and one of the most popular Earth Reds. Originally a natural pigment found near Venice, but a now synthetic iron oxide, Mars Red, with calcium sulphate.

POZZUOLI EARTH

Traditionally the pinkest of the reds, it is sometimes not quite so bright and also a little darker. It was originally a natural volcanic earth from the Naples area. The current Pozzuoli Earths are made with synthetic iron oxides.

MARS RED

The Mars colours are the standard synthetic iron oxides, produced in successively deeper shades by heating Mars Yellow until the desired end colour is reached (see panel opposite). Mars Red is the colour frequently used for Venetian Red and Pozzuoli Earth, and therefore almost identical to them, but it can produce slightly darker tones at full strength.

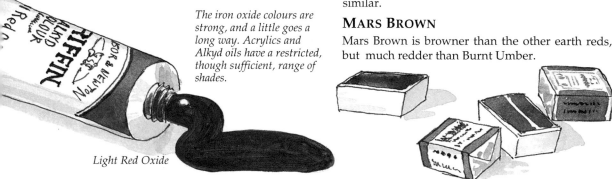

The iron oxide colours are strong, and a little goes a long way. Acrylics and Alkyd oils have a restricted, though sufficient, range of shades.

Light Red Oxide

CALCINED RED OXIDES

These colours are very similar to the previous group in appearance, but are derived from natural ingredients, some of which contain clay or silica as well as iron. Intense heat darkens and reddens the initial colour. Their lighter tones tend more towards the orange rather than pink.

LIGHT RED

The best-known variety of this group. It is an ancient colour, produced by heating Yellow Ochre. It is powerful, opaque and absolutely permanent. The principal colouring agent is natural hydrated iron oxide with clay and silica. Burnt Light Ochre and Red Ochre are similar.

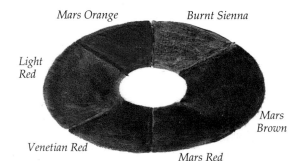

Mars Orange *Burnt Sienna*

Light Red

Mars Brown

Venetian Red

Mars Red

MARS ORANGE

The first stage of heating Mars Yellow produces the most inclined to orange of the Mars colours, and is one of the lightest in tone of the earth reds. It is redder than Burnt Sienna, but can replace it in oils where its opacity is useful. Brown Ochre, (Blockx), and Brown Ochre Light, (Old Holland), are yellower than Mars Orange, between orange and red-brown in colour.

BURNT SIENNA

A very variable colour, made by roasting Raw Sienna until the desired colour is obtained. The best versions possess a fiery red-brown colour and the colour is indispensable in watercolour for its transparency. Red Brown from Sennelier is a mixture of mainly synthetic red oxide and a little natural Sienna and Yellow Ochre. Transparent Oxide Red is made from synthetic materials but is similar.

MARS BROWN

Mars Brown is browner than the other earth reds, but much redder than Burnt Umber.

DARK RED IRON OXIDES

A distinct group of darker colours tending towards the violet and blue. They all contain high proportions of the dark anhydrous iron oxides.

INDIAN RED

This is the most common of the dark red earths. A strong and useful colour in mixtures for dark tones; it is notably darker than English or Venetian Red, and reduces towards a dusky dull pink in thinner washes or layers. Persian Red is a natural red oxide of similar colour, from Old Holland.

MARS VIOLET

An intense dark colour slightly bluer than Indian Red, intermediate between this and the following colour. The violet comes out strongly in mixtures with White. It is especially useful in tempera to give strength and depth to the darks.

CAPUT MORTUUM

The darkest colour of this range, an intense dark violet-brown, slightly bluer and darker than Indian Red. It is very useful in making up dark mixtures and makes attractive violet-browns in mixture with White. The curious name recalls its early mediaeval origins when a pigment of similar colour was believed to be extracted from dead heads.

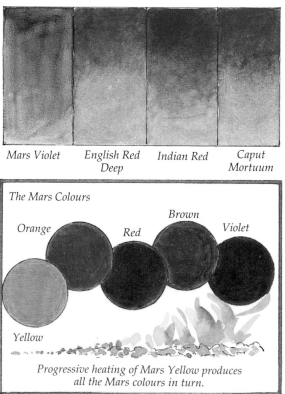

Mars Violet   English Red   Indian Red   Caput
Deep   Mortuum

The Mars Colours

Orange   Red   Brown   Violet

Yellow

Progressive heating of Mars Yellow produces all the Mars colours in turn.

REDS

A large number of reds are offered to painters in a bewildering combination of names and ingredients, of which a number are impermanent. The most important bright red, except in watercolour, is still the reliable Cadmium Red in its many varieties. For the dark reds there are practical replacements for the doubtfully permanent Alizarin Crimson, so some alternatives are suggested, but they may not be available everywhere.

CADMIUM RED

A very useful basic red for your collection, coming in a long range of shades. Especially good in all mediums except watercolour where their heavy opacity dulls their effect. Cadmium Red Light and Cadmium Red Orange are inclined towards the orange and Cadmium Scarlet is slightly redder. Cadmium Red itself is usually a deeper colour than expected at full strength. Cadmium Red Deep and Cadmium Red Purple are darker and more subtle. These colours are made from the red cadmium seleno-sulphides and first became available around 1910.

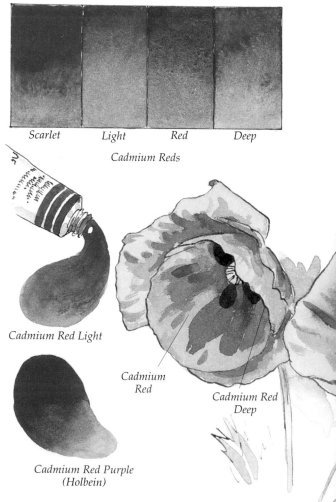

Scarlet   Light   Red   Deep

Cadmium Reds

Cadmium Red Light

Cadmium Red

Cadmium Red Deep

*Cadmium Red Purple
(Holbein)*

SCARLET LAKE

The original Scarlet Lake was a rather dull red, and a wide variety of reds is still sold under this name, almost all of which will fade. The exception is the excellent Winsor & Newton colour, a fine bright red made from the permanent pigment, Naphthol AS, (PR188). In watercolour its clarity and brightness is superior to the heavier-looking Cadmium Red. A surprisingly clear pink results from dilution with water. In oils the mixture of white can affect the permanence of considerably thinned colour. Old Holland's Scheveningen Red Light uses the same pigment. They also make the darker Scarlet Lake Extra.

VERMILION

The traditional bright red has been in use from the earliest times when it was discovered as a naturally occurring mineral in the form of cinnabar. True Vermilion, red mercuric sulphide, is now manufactured, but after Genuine Ultramarine, Vermilion is by a long way the most expensive of all pigments, while its occasional tendency to partially mutate into its black form makes it risky to use. Few makers now supply it in its original form. There are excellent substitutes in Cadmium Scarlet or Cadmium Red. In colours labelled as Vermilion, those by Liquitex and Holbein and Old Holland contain reliable alternative pigments.

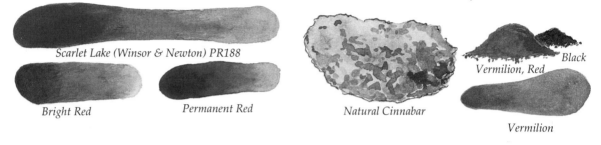

Scarlet Lake (Winsor & Newton) PR188

Bright Red   *Permanent Red*

Natural Cinnabar

Vermilion, Red   *Black*

Vermilion

PERMANENT RED

An umbrella name for a range of fairly bright orange-reds, by no means all permanent. New Permanent Reds by Schmincke and Maimeri are reliable replacements for less dependable colours.

MISCELLANEOUS BRIGHT REDS

There are a considerable number of bright reds made from modern organic pigments, mostly unreliable, but the new Winsor Red is safe to use.

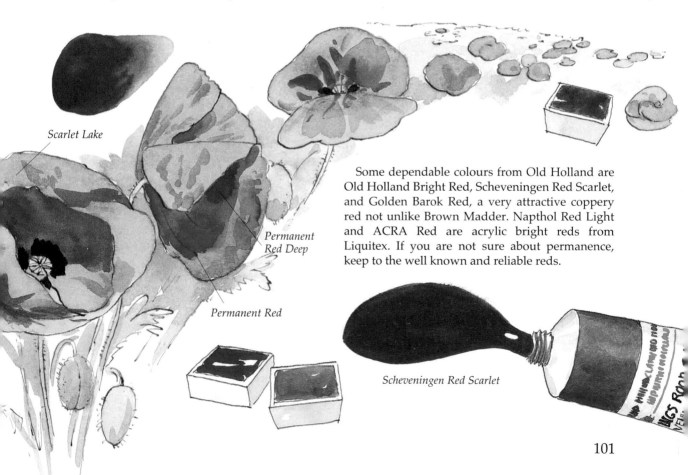

Scarlet Lake

Permanent Red Deep

Permanent Red

Some dependable colours from Old Holland are Old Holland Bright Red, Scheveningen Red Scarlet, and Golden Barok Red, a very attractive coppery red not unlike Brown Madder. Napthol Red Light and ACRA Red are acrylic bright reds from Liquitex. If you are not sure about permanence, keep to the well known and reliable reds.

Scheveningen Red Scarlet

ALIZARIN CRIMSON

Since its discovery in 1826 Alizarin has become the standard crimson, but has recently has failed the ASTM tests for light-fastness in watercolour and acrylic, and is in the borderline Category 3 for oils. It is safest when used strongly, but in spite of its advantages as a strong dark red, it is better to replace it if you can with more reliable pigments.

This watercolour sample was kept on a windowsill for 11 months, with the left side covered, so was subjected to much stronger light than usual. However this only speeded up the natural processes which would still take their course. The lighter tones fade and become duller more quickly than the darks.

ALTERNATIVES TO ALIZARIN CRIMSON

Single colours based on quinacridone are Permanent Alizarin Crimsons from Winsor & Newton and Liquitex, Alizarin Crimson Lake Extra, from Old Holland, Ruby Lake Deep from Schmincke, and Talens's Rose Madder, all transparent violet-reds. Old Holland offer several other permanent dark reds. Brown Madder from Holbein is the only currently light-fast Brown Madder, and is yellower than the true crimsons.

ROSE MADDER

The genuine pigment came into prominence in the 17th century, and is mainly alizarin extracted from the roots of the madder plant. It is prone to fading, so a permanent pigment, Quinacridone Violet, (PV19), replaces it in reliable versions.

CARMINE

Paints containing the genuine ingredient, cochineal, fade with amazing speed, as do the Crimson and Purple Lakes derived from the same source. Liquitex and Schmincke make reliable Carmines.

PERMANENT ROSE

This replaces all the romantic but impermanent old colours like Rose Madder and Madder Lake. In flower painting it is indispensable as the only pink bright enough to approach a common colour in flowers. Introduced in the 1950's, this Quinacridone Red, PV19, is the brightest of them all.

Permanent Rose PV19

MISCELLANEOUS PINK REDS

The brilliant violet-pinks are nearly all unreliable. Madder Lake Light from Talens is a reliable pinker variety of their Rose Madder. Winsor & Newton's Rose Doré is a mixed soft colour suitable for some flowers. Rose Doré is a rather weak colour. If possible, check the ingredients of colours you are not sure of. Many are made with the organic chemicals called quinacridones.

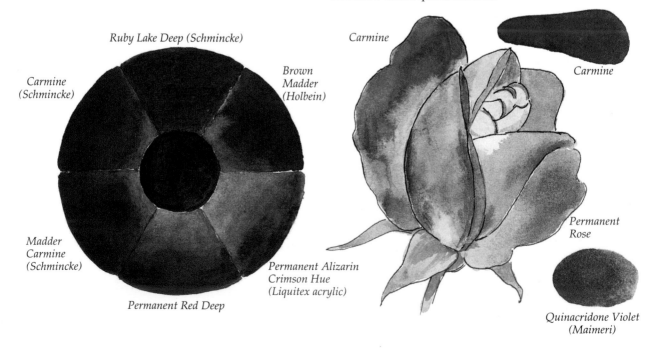

Ruby Lake Deep (Schmincke)

Carmine (Schmincke)

Brown Madder (Holbein)

Carmine

Carmine

Madder Carmine (Schmincke)

Permanent Alizarin Crimson Hue (Liquitex acrylic)

Permanent Red Deep

Permanent Rose

Quinacridone Violet (Maimeri)

VIOLETS

The more brilliant and attractive the colour in this section, the less likely it is to be permanent, so care is needed in selection. Single colours are nearly always brighter than mixtures, but only flower painters normally need these. Manufacturers are working to improve the range and permanence of violets.

PERMANENT MAGENTA

A useful strong colour made with quinacridone. It is not brilliant in colour and can appear heavy. In mixtures it can help to replace Alizarin Crimson.

Permanent Magenta PV19

COBALT VIOLET

A red-violet, clear and permanent, but weak, grainy and gummy in watercolour; it is more satisfactory in oils, but expensive if genuine. Sennelier and Maimeri supply reliable substitutes.

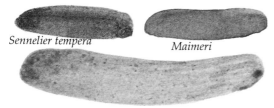

Sennelier tempera   *Maimeri*

Cobalt Violet – genuine (Winsor & Newton)

PERMANENT MAUVE

This is made with a pigment called Manganese Violet, PV16, and the only colour labelled as a "mauve" that is light-fast, Permanent Mauve is a very satisfactory colour for flower painting, although not very strong or dark. Sennelier's Mineral Violet also employs the same pigment.

Permanent Mauve PV16

VIOLET ULTRAMARINE

Ultramarine comes in a wide range of shades, and further chemical treatment produces the redder shades; the reddest of these just tend towards the violet, and are so labelled by a few makers. They are very permanent. Holbein's Mineral Violet is made of Ultramarine, and a redder version of the same is Lukas's Ultramarine Red.

MISCELLANEOUS VIOLETS

Paint makers are gradually replacing fugitive materials with more dependable pigments while retaining the well-known names for convenience, but currently only a few have been proved to be permanent.

A number of popular and attractive Violets contain Dioxazine Violet, a borderline pigment for permanence if used thickly, but less reliable as a tint.

Reliable violets are mostly based on the preceding pigments.

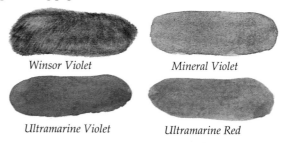

Winsor Violet   *Mineral Violet*

Ultramarine Violet   *Ultramarine Red*

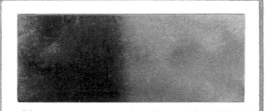

Mauve, a strong attractive colour, with the left half protected from the light, faded dramatically in just two weeks; the red component almost disappeared, leaving a dull permanent blue. Many violets are prone to fading, especially in watercolour.

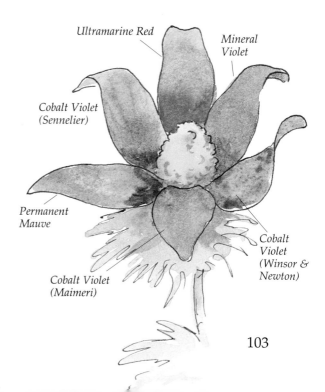

Ultramarine Red

Mineral Violet

Cobalt Violet (Sennelier)

Permanent Mauve

Cobalt Violet (Winsor & Newton)

Cobalt Violet (Maimeri)

BLUES

The most useful and popular Blues are very permanent and fine colours. It is convenient to divide them into the "warm" blues, represented by Ultramarine, and the "cool", or green blues like Prussian or Phthalocyanine Blue. Phthalocyanine is the name of a powerful pigment, and is the chief ingredient of many mixed blues and greens.

ULTRAMARINE

Genuine Ultramarine, spreading into Europe after 1200 AD, is extracted from the semi-precious stone lapis lazuli by chemical precipitation, so the price has always been very high. The first extraction brought out the deepest and best colour, each further repetition giving a lighter colour, ending with the pale Ultramarine Ash. The greater transparency of the ground crystals of genuine Ultramarine is one difference between it and the more powdery and intense, but chemically matching, artificial Ultramarine, discovered in France around 1830. This is a sodium aluminium silicate with some sulphur, giving a range of blues and violets. Ultramarines, from Schmincke, Rowney and Lukas, are among the most beautiful, but all are attractive and completely permanent. Some, but not all Ultramarines, settle out in watercolour to give a grainy effect.

Paler Ultramarines are available under different names such as New Blue; King's Blue and Royal Blue are Ultramarines with White.

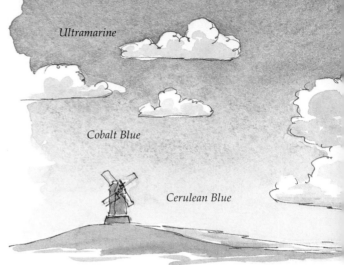

Ultramarine

Cobalt Blue

Cerulean Blue

COBALT BLUE

This bright medium blue pigment is a combination of cobalt and aluminium oxides. It is completely permanent, and is a fast dryer in oils and tempera. It has a clearer colour than Ultramarine and a suggestion of comparative greenness is valued in it. Deep and Light versions are sometimes offered, and different makers' versions of Cobalt Blue also vary in strength and brightness. Like the other colours based on metals, such as the Cadmiums and Cerulean Blue, it is expensive. It was introduced in 1802 in France.

Some Cobalt Blues settle out into a grainy texture on rougher watercolour papers, while others tend to retain the shapes of the brush-strokes, making them tricky to use for smooth skies.

Ultramarine (Lukas) PB29

Cobalt Blue PB28

Ultramarine (Lascaux acrylic)

Cobalt Blue Light

Ultramarine Violet PV15

Ultramarine

Cobalt Blue

The two Blues mixed with Permanent (Titanium) White.

The brilliant blues of the peacock need clear shades to match them.

Phthalocyanine Blue

Manganese Blue

PHTHALOCYANINE BLUE

Alternative names:

Thalo Blue, Winsor Blue, Blockx Blue, Brilliant Blue, Helio Blue, Mineral Blue, Monestial Blue, Old Holland Blue, Scheveningen Blue, Blue Lake, and Rembrandt Blue.

Many makers avoid the chemical name, copper phthalocyanine, pronounced simply "thalo-cyanine". It is a rich colour, available in varying shades, inclined slightly more towards the green than the red. Phthalocyanine Blue was discovered in the 1930s, since when it has tended to supersede the older Prussian Blue. It is transparent, permanent, and the strongest of all colours for tinting strength in mixtures. It is an ingredient of numerous mixed colours, and mixtures with white bring out its tendency towards green.

Phthalocyanine Blue   PB15

PRUSSIAN BLUE

A somewhat greenish blue, very powerful and transparent, almost with a suggestion of greyness compared to Phthalocyanine Blue. It consists of ferric ferrocyanide and was first produced in 1704 in the Prussian city of Berlin. A very finely divided pigment that can stain hogshair brushes. Doubts have been expressed about its permanence but it is perfectly reliable.

Paris Blue and Milori Blue are names of good grades. A paler variety is called Antwerp Blue.

Prussian Blue PB27

CERULEAN BLUE

A bright and permanent blue with a suggestion of green, useful for skies, especially in oil painting. The expensive pigment is a combination of the oxides of cobalt and tin. In some watercolour versions it settles out into the grain of the paper, producing a speckled appearance. The colour was introduced in 1820. Cerulean Blue from Sennelier and Cerulean Blue Tone from Schmincke are bright mixtures of Phthalocyanine and White.

Cerulean Blue PB35   *Manganese Blue PB33*

MANGANESE BLUE

Manganese Blue is like Cerulean, but brighter, greener and much more transparent. It was introduced around 1910, and is most effective in tempera. In watercolour it is weak in colour.

INDIGO

Originally a dark blue dye extracted from Indigofera plants in India. Natural Indigo fades, so it is currently prepared from mixtures of more light-fast modern pigments. Rowney make a colour that replaces it well, and Old Holland supply the warmer Old Delft Blue.

Indigo (Rowney)

Old Delft Blue (Old Holland)

MISCELLANEOUS BLUES

A number of blues are mixtures. A few permanent bright blues, such as Zürich and Brilliant Blue, contain a small proportion of White.

Mountain Blue (Schmincke)

Zürich Blue (Sax)

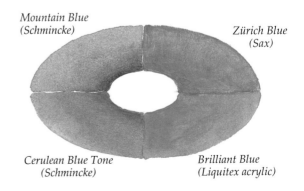

Cerulean Blue Tone (Schmincke)

Brilliant Blue (Liquitex acrylic)

GREENS

Most permanent green pigments tend towards clear blue-greens that need the addition of other colours before use. A considerable number of ready-mixed Greens are also available, but not all are permanent although manufacturers are steadily improving their ingredients. The word "permanent" on the label doesn't always mean what it says. The most useful greens in practice are the few Olive, Golden, and Sap Greens that are permanent mixtures.

OXIDE OF CHROMIUM

A very permanent and opaque dull green, never very dark, but a powerful force in mixtures. Useful in small amounts, but it can look heavy if painted thickly. Introduced around 1860, this colour is also sold as Lamoriniere Green by Blockx.

Oxide of Chromium

VIRIDIAN

A clear brilliant transparent green, requiring discretion in its use, but very useful occasionally in small amounts. Viridian is the same chemical as oxide of chromium, but incorporating a water molecule in its crystals, making it transparent and much brighter than the former. Viridian has been available since 1830. Emerald Green from Blockx is made of Viridian.

Viridian PG 18

EMERALD GREEN

This is a colour name for a pale bright green, nearly always based on Viridian or Phthalocyanine Green. The original pigment, discovered in 1814, was one of the few that were genuinely dangerous as it contained arsenic: true Emerald Green is no longer sold.

Winsor Emerald

COBALT GREEN

A light sea-green, opaque and permanent, but weak as a watercolour, introduced around 1850. Schmincke and Holbein substitute opaque and bright mixtures which are more amenable to handling.

Cobalt Green (Holbein)

PHTHALOCYANINE GREEN

Alternative names:

Thalo Green, Phthalo Green, Winsor Green (Blue and Yellow shades), Blockx Green, Helio Genuine Green Deep, Monestial Green, Scheveningen Green Deep.

The pigment is chlorinated copper phthalocyanine, PG7, (a shortened form of Pigment Green no.7). It is completely permanent and was introduced in 1938. The colour is rather like Viridian, but much more powerful and intense. There is a range of shades, some slightly yellower, some bluer. Although very transparent, its sheer strength gives it good covering power, but it is most useful in small amounts, either to make olive greens in mixtures with colours like Burnt Sienna, or in combination with a bright yellow to brighten over-dull greens. Phthalocyanine Green also appears as Emerald Green from Lukas and Sennelier. Warm Green Imitation is a slightly yellower variety, (PG36), of the same pigment. Phthalocyanine Green is a component of many mixed greens.

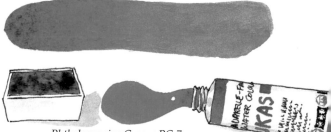

Phthalocyanine Greens PG 7

GREEN EARTH (TERRE VERTE)

Green earths are all permanent, coming in a very wide variety of colouring. They are relatively dull and weak but these qualities make them especially suitable in oil painting for modelling the flesh tones in figures and portraits, providing neutral shadows in combination with the pink flesh tones. Genuine Green Earth makes a very poor and thin watercolour pigment, so is often bolstered with more manageable colours, but these change the colour as well; the most pleasing to use are the mixtures without genuine Green Earth such as Holbein's.

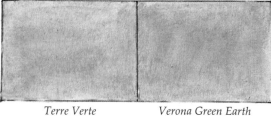

Terre Verte
(Winsor & Newton)   *Verona Green Earth*
(Schmincke)

Natural green earth (Terre Verte, PG 23) is a weak colour. Small amounts of stronger greens are often added to manufactured paints.

SOME OTHER MIXED GREENS

Permanent Green is the name for a range of made-up cool greens, based on Phthalocyanine Green or Viridian, and mostly permanent. Cadmium Green is a light bright and permanent mixture of Cadmium Yellow with either Viridian or Phthalocyanine Green. Hooker's Greens in permanent versions are made by Talens and Schmincke, (Hooker's Green 2). Prussian Green is a strong, almost metallic blue-green, in a reliable version from Liquitex. Other strong blue-greens are Talens Green and Brilliant Green 2, (Schmincke).

Distinctly yellow-greens include Green Gold (Winsor & Newton), Yellowish Green (Talens), Cinnabar Green Pale Extra (Old Holland), and Holbein's Green Grey, which is opaque.

Check the ingredients of mixed greens if you can.

Cadmium Green Deep

Cadmium Green Light

Brilliant Yellow Green (Liquitex acrylic)

Cinnabar Green Deep (Schmincke)

Golden Green (Roberson)

Genuine Emerald Green doubled as an effective insecticide called Paris green.

It was also effective on people.

Greenish Yellow (Holbein)

OLIVE GREEN

In oils, Roberson and Old Holland supply strong dark colours, only just green, but very valuable in giving depth to your own green mixtures. In watercolour, Winsor & Newton's version is the only completely permanent one currently available, but is not a strong colour.

Roberson

Olive Greens

Winsor & Newton

SAP GREEN

An attractive mixed bright green colour, only a few of which are permanent. Reliable versions currently come from Liquitex, Talens, Winsor & Newton and Blockx. Sap Green was originally made from a fugitive dye extracted from buckthorn berries.

Permanent Sap Green (Liquitex acrylic)

A very wide range of mixed greens is available. Check for permanence if possible.

BLACKS

All the blacks are effectively permanent and the minor differences between them show up best in mixture with White and where the binding medium is least obtrusive, such as in egg tempera. Black was used by Titian, Rubens and the other Old Masters in combination with white lead, (Flake White), for tonal underpainting, and also for glazing deep shadows.

IVORY BLACK

The most intense and popular black, a little warmer than Lamp Black. It doesn't flow very freely in watercolour and dries with a slightly uneven finish. Slow drying in oils, where it can now be avoided by using Mars Black instead; however, it should never be used so thickly as to cause this problem. Nowadays it is made by charring bones, rather than ivory which is no longer available.

LAMP BLACK

Lamp Black is nearly pure carbon, collected as the soot from an oily flame. A strong reliable pigment giving a fine pearly grey in watercolour, where it dries more smoothly and attractively than Ivory Black.

SPINEL BLACK

A new and expensive Black, only available as a pigment. Somewhat transparent, but builds up to make the most intense of Blacks. Shows a cool violet tinge in mixture with Titanium White. Well suited to tempera, as it mixes well with water, unlike most other blacks.

MARS BLACK

A dense and opaque black consisting of synthetic black iron oxide, and completely reliable. Sold as Mars Black in oils and acrylic, but in watercolour available as Neutral Tint from Rowney.

OTHER BLACKS

Peach Black used to be made from burnt peach or almond stones, but is now a mixture of other blacks. Vine Black is a colder mixture of Black and Blue. Blue Black is also a mixture. These colours are listed by a few makers and are generally reliable.

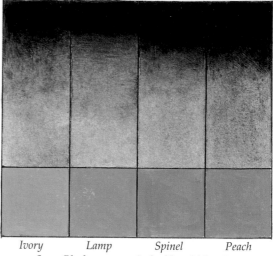

| Ivory | Lamp | Spinel | Peach |

Some Blacks, progressively diluted (above),
and mixed with White (below).

GREYS

Most of the Greys are almost indistinguishable at full strength from the Blacks as they are usually mixed colours containing a preponderance of black.

PAYNE'S GRAY

Payne's Gray was originally a mixture of Indigo, Ivory Black and Crimson Lake, invented by the watercolourist William Payne. This impermanent colour is now replaced by reliable mixtures that vary according to maker and medium. Bluer versions come from Winsor & Newton, Maimeri, Holbein, and Liquitex; at the other end of the scale are cool neutral blacks. Blue Black is almost indistinguishable from the more neutral Payne's Greys.

OTHER GREYS

Davy's Grey is a light greenish grey that used to be made from finely ground slate. All the current colours are mixtures of standard pigments. Because of its weak colouring it can be useful for retaining a clean looking effect when used for shadows on pale pinks.

Charcoal Grey is a warm black made from willow wood, which dries with a somewhat rough and gritty finish. Neutral Tint is usually a black with a tendency towards the blue-violet,

Old Holland Warm Grey Light is a useful warm stone colour. Slow drying.

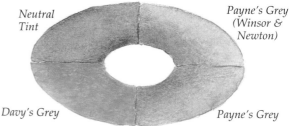

Neutral Tint

Payne's Grey (Winsor & Newton)

Davy's Grey

Payne's Grey

WHITES

All mediums except watercolour use considerable quantities of Whites. They are few in number but very dependable and long lasting.

FLAKE WHITE

This is made of basic lead carbonate, usually with a little Zinc White. White lead is opaque and a quick drier which brushes out very pleasantly in oils, and doesn't need much oil for grinding when the paint is being made, so reducing potential yellowing. Lead White has been one of the foundations of oil painting since it began, drying to a tough, flexible permanent film that has much to do with the longevity of the old masters' work. As an Alkyd paint, Flake White loses most of its opacity and is best replaced with Titanium White. Compared with Titanium White, Flake White is creamy-white in colour.

TREAT WHITE LEAD WITH CARE

White Lead oil paint is quite safe to use with reasonable care, because each grain of the poisonous powder is safely enclosed in a coating of oil. However, if you frequently get paint onto your hands or where it might indirectly be eaten, it is safer to use Titanium or Zinc White.

CREMNITZ WHITE

This is the name of the best grade of the white basic lead carbonate, a pure dense form of lead white. Compared to Flake White it appears slightly greyish.

TITANIUM WHITE

The most opaque white is used extensively in water-based mediums where its non-toxic nature and good handling properties are advantages. It is also good for oil painting but slow drying. The pigment is titanium dioxide, introduced in 1920. It is sometimes sold as Opaque White.

ZINC WHITE

In mixtures Zinc White produces cooler tints than Flake White, for it is a very pure white, but not so opaque as the preceding whites.

MIXED WHITES

Whites made of Titanium and Zinc White together are available, and exhibit the good properties of both ingredients.

Availability of Pigments and Paints

All the pigments or paints described in this ssection are available from various sources in Britain and Europe, and the names of retailers and mail order firms are listed on p. 252. The retail shops will promptly post materials ordered by phone or fax; mail order firms can be slower. Among oil paints in particular there is a great variation in price; higher prices are mostly due to the use of pure and expensive ingredients, without the use of extenders or fillers, and ground with higher quality oil. Without unduly altering a colour, a proportion of cheap extender in a tube can dramatically lower the cost to the makers. The most expensive pigments in general use are all the Cobalt and Cadmium colours, Cerulean Blue, and a few of the new synthetic colours.

THE MEDIA

INTRODUCTION

Availability and cost often dictate the choice of medium, and some artists find themselves using a medium without ever having made a conscious decision to use it as the most fitting for their needs, wondering later whether there is a better way. Oils and the water-based media, watercolour, acrylics and gouache, are all on sale in almost every art shop. Cheaper, or student's, versions of the first three are also available, but except in case of real need, you will find the artists' quality materials more rewarding and easier to use.

Drawing is fundamental to all art, and so comes first in this section. At the highest level, painting itself becomes a form of drawing with the brush; in oil painting the initial drawing on the canvas is often executed with a fine brush. In these two pages the characteristics, advantages and disadvantages of the main media are briefly outlined. Each is then dealt with more fully in its own chapter. Many alternative versions and hybrids of the media have been developed in recent years, but at present none of them poses any serious competition to the traditional media, and are not considered in detail in this book.

WATERCOLOUR

The pearly transparency of the single watercolour wash is currently valued as the artist's highest accomplishment in this medium; the aim is to retain its insubstantial airiness as far as possible. Considerable depth and contrast are also available, so there is no reason why watercolours should look pale or lacking in depth.

Small to medium-sized pictures are the most suitable, up to about 55 × 76cm. Certain papers can be bought from a roll, so increasing the possible width to 150cm.

Convenience is one of the chief attractions, as a complete outfit can be very small and portable. Bulk is minimal, also the time needed for setting up and clearing away. The paints are cheaper than their equivalents in oil or acrylic, but brushes need to be good and are expensive. The cost of paper is low, compared to the cost of canvas or to the time taken to work on it.

ACRYLICS

In skilled hands, acrylics are very versatile and can match the effects of almost any water-based medium, even bearing a superficial resemblance to oils. The initial layers can be overpainted without disturbing them, a convenience that allows great realism to be achieved. It is widely used by commercial artists, but the medium requires considerable skill to control. There is no reason for acrylics to look hard or garish other than through misuse or lack of instruction. Acrylic resin is a form of plastic, and thickly applied paint can look like plastic. Its quick drying time leaves little opportunity for considered manipulation, which makes it an unsatisfactory substitute for oils.

There is no limit to picture size. Some of the world's largest paintings, on the sides of buildings in the USA, are in acrylic.

Acrylic paints are moderately expensive.

GOUACHE

Gouache dries to a very matt finish, somewhat akin to the surface of pastels. The surface is relatively fragile and easily marked. Stretched pastel or watercolour paper is used, so small to medium-sized pictures are the most frequent. For large paintings, acrylic is a more resourceful medium with a tougher surface.

As long as the paint is not applied too thickly, gouache is versatile, and under-rated. The paints are cheap, but take care in selection as many bright colours are not permanent.

EGG TEMPERA

Tempera has a flat silky finish, more like an oil than a water-based medium, with a softer effect than acrylic or gouache. Strong darks are not easy to produce, so most tempera paintings have a relatively high-key appearance. Tempera lends itself to a very fine finish with sharp detail, but is slow in use.

Panels or very thick paper are the supports, so picture size is determined by their availability and weight. The paint can be made up as you go along, but tubes are available. Once you have located and bought the pigments, running costs are minimal.

The simple ingredients of Egg Tempera.

OIL

Oils have long been the premier medium, capable of almost any pictorial effects, other than those characteristic of watercolour and pastel. The paint, when correctly used, dries to a satin sheen or gloss finish, although a matt finish can be obtained with a suitable medium and matt varnish. There is no real limit to picture size, either small or large.

The paint on its own takes a considerable time to dry, but the use of a suitable painting medium speeds it up considerably. The alkyd oils with their medium dry overnight. The paints vary greatly in price according to content and manufacturer, but all are compatible with each other. Oils can be easy to use, although messy if approached misguidedly.

Canvases are an expensive item, but the cost can be notably reduced by preparing your own, or even further by using canvas boards, but these are much less permanent.

Oil paints come in great variety, but can all be mixed with each other. The colour range is much more extensive than in any other medium.

Le Chapeau de Paille by Rubens. Oil.
Rubens was one of the supreme masters of technique, and developed a painting medium ideally suited to his methods. He could paint very quickly, as could Van Dyck, who was said to be able to paint a head in half an hour. This portrait shows the brown tone of the panel showing through the thinly painted background. The flesh colours are opaque and finely blended, contrasting with the transparent shadow.

All oil paints can be safely mixed together.

PASTEL

Pastels are famed for their intense and vivid colours, due to the thickness of the applied pigment and the scantiness of the binder. A powdery matt finish is characteristic. Medium to large picture sizes are possible according to the paper size available. There is little scope for colour mixing and this can be compensated for by collecting as many different coloured pastels as possible. This makes it possibly the most expensive medium to start up. The work is quick and immediate, but produces much pastel dust, so is messy.

ALTERNATIVE MEDIA

Several have appeared in recent years, such as oil sticks or pastels, oil paints compatible with water, liquid acrylic inks, liquid watercolours and water-soluble crayons among others. These are specialised versions of the standard media, designed to overcome particular problems or objections to them. Liquid acrylic inks, liquid watercolours behave like their standard counterparts when sufficiently diluted, but the colours are relatively more intense. The artist still has to learn how to use them to their advantage. The traditional media are generally more versatile and resourceful, but the alternatives offer a few extra techniques that can be very useful.

111

DRAWING

INTRODUCTION

The drawing media are generally easier to apply than paints, so they are especially useful for studying and developing your skill in the perception and observation of the world. The materials are readily available, and in considerable variety beyond the usual "pencil and white paper". There are several alternatives worth experimenting with by anyone wishing to expand their range of expression or inject new life into procedures that may have become routine over the years.

Raphael's drawing is made with a sharply pointed sanguine chalk (see p. 118). By maintaining a point, the range of expression is enormously enlarged as a refined line can be combined with broad effects of shading. See how finely the hands are drawn, with no hint of clumsiness.

Drawing today is mainly associated with the pencil, but the graphite, or "lead" pencil as we know it only appeared in the 17th century, and its closest equivalent before that was silverpoint, a difficult medium giving results similar to a hard pencil. Before then, drawings showing light and shade as well as line were made with an imaginative use of coloured paper with charcoal, chalks and pen, with some of the more elaborate examples differing from paintings only in their lack of colour.

Conté (see p. 118) enlarges the scope of drawing by introducing tone. It is very sensitive to pressure, so gradations appear almost automatically.

The drawings of the old masters were executed with a wide range of materials, including silverpoint, a recalcitrant instrument consisting of a fine point of real silver wire in a holder that makes a faint line on specially prepared paper. It is always delicate in effect, but becomes easier to see after a time when it darkens by tarnishing. Other types of metal, especially lead, also make a mark on paper, and were occasionally employed, but all these are limited to small-scale work. Charcoal lends itself to larger scale tonal effects, and is one of the very oldest materials. It was frequently used for preparatory studies for oil or tempera paintings, and is still a most suitable medium for drawing on canvas as a preliminary to painting because it is easier and cleaner to work with than pencil.

Conté, chalk and charcoal easily combine line and tone; their softness allows a three-dimensional quality to be quickly conveyed. The same softness means that they need to be sharpened frequently to maintain a good point.

Conté crayons

Charcoal

112

"Chalk" is a word used to describe any black, coloured or white conté-type stick, although true chalk is white; chalks are made with a mixture of pigment with wax or oil in a similar way to the modern pastel, which uses gum as a binder. The borderline between chalks and pastel isn't clear and some authorities include pastels as a drawing medium while others continue to regard their use as a form of painting. Conté crayons also provide a full colour range, and the distinction between drawing and painting depends on whether you look on drawing as anything applied dry manner as against the fluid media used in true painting.

Chalk was widely used by the Old Masters, but no modern material is sold as "chalk", and its modern descendant is the Conté crayon, which now comes in a complete range of colours besides the traditional black, white, and sanguines, which are earth red colours. All of the chalky media are especially effective on tinted paper with the addition of white to bring out the highlights.

Entirely different effects are produced by the crisp thin lines of pen and ink. The earliest pens were made of reed stems or the quills of feathers, largely giving way to the metal nib today. These drawings were often elaborated with watercolour washes and white bodycolour, and drawn on tinted paper.

The present-day emphasis on pencil drawing is due to the convenience and ability to produce an extensive tonal range from a selection of 19 grades of hardness and softness.

Pencil shows to advantage where clear line is more important than tone. Shading can easily be added to emphasize any part, but usually plays a minor role.

The softer pencils are smooth to use and make strong drawings that equal the impact of Conté and charcoal pencils in depth of tone. Hard pencils on the other hand produce fine and delicate lines and tones that cannot be matched by any other drawing medium. Pencils retain their points for longer than the chalks, giving an advantage where clear lines are important.

Drawing implements such as pens, pencils, charcoal or Conté crayons are media in their own right, able to produce fine finished pictures, as well as performing their more familiar roles as the early stages in other techniques. The great majority of paintings start with drawing, so some ability in this field is essential for further progress, and this section tries to show how to acquire it.

Pencils

Steel pen

Copse near Trompenberg by Rembrandt.

Pen and ink make dramatic drawings with no half-tones. Shading has to be executed with thicker lines or with hatching, but line is the main strength of pen and ink. A reed pen and two shades of brown ink were used, and the width of the reed nib leads to a solid looking drawing.

Reed pen

113

THE USE OF TONE IN DRAWING

Where tone is employed in a drawing, its purpose is the revelation of form rather than implying depth of colour. Dark areas in a drawing appear to recede back behind the surface of the paper, while the lights advance towards you. This works well in helping to achieve three-dimensional form, but if a dark area doesn't coincide with a receding plane it can look like a hole in the paper. This is why you so seldom see cast shadows on a drawing: their unusual shapes give little information about form, and can be difficult to interpret as only the most obvious look fully convincing.

Tone was used very widely in drawings by the Old Masters, who often added washes of paint or ink, but with the growing predominance of pencil, which is more suited to line than to covering areas, the practice of tonal drawing has declined. The appropriate addition of tone, based on the use of tinted paper, charcoal, conté or pen, helps the illusion of depth and perspective and can quickly convey the impression of a full tone range. Contrast is strongest in the foreground where the strongest darks are naturally found, made by increased pressure of the drawing instrument or by shading.

Sketching out of doors needs adaptable materials – tinted paper, charcoal, soft pencils – to produce satisfactory results quickly.

When you intend to shade with pencil, first make a normal line drawing using lines of varying thickness to suggest differences of tone. Then develop the texture carefully before adding any general shading. Only apply the minimum of tonal shading necessary to convey the form, otherwise the effect can become heavy and overworked.

Working on toned paper allows you to approach a full range of tones more closely, and in these circumstances cast shadows can be more successful.

Shading for colour implies the blocking-in of areas just to build up weight of tone, with a consequent loss of clarity and time. Where colour and an associated pattern are necessary for identifying your subject, they have to be indicated lightly and carefully so their shapes are distinct, avoiding any confusion with the light and shade of modelling.

The finely graded tones of white flowers lend themselves to pencil rendering. A range of hard pencils conveys the smooth textures. The light tones can be erased with a sharpened or pointed rubber if necessary.

Materials

PAPER

The surface of the paper, its quality and texture, can be said to exert the strongest single influence on the overall look of a drawing. The texture, or grain, determines the way in which the pencil lead, or charcoal, is sheared off as it is drawn across it. Under strong magnification, paper is an interwoven mat of fibres, and the fibres, aided by the small amount of wax in the lead, hold the medium in place.

The features of paper that affect the artist, in addition to its texture, are permanence, surface hardness and colour. Paper made with rag, rather than wood-pulp, is the best for quality and permanence. Surface hardness has a direct bearing on the amount of repeated erasure it can stand before roughing up; you can feel a paper's hardness and grain with your finger-tips. In general a hard paper is easier to use than a soft one, but try a few to see the different results produced.

WHITE PAPER

Bristol boards are the hardest and most durable of all papers, so are a good first choice for your drawings. They are available in a wide range of thickness. If you have never made a drawing on good quality rag paper you will be pleasantly surprised at the difference it can make. Their harder surfaces are more responsive and take a stronger line than softer papers from any grade of pencil. A fairly smooth type of paper called cartridge paper is well adapted to pencil and the other drawing media, and is the most common type sold for drawing: it varies a lot in quality and thickness, so use the best you can find.

The smoother sorts of watercolour paper can also be used, and can be coloured to suit yourself if stretched and tinted. Hot-pressed paper is good for pen, or pen and wash, and for most other drawing; some of the not-, or cold-pressed, versions of most papers can be too grainy, so besides wearing down points quickly the results can look rough.

Try out a small piece first before you commit yourself. The rougher types of watercolour paper lead to a coarse and grainy look, so are best avoided for drawing unless you want such an effect.

COLOURED PAPER

Pastel papers come in a large range of colours, and their tints imply the use of white for heightening the lights; this makes the paper tint into a middle tone and increases the illusion of three dimensions. Ordinary HB pencil doesn't show up well on most coloured papers, so use a softer pencil, 3B or 4B; alternatively, pen, charcoal or conté could show up better. The addition of white increases the effect of three-dimensional form.

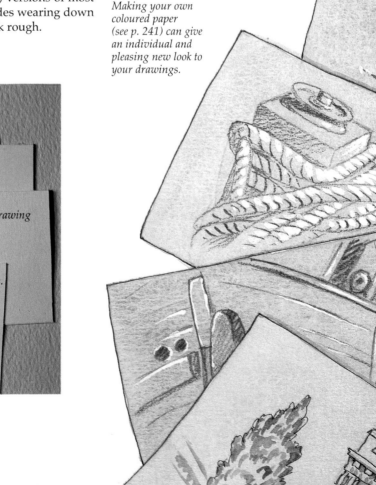

Making your own coloured paper (see p. 241) can give an individual and pleasing new look to your drawings.

Cartridge

Heavyweight Cartridge, more agreeable to draw on.

Hot-pressed watercolour, makes drawing of finer quality, takes washes.

Bristol board, hard surface flatters some drawing materials.

Layout paper, for working out designs, semi-transparent.

PENCILS

Graphite, the black material used in pencils, was first thought to be a form of lead, and so the name of "lead" has persisted even though graphite is actually a form of carbon. Pencil leads are made from a mixture of graphite and clay; the clay holds the graphite together; the more graphite there is in the mixture, the softer it is and the blacker it comes off onto the paper. Pencils are made in a range from 9B, the softest or blackest, to 9H, the hardest. B stands for Black and H for Hard. The pencil marked F, for Firm, is slightly harder than HB. Some pencils are graded by number rather than letters, in which case 1 is the softest grade. There is not a lot of difference in quality between the cheaper and more expensive pencils.

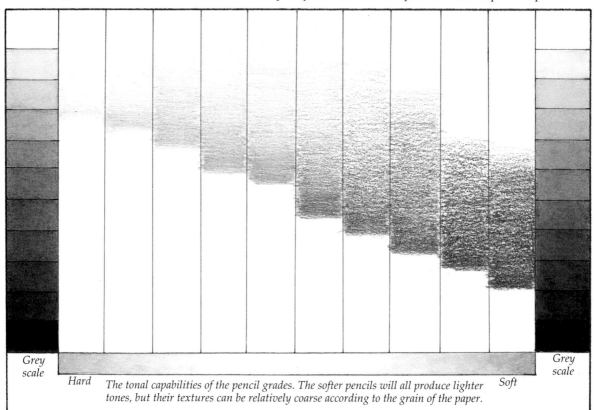

Grey scale   Hard

The tonal capabilities of the pencil grades. The softer pencils will all produce lighter tones, but their textures can be relatively coarse according to the grain of the paper.

Soft   *Grey scale*

HOW TO SHARPEN A PENCIL

For accurate drawing you need to know exactly where your pencil is going to touch the paper, so the aim of sharpening is to produce a very long point which gives the maximum visibility and accuracy. The point on a new pencil looks smart, but it slopes so steeply that even a few minutes drawing will have worn the tip back, thickening the line and making it harder to see what you are doing.

Much drawing is made unnecessarily harder by the bluntness of so many pencils, which makes the lines insensitive and inaccurate. The time spent on making the points longer is more than made up for by a new-found pleasure and precision. The points last for much longer, so re-sharpening is infrequent.

Sharpening by hand with a hobby-knife or safety-razor is preferable because you are free to shape a longer point. If you haven't drawn with a long point before, you will be pleasantly surprised by how much easier it is to see what you are doing.

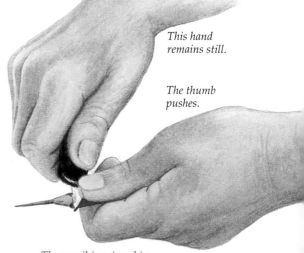

This hand remains still.

The thumb pushes.

The pencil is gripped in the curled fingers.

Cut into the wood first and remove it evenly.

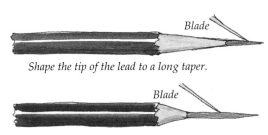

Shape the tip of the lead to a long taper.

Cut back the wood to expose more lead.

Slide the knife sideways at a slight angle along the length of the exposed lead to improve the overall taper. Avoid downward pressure.

If you are unfamiliar with a pencil sharpened like this, don't worry about it snapping while you draw, as you will instinctively refrain from pressing too hard. The softer pencils aren't so strong, so the points need to be a little shorter.

SANDING BLOCK

A sanding-block makes it easy to produce a good taper on the harder leads which resist the blade of your sharpener. Slide the lead sideways, back and forth, with as little downward pressure as possible.

Sanding block

PENCIL EXTENDERS

The cost of pencils is no longer negligible, so an extender can be a worthwhile accessory. Besides prolonging the life of a pencil, they help to balance shorter ones, which are more difficult to manipulate.

Pencil extender

To avoid exaggerated movement of the pencil, it should be long enough to rest comfortably on your hand. An extender will give sufficient length to old pencils.

SKETCHING PENCILS

For quick results squared points can shade sizeable areas, blocking in shadows before they move, which is invaluable in capturing the effect of sunlight. The tips at each corner of the square can do the thinner drawing lines. Keep a sanding block handy to maintain the corners, otherwise the lead can become impossibly blunt. It can be difficult to see which part of the pencil is touching the paper.

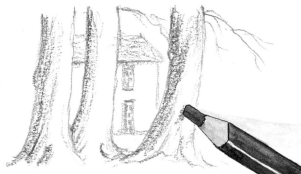

Quick shading with broad pencils.

GRAPHITE STICKS

These come in a variety of shapes and sizes, produce a thicker line, and are good for free sketching. The graphite is in a large solid piece; some sticks are the same shape as a pencil but with a plastic covering instead of a wood surround, which makes them more fragile. The round 6B has a smooth silky feel on the paper that makes drawing a pleasure, and the range is from 6B to H. They need frequent sharpening.

Some graphite sticks and the lines they draw. Shading is easy with the broader shapes, but accuracy usually has to be sacrificed to speed unless there is a good point on them.

AUTOMATIC PENCILS

Automatic, or clutch pencils are alike in their ability to lengthen or retract the lead, and their instant adjustability saves sharpening. The metal tube on the end adds to the apparent lead-length to give good visibility. The smallest pencils take a .3mm lead, while the larger clutch pencils go up to a diameter of .9mm. Most automatic pencils are .5mm.

RENEWING THE LEADS

Automatic pencils contain spare leads inside the barrel, which feed down automatically. When a lead is used up, it slips back into the pencil when you touch the paper; press the button at the top repeatedly and the remaining lead will eventually drop out. Carry on pressing the button until a new lead appears.

CLUTCH PENCILS

These hold a single, replaceable, long lead. Pressing the button will cause the lead to slip out as far as you want it to. The softer leads are thick and benefit from a special sharpener like the Staedtler one. Have it with you when you are drawing.

Staedtler sharpener

CONTÉ CRAYONS

Conté crayons are named after their inventor, Nicolas-Jacques Conté, who also invented the pencil. They are available in square sticks which can be sharpened to a point with a hobby knife. Their advantage is the ability they give you to draw on tinted paper and quickly establish a tonal effect, aided by the use of highlighting with white or light grey. The white is made of alumina chalk, and like the black is produced in differing degrees of hardness. The colour range has been greatly extended, but the traditional conté colours were black, grey, white and a short range of earth reds called sanguines, especially suitable for figure drawing, producing effects similar to the drawings of Raphael and Michelangelo.

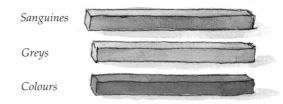

Sanguines

Greys

Colours

The colouring material of the greys and blacks is graphite, so they are related to the graphite sticks rather than to the pastels, although the large and bright colour range now available in conté crayons blurs the practical distinction between them and the harder varieties of pastels.

Conté sticks are ideal for sketching as well as figure drawing. If the points are sharpened, very accurate lines are possible.

The relative softness of most conté crayons means that if you want a fine drawing you need a good sharpening knife at hand to maintain the points while you draw. Keep a light touch at first until you have established the shapes because conté is slightly waxy, and doesn't respond as well as pencil or charcoal to rubbing out. A putty rubber is the most likely to succeed. Harder rubbers can smear the crayon into the paper.

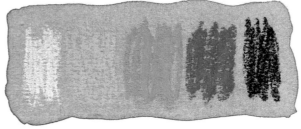

The range of greys

Sanguine, white and black on tinted paper

White highlights

White applied thinly

Black for accents

Shadows in 3 shades of sanguine

COLOURED CONTÉ

The range of colour tends to the brighter side, so restraint is necessary in colouring natural scenes. A certain amount of direct mixing is possible until the crayon builds up too much to take any more. A handful of harmonious colours will produce a more satisfying and useful sketch than an attempt to match real colours exactly.

A scene with a handful of muted colours. Conté is very quick for recording and sketching, and is better with just a few colours.

PASTELS
The Conté colour range bridges the gap between drawing and pastels. Whether the use of pastels constitutes drawing or painting is a matter of opinion. Pastels and their techniques are described separately in a later section, and conté crayons can be used in the same ways in conjunction with pastels. See p. 238 for more on pastels.

Charcoal

Although charcoal drawings resemble chalk and conté in appearance, charcoal, like the graphite of pencils, is carbon. Natural charcoal comes in sticks about 15cm long, made from twigs of vine or willow which have been carefully roasted in air-tight kilns. It was the earliest of all drawing instruments, and is suited to a loose style incorporating light and shade, where the broad tip helps in covering large areas with tones. It adheres lightly to the paper and is the easiest of all materials to remove. It is supplied in three grades, soft, medium and hard.

Charcoal will not only make ordinary marks on paper, but it can be rubbed. For a finer finish to your charcoal drawings, soft modelling can be achieved by careful blending with your fingertips or with a stump. Fingertips are the most available and flexible instruments, so for a small amount of rubbing they are sufficient. Have a damp flannel at the ready for cleaning your fingers, for the charcoal can find its way back onto other parts of your drawing

Heating willow twigs to make charcoal sticks

Charcoal sticks

Natural vine charcoal from Zecchi

Developing a point on rough paper

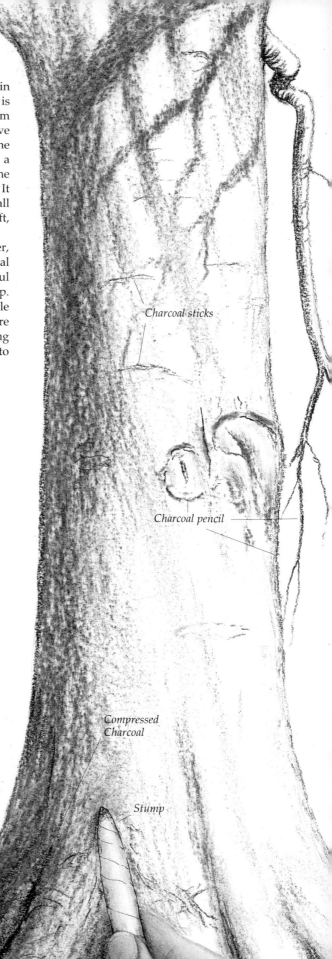

Charcoal sticks

Charcoal pencil

Compressed Charcoal

Stump

CHARCOAL PENCILS

Compressed charcoal is re-formulated, with the addition of a little linseed oil, into regular sticks and made into pencils of different grades. They can produce a blacker tone than most ordinary charcoal and the pencil form keeps your fingers clean.

They need regular sharpening while you work, but the oil hardens them slightly so that they are not so crumbly as charcoal and need less sharpening. They are also much cleaner to handle. They are made in a few grades of hardness and are similar to black conté in use.

OIL CHARCOAL

Charcoal is porous, and can be made to soak up oil by standing sticks in a jar of linseed oil for a short time. After taking them out and wiping the surface dry, the sticks will draw with a blacker line, and dry firmly attached to the paper. Sticks can be stored by wrapping them up tightly with thin kitchen foil to prevent the oil drying out.

COMPRESSED CHARCOAL

Compressed charcoal is made from charcoal powder with a binder into hard-feeling 10cm cylindrical sticks. It can produce a blacker line than ordinary charcoal, and unlike soft graphite pencils there is no waxy shine, so its blackness registers at full value. It can be used in conjunction with ordinary charcoal or with other drawing media.

Charcoal is ideal for outdoor sketching and builds up textures and tones very quickly. Keep a separate sharpened stick for important dark lines. They bear the same relationship to charcoal pencils as graphite sticks to ordinary pencils.

STUMPS

Stumps are made for rubbing small areas. You can buy them in several sizes or make your own with blotting paper to a pattern, shown below. Roll up the paper as tightly as you can and hold it finally with sticky tape.

Tapered end　　　　　　　*Round end*

10cm

Wet the blotting paper first to soften it, otherwise it is impossible to begin the roll tightly enough.

23cm

Fix outer end with tape when dry.

A pattern for making a stump.

POWDERED CHARCOAL

This can be rubbed into the paper with fingertips or stumps to produce tonal effects. Further drawing is possible over a rubbed area, so detail can be added as well as further weight of tone.

Compressed charcoal sticks

Powdered charcoal

Rubbing with a finger-tip

PEN AND INK

The earliest pens were made of bamboo reeds cut to shape, followed by quills made from the feathers of large birds such as swans, geese and crows. All of these are still available ready-made, or can be cut at home with a scalpel or sharp knife. The lines they make are softer than those made by a metal nib, and frequently broader. Metal nibs are the most popular as they are readily available and need no maintenance. The range of line-widths is large, from small mapping-pens to large italics. Italic nibs can give two line widths, so the narrower nibs are more consistent.

PEN NIBS

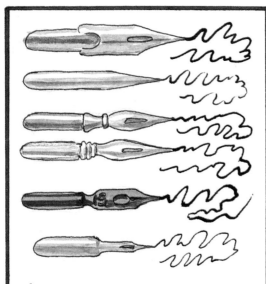

The metallic pen-nib, made of brass or steel, was invented in the late 1700s and has become, in its many varieties, the main type of nib in use today. The strength of the line is always the same, but can vary in width according to the pressure you put on your nib; many artists prefer this flexibility compared with the modern technical pen. Given their cheapness, it is worth trying several sorts and sizes to see which you prefer.

Metal nibs give great variety of line. Several sorts can be used in any one drawing, thicker nibs to give emphasis to the foreground and strong shadows, flexible ones for the foliage, and small or mapping pens for very fine distant landscape detail. When changing over to another nib, wipe the previous one clean with kitchen-roll paper.

QUILL PENS

It is most convenient to buy a ready-made pen and use it as a model in shaping your own nib. The system of shaping is the same as for the reed pens shown below. First heat the quill end carefully to drive off the oils. Use a scalpel or narrow hobby knife for shaping, so that cuts are clean.

Slip to hold ink

REED PENS

Reed pens are seldom used because they need frequent re-shaping, but like the quills give a softer line than metal nibs. The tips are shaped from reeds of the common reed or any strong hollow stalk.

Cutting a reed pen nib

The crisp lines of these working boats and barge make them ideal pen subjects. The shading of the barge was added to make a strong contrast with the white boats rather than for its own sake.

INK

Inks have developed over the years, from the classic black India ink to the complete range of coloured inks available today. For drawings that are meant to be permanent, make sure the ink comes from an art manufacturer or similar reliable source, because many will quickly fade, even some of the blacks. Inks can be diluted for washes to add to pen drawings.

Indian ink

Chinese ink stick

TECHNICAL PENS

The standard line width is .35mm, and this size has a smooth feel to the tip as you draw. For the finer points, .18 and .13, you may need some special cleaner to dissolve clogging dried ink. The ink is lightfast and waterproof when dry, so you can add washes of tone afterwards without disturbing your drawing.

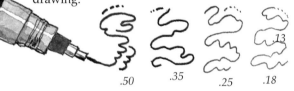

.50 .35 .25 .18 .13

To clean: unscrew, pull off the cartridge and run cold water slowly through the nib section. The cartridge can be refilled with a certain ingenuity. Stand the tip section in special cleaner if the ink has dried inside.

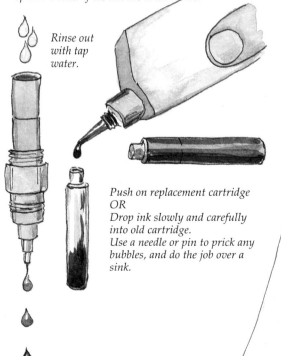

Rinse out with tap water.

Push on replacement cartridge OR
Drop ink slowly and carefully into old cartridge.
Use a needle or pin to prick any bubbles, and do the job over a sink.

FELT-TIP PENS

Only dye can work its way through a felt tip, and dyes are seldom lightfast, so their best use is in sketch-books, where their speed and versatility can save a lot of time. The word "permanent" on some pens may mean that it won't wash out of your clothes, rather than permanence to light. Felt-tip pens usually have round points like a pencil; decide on what sort of line you want, explain it to the shop assistant, and try out in the shop.

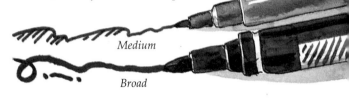

Medium

Broad

MARKER PENS

A specialised type of felt-tip with a chisel-shaped felt nib. They are also good for sketching, and the same provisions as for felt-tips apply. As well as many colours they include a range of greys, which is useful because you cannot control the depth of colour from a marker pen; you need one for each colour.

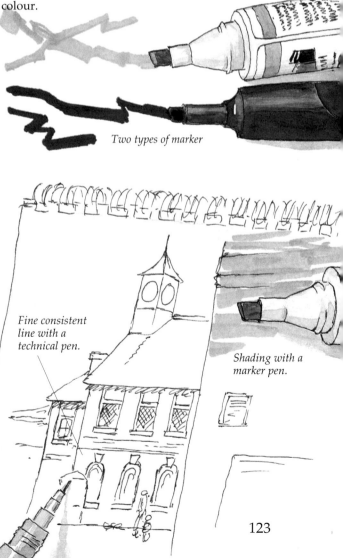

Two types of marker

Fine consistent line with a technical pen.

Shading with a marker pen.

123

ACCESSORIES

A number of aids to drawing can make life easier, others are essential for accuracy.

FIXATIVE

Pencil and the other drawing media are prone to smearing, which happens most often from handling afterwards while the drawing is being shown around. A fixative will seal in the pencil or other medium by coating the surface with synthetic resin; this is usually sprayed on from a can supplied by a regular paint manufacturer. The older sprays have a strong and lingering smell that is not unpleasant, but toxic, and best avoided by doing the spraying outdoors on a still day. Some newer fixatives are much safer, but are still better used out of doors. The paper soaks up the fixative and needs some time to dry. Keep the can itself warm so it sprays finely and evenly.

DRAWING BOARDS

The drawing paper needs a firm surface to rest on, and one that is large enough to support your wrist, so if you are not using a table, a light drawing board will serve to hold the paper. For dry instruments such as pencils and chalks, pinning or clipping the paper to the board is sufficient, but if any ink, watercolour or gouache washes are to be used then it is advisable to stretch the paper on to it first.

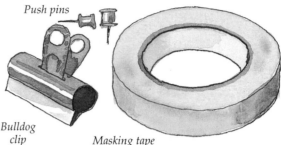

Push pins

Bulldog clip

Masking tape

ERASERS

The best of the older, more natural rubbers are excellent cleaners and safe on watercolour paper. They have a tendency to harden with time, but regular use keeps them in condition.

Magic-type rubbers are made of plastic, are valuable alternatives to natural rubber, and are quite safe on watercolour paper. Avoid the harder sorts; feel them in the shop.

Putty rubbers are the safest for preserving the paper surface, are good for a general clean up, and the most successful removers of conté or pencil on canvas.

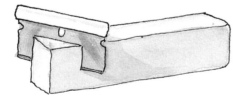

SHAPING A RUBBER

Cut off a triangle from one end to make a sort of chisel edge; it is easier to see what you are doing with a tapered end, to enable you to rub out more precisely.

CLEANING

Rub the eraser firmly over some strong grainy paper to remove the blackened surface.

SHARPENERS

Safety razor

Retractable ◁ hobby knife

The old safety razor is harder to find now, but a retractable knife with disposable blade tips is a good substitute.

124

DRAWING AIDS

Mechanical drawing aids have been used since the beginning of drawing, so there is no need to feel guilty about their use. Dürer, over four hundred years ago, published a drawing showing how to use a squared grid placed between artist and model to assist in the drawing and foreshortening of figures. Great artists have always used whatever means will help them to make their pictures. The judicious use of these implements will improve your drawing and enable you to tackle more mechanical subjects. Their use should not be obtrusive, or cause parts of the drawing to look more perfect than the rest.

RULERS

You will need a ruler, especially in architectural work, for lines of perspective and actual lines on buildings. Particular care should be taken to avoid digging in with the pencil when ruling straight lines. If you combine ruled and freehand straight lines in the same picture, check that they are not too different in character.

FLEXIBLE RULE

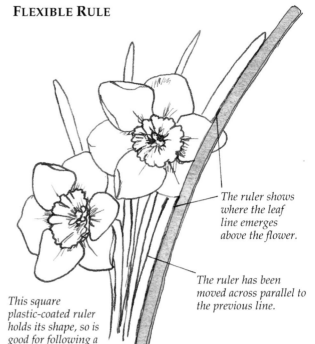

The ruler shows where the leaf line emerges above the flower.

The ruler has been moved across parallel to the previous line.

This square plastic-coated ruler holds its shape, so is good for following a curve behind a shape.

Going freehand over ruled lines.

SET-SQUARES

These are essential for checking verticals in architecture, and horizontals for the sea's horizon.

Check verticals by aligning the set square.

Align the set square with the bottom edge of the paper.

Checking that the sides are equal.

DIVIDERS

Use them to check matching distances, and sometimes to measure directly from the subject, a method employed by some botanical artists.

ELLIPSE GUIDES

These come at particular angles, so a 20° guide gives a range of sizes of a circle viewed from an angle of 20°. They have many uses and are essential for accurate work but are expensive.

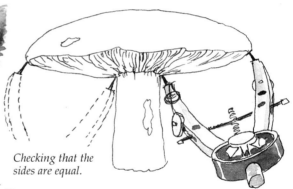

125

How to Draw

Drawing depends on accurate observation and can only be learned with practice. A very few people have a natural facility for drawing quickly, but this is unusual and doesn't show in the final result, so take heart if you find drawing difficult. With patience you will succeed even if it does take a little longer.

Drawing can be learnt like any other skill, and it needs the same rational approach. The first step is to look at everything as if you had never seen it before, forgetting any ideas of what things ought to look like. A pre-conceived picture in your mind, of which you are probably unaware, can easily obliterate reality, and can be responsible for the great majority of errors and difficulties in drawing and one of the biggest barriers to seeing clearly. The paintings and drawings of the old masters reveal little of their methods, but clearly demonstrate their ability to see; the perfection of line and command of tonal range is the result of observation, which is afterwards translated to the paper through technique. The greater part of drawing is to learn to judge lengths and angles. The manipulation of your drawing materials is relatively simple.

JUDGEMENT OF LENGTH

Start with the simplest and most "obvious" features of overall size and proportion. The basics are often overlooked in the search for lesser information that is harder to see – an indentation halfway along a smooth curve, or the exact shape of a nose. The important facts to start with are the overall height and width of your subject. Within their limits, which can be adjusted as the drawing develops, everything will fit comfortably.

- Put in a mark where you want the top of your drawing to come to.
- Put another mark where the bottom will be.
- Place two more marks, one at each side to show the width.
- Within these boundaries, simple sub-divisions can be estimated and marked.

The main proportions are squares

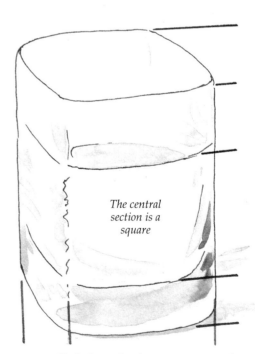

The central section is a square

Divisions are usually halves, thirds or quarters, and should never become too many – if necessary each division can be divided in turn. The four parts into which the height of the glass is divided ensure the overall accuracy, within which the details fit comfortably.

Regular shapes can be detected even when disguised under the flowing curves of the modern car, as long as there are fixed points in suitable places. The door joins and the bottoms of the wheel arches give a start. Natural shapes have less in the way of fixed guides, but there are always some. For the drawing of the dog, the head, body, tail and legs need their proportions estimating correctly before beginning, and by doing this the common fault of making the head too large can be avoided.

Within the divisions already marked, further subdivisions can easily be found.

The flower head below, without obvious regular shapes, is an example where it is useful to compare the balance on each side of the stalk: this shows that the width of the flower head is twice the height. The leaf below has five lobes altogether, three of them equally spaced on the right. The church tower, below right, divides easily into four vertical sections, while the little tower in front occupies about half its width. The width of the porch is the same as that of the main towers. Carefully estimate and mark these proportions out before beginning the drawing.

Irregular shapes also consist of simple proportions.

Foreshortening of the body reduces its length.

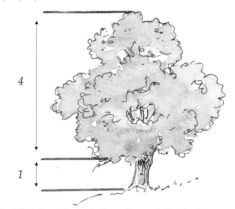

Mark height and width first, then subdivide them.

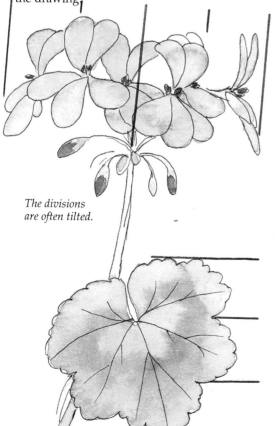

The divisions are often tilted.

Mark the intended bounds of the drawing and estimate overall proportions, then work down to the smaller details last of all.

127

JUDGEMENT OF ANGLES

After size and proportion, direction determines the balance and character of your picture. Stability, action, and the whole feel of a picture depend on the angles of a few critical parts. Look for the simplest, the verticals and horizontals first. From these, other more difficult angles can be more easily estimated. Genuine verticals are frequent, except in the countryside, and are useful for estimating the slopes of other steep angles.

If there is no clear guide nearby, take especial care over angles near to the vertical, because they are frequently drawn tilting in the wrong direction; a plumb-line is an infallible guide if in doubt. True horizontals are much less common because the effects of perspective cause most of them to slope to some degree. If all true guide-lines for angles are absent, hold your pencil vertically or horizontally in front of you to compare with the angles you are drawing (see p. 126).

HORIZONTAL ANGLES

The bases of the clouds are horizontal and unaltered by perspective. The distant hills have slight slopes; there is sometimes a tendency to exaggerate the steepness of distant hills and particularly of mountains.

VERTICALS

Until you can judge them confidently, use a set-square, aligned with the bottom of the paper, to check your verticals after you have drawn them.

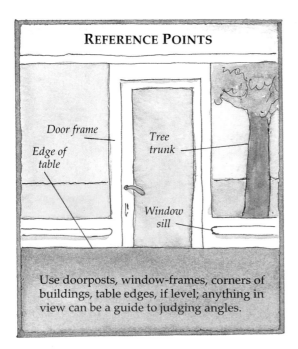

REFERENCE POINTS

Door frame

Edge of table

Tree trunk

Window sill

Use doorposts, window-frames, corners of buildings, table edges, if level; anything in view can be a guide to judging angles.

True vertical

The slight angles at which the flowers grow require careful observation and judgement. The flat, but not level, bases of the flowers provide a foundation for drawing the slopes of the sides.

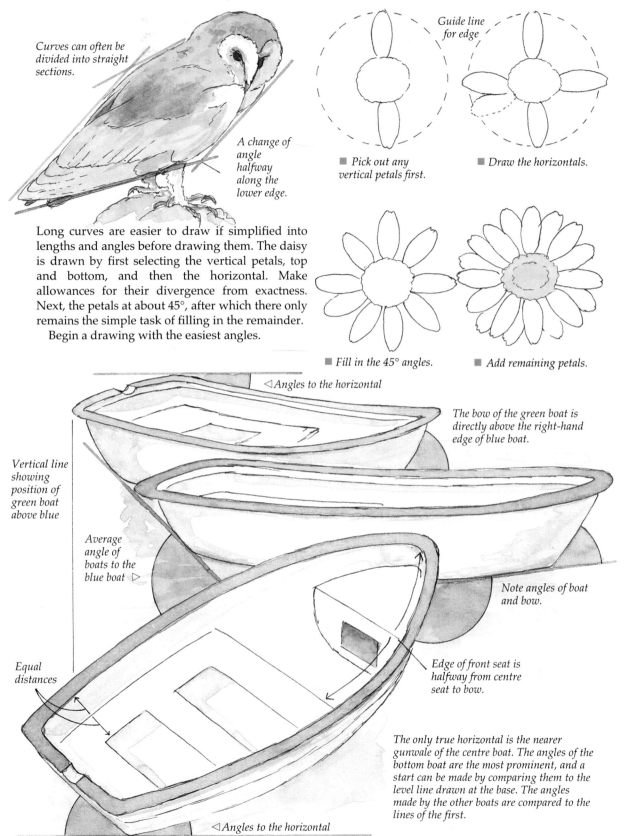

Curves can often be divided into straight sections.

A change of angle halfway along the lower edge.

Long curves are easier to draw if simplified into lengths and angles before drawing them. The daisy is drawn by first selecting the vertical petals, top and bottom, and then the horizontal. Make allowances for their divergence from exactness. Next, the petals at about 45°, after which there only remains the simple task of filling in the remainder.

Begin a drawing with the easiest angles.

Guide line for edge

■ *Pick out any vertical petals first.*

■ *Draw the horizontals.*

■ *Fill in the 45° angles.*

■ *Add remaining petals.*

◁ *Angles to the horizontal*

The bow of the green boat is directly above the right-hand edge of blue boat.

Vertical line showing position of green boat above blue

Average angle of boats to the blue boat ▷

Note angles of boat and bow.

Edge of front seat is halfway from centre seat to bow.

Equal distances

The only true horizontal is the nearer gunwale of the centre boat. The angles of the bottom boat are the most prominent, and a start can be made by comparing them to the level line drawn at the base. The angles made by the other boats are compared to the lines of the first.

◁ *Angles to the horizontal*

RECOGNISING THE BASIC SHAPES

Most people can easily draw the four simple forms below even in the absence of models; the same simple forms underlie many of the objects we draw. Recognition of them simplifies drawing: if we can clearly understand the shape of an object then we are half-way to drawing it correctly. Experienced artists recognise the basic shapes as an underlying framework below the disguise of the surface details. The shapes appear in many variations, which are more often seen than their basic forms; some of the easiest are illustrated on these pages.

As you practise so you will also become aware of others, such as the long solid triangle of the windmill roof opposite. Besides their value in clarifying form, they also serve as a guide for the play of light and shade, which is described more fully in the Lighting section. Every shape cannot be included, as their variety is infinite, and others are less frequent and you can nearly always break down the more complex into the simpler well-known shapes.

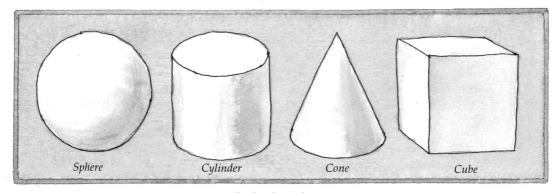

Sphere   *Cylinder*   *Cone*   *Cube*

The four basic shapes

HOW TO IDENTIFY THE SHAPES

Memorise the simple shapes first and look out for them. Flat shapes without any complications of three-dimensional form are easy to see, and appear all over buildings as well as making up the sides of rectangular objects. Three-dimensional forms are often half hidden, like the cylindrical roofs of the railway station below, or merge into others like the cones and spheres that make up the hot-air balloons opposite. The top of the flattened cone below the windmill housing is disguised by being cut off, and stands on a very short cylinder. The cat shows how the dividing line between cylinders and cones is often unclear, but recognition is more important than classification. Once you see any form for what it is, the way to drawing it becomes clearer.

FLAT SHAPES

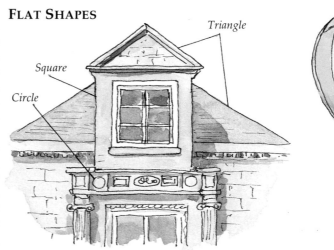

Triangle

Square

Circle

Many shapes, like the chair, appear just as a frame. The legs encompass a cube, and although the cube itself is empty, its form is there. By first sketching in the cube accurately, the chair legs can easily be given their proper lengths and positions.

The underlying shapes are easier to see in man-made objects.

Heavily disguised shapes in a cat.

IRREGULAR FORMS

An understanding of the basic shapes still leaves much that is apparently unclassifiable, but everything that lives has form of a sort and you will soon begin to notice many more uncommon but regular shapes. With developing skill, the field of purely irregular forms will diminish, for to be able to draw something it is essential to impose some sort of order on it.

A holly leaf may seem the ultimate in disorder; draw the centre vein first to give it direction, space out the points on each side and join them up.

131

SYMMETRY

Lop-sided pots and vases detract from many pictures, perhaps because their artists were nervous of taking advantage of any assistance. There is no virtue in going back to the days before the invention of rulers and other aids, or in feeling guilty about doing what every professional takes for granted. Well-drawn symmetrical objects give authority to a painting, and take their place in the composition without drawing attention to themselves by their failings.

There are two ways of ensuring symmetry; one only needs a ruler but is less accurate, the second is easier and more reliable. For both methods you need to do a light freehand drawing first to fix the position, size and accurate general appearance.

TWO METHODS OF ENSURING SYMMETRY

MEASURING

■ Draw the complete shape lightly.

■ With a ruler draw the centre line very lightly.

■ Choose one side and re-draw it as accurately as possible.

■ From the centre-line, measure selected points on the drawn side and mark matching distances on the opposite side with light dots.

■ Match the first side by joining up the dots smoothly, and rub out the centre-line.

TRACING

■ Draw the complete shape lightly.

■ With a ruler draw the centre line very lightly.

■ Choose one side and re-draw it as accurately as possible. Rub out the other side.

■ Lay tracing paper over the drawing. Draw a matching centre-line on it over that of the drawing. On this line, mark the top and bottom of the pot. With the centre-line and marks in position over the drawing, trace the side you have just drawn.

■ Turn the tracing paper over, and position it so the centre line and marks register exactly. Hold or tape it firmly, and rub over the back of the tracing paper with your finger-nail or burnishing instrument to transfer the line.

■ Tidy up the traced line to match the first side, and rub out the centre-line.

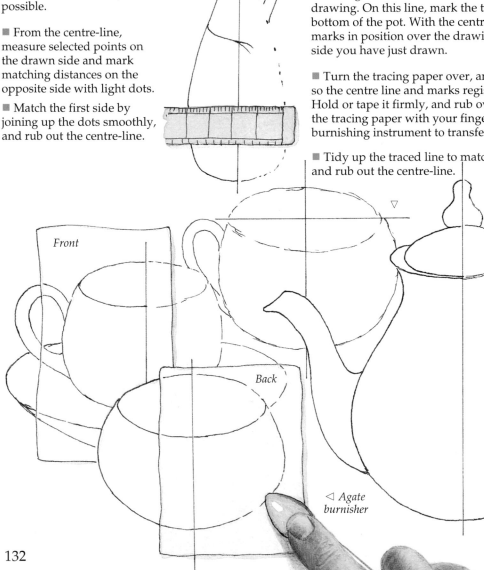

Front

Back

◁ *Agate burnisher*

CONSTRUCTING ELLIPSES

An ellipse is a circle in perspective, so the circle's regularity, and the continuity of its curve has to be retained. Most ellipses can be drawn freehand or, if small enough, with an ellipse guide, p. 125. For larger and more important ellipses, an accurate method using dots and lines works well. You will need a ruler for the cross lines of the axes, and a straight-edged piece of good paper or thin card. The intended ellipse needs to be roughly drawn, and the long and short axes lightly ruled in at right-angles to each other.

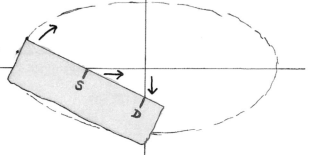

■ Slide the D mark downwards a short distance and the S mark sideways, keeping the marks on the axes. At the corner, put a dot. Continue sliding the marks along the axes and adding dots.

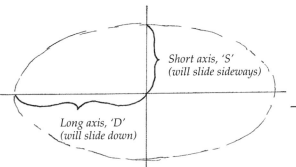

Short axis, 'S'
(will slide sideways)

Long axis, 'D'
(will slide down)

■ Draw the ellipse lightly in position, then, with a ruler, draw the long and short axes.

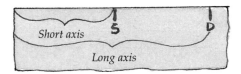

Short axis   S   D

Long axis

■ Find a piece of stiff paper or thin card with a straight edge. Lay it along the long axis with the corner at the edge of the ellipse (as below). Mark the centre of the ellipse with a D. Do the same with the short axis and mark the centre S.

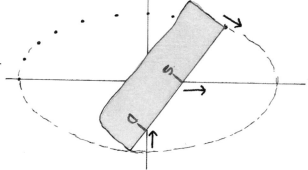

■ After passing the top of the short axis, continue round, as the D mark works its way up the short axis again. Finally, join the dots smoothly and rub out the lines.

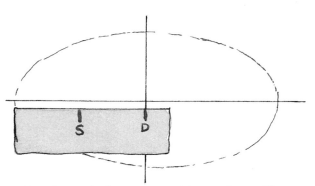

S   D

■ Lay the marked paper in position as shown. The left-hand tip of the card will follow round the edge, and each successive position will be marked with a pencil dot. The marks S and D will at the same time be kept on their axes.

Ellipses are not always large, but are always important.

PENCIL SHADING

PENCILS AND THE CONTROL OF TONE

Partial shading emphasises the third dimension without being committed to a full-scale tonal rendering, although pencils are quite capable of this. A full tonal drawing will use a range of grades. Medium pencils, HB-2H, do the middle and light tones well, without reaching the real dark tones. The hard pencils, 2H-9H, give a fine finish and are ideal for light tones, but lack strength for the darks. In a tonal drawing, apply the hard pencils first, because the soft can be worked over them. With the hard pencils you can go back and forwards over the work until all the gaps are filled in, as the paper will pick up the lead while none will be added to the parts already covered. Hold the pencil well back from the point and avoid pressing – the long sharp points that make drawing easier should help here. When a soft B pencil is used, the paper grain can show strongly, especially if the point is blunt. In tonal drawing they are most useful for reinforcing the strong darks.

B PENCILS

A full range of tones is to hand with a soft pencil, and considerable speed, as its marks are immediate and strong. With a B pencil, a sharp point will increase accuracy and minimise graininess.

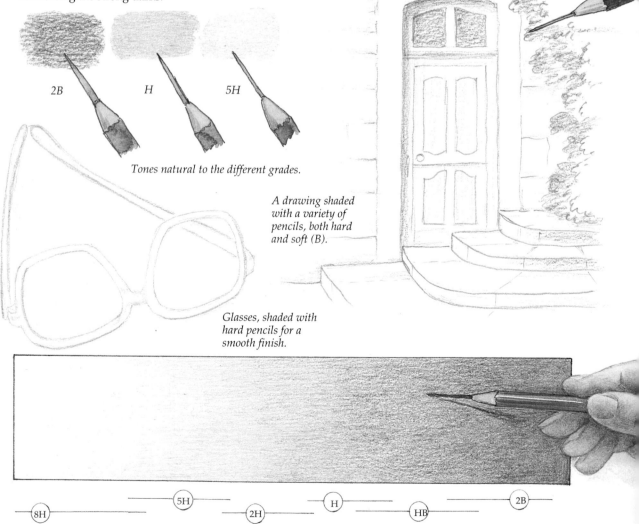

2B   *H*   *5H*

Tones natural to the different grades.

A drawing shaded with a variety of pencils, both hard and soft (B).

Glasses, shaded with hard pencils for a smooth finish.

(8H)   (5H)   (2H)   (H)   (HB)   (2B)

Making an evenly graded panel is a useful exercise from which one can learn a lot about pencil handling. Start with the hard pencils, working from the light end.

LINE AND WASH

Line and wash is a combination of drawing and painting, in which a wide range of expression is possible. Either the drawing or the painting can be done first, although the drawing is more usual. A technical pen or steel nib with Indian ink gives the best results as the washes can dissolve ordinary ink and spoil the drawing. The difficulties of first-time drawing without being able to rub out suggest the insurance of a few pencil guidelines before continuing with ink. Rub out the pencil completely before painting over the washes. Further washes or pen detail can be added at any stage, but line and wash is mainly a sketching technique.

Waterproof ink gives you freedom to develop the washes without spoiling the lines. For the washes, the ink can be diluted; alternatively, watercolour does very well and can be worked over.

Dry-brush for smoke and steam

Wash for large flat shadows

◁ *The effects of strong sunlight are quickly captured by strong broad washes.*

Washes rapidly convert outlines into 3-dimensional forms.

◁ *Sunlight captured with watercolour washes over a pen drawing. There is always a hurry in sunlight as the shadows move so quickly and look their best when you start (which is why you choose the subject). As soon as enough drawing is done, paint in the shadows directly with a brush. Later on, further pen drawing can be added.*

SKETCHING

The object of sketching is usually to record information for later use, not just by drawing detail, but by capturing lighting or even colour effects. Sketching enjoyment is dependent on the weather and available time, but also on your choice of materials. The widespread popularity of the pencil has obscured the benefits and advantages of toned paper and a wider range of materials. If pencil is used, the soft Bs, 3B-6B, provide an immediate effect, especially on good heavyweight cartridge or watercolour paper.

Lighter pencils, like an HB, can fill in details later. The alternative of using toned paper gives you a flying start, as a basic tone is already there and doesn't have to be worked up patiently from white paper. Soft pencil, charcoal, sharpened conté all work well for the basic drawing, which then comes alive with the application of either white conté or white gouache. This employment of mixed materials dates back to the beginning of drawing and probably captures more information in the shortest time than any other method.

Make sure you are comfortable before you start as external annoyances will affect your concentration and shorten your sketching time. A combined stool and easel, or a camping chair, is the best outdoor seat. The ground, if dry, is also suitable, but may give too low a viewpoint. In a sketch, all you know about drawing and painting has to be pressed into service within a limited time. A certain amount of accuracy has to be sacrificed for speed, but be careful of careless or hasty scribbling, because every mark or wash will need to be an intelligible reminder later.

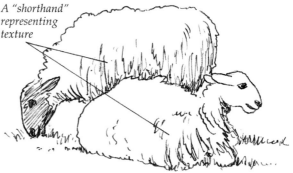

A sketch, recording position

A "shorthand" representing texture

SKETCHING OUTFITS

The canvas bag is the basis of all expeditions, and holds useful extras, such as a flask. The sketching outfits below and opposite are shown in order of the speed of use, so the pencil may be best when time is short, but the coloured paper and conté outfit is nearly as quick to use and makes for a more informative result. Pen, charcoal, chalks and white will give you everything except colour and is a very satisfying combination. The watercolour outfit can produce a finished picture, given time.

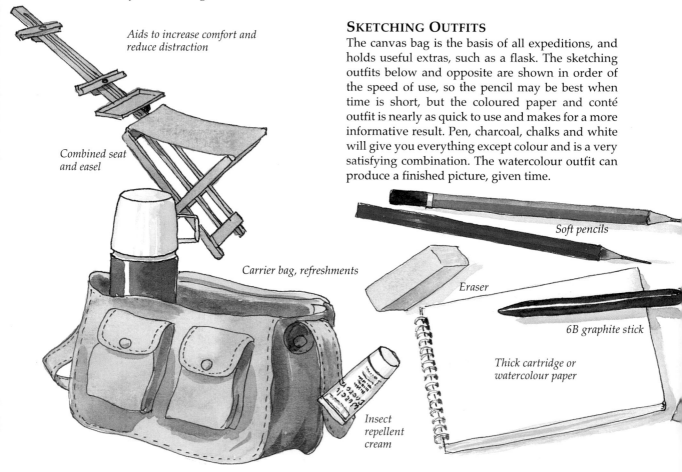

Aids to increase comfort and reduce distraction

Combined seat and easel

Carrier bag, refreshments

Insect repellent cream

Soft pencils

Eraser

6B graphite stick

Thick cartridge or watercolour paper

A sketch on blue-grey paper heightened with white

Darker wash over shadows

Sunlit areas put in with white paint or conté

SKETCHING TO AID THE MEMORY

Outline and sample detail

Carefully drawn seed-head

Majority roughly drawn

Until you are experienced, monochrome line and wash will give better results than colour sketching, where paint mixing can take up too much time. For colour sketching:

■ Employ a good range of colours. Don't waste time in mixing with too limited a palette unless you are very experienced.

■ Use paints that are fresh enough to mix strongly in quantity. Discard old dried-out pans.

■ Keep to a large wash brush and a sable, about size 5, with a good point for details.

■ Use a modest paper size that your brushes can cover quickly.

■ Know some strong and quick 2-colour mixtures that look good and save time, for instance Phthalo Green with Burnt Sienna for trees.

Equipment for line and wash ▷
▽

Small paint-box

Thick paper

White conté

Thick coloured paper

.35 technical pen

Pen

4B pencil

Pencil, HB

Eraser

Camping water bottle

137

WATERCOLOUR

INTRODUCTION

Watercolour is an exciting medium, based on transparency but capable of strong tone and colour. In skilled hands it can also yield an airy and intangible appearance unmatched by any other medium.

Over the years watercolour has come to mean transparent painting without the use of white, but it originated from a technique that included the regular use of body-colour, and there can be no clear dividing line between watercolour with the occasional use of white, and gouache, where white plays a major role. The addition of white in any quantity changes the appearance of watercolour, and the section on gouache describes the different techniques its use requires. Not all watercolour pigments are fully transparent, and a few paints are mixtures containing white, but generally their thin application renders them effectively transparent. In watercolour light travels through the paint film and

is reflected back again by the paper, rather like light passing through a stained-glass window.

The early watercolourists had few permanent colours and worked in a method similar to line and wash, where colours were used to embellish the drawing with tone, introducing light and shade. Improvements in the quality of the paints themselves freed artists from reliance on line and allowed the development of the traditional and modern styles.

The medium's many useful qualities include lightness, portability and cleanliness, making it very suitable for outdoor sketching as well as for more finished paintings.

Watercolour requires a considerable level of skill and technique to be successful, and its transparency means that everything you have done on the painting shows, making corrections difficult.

Shallow Waters, by Barbara Leubke Hill.
A restrained use of colour, such as the gold, brown and violet colour scheme here, is very satisfying in watercolour.

Some modern paints and a watercolour sketch.

Landscape and Meadows by Van Dyck. Its colours may have faded over the years.

The transparency of the paint reveals much of your technique; so good materials will greatly help by making watercolours easier to manage. Fine paper improves the look of the painting, as well as being able to stand a fair amount of abuse. Good paper also allows considerable latitude for building up a painting with successive washes, (a wash is an area of paint applied in one operation). These are easier to apply and manipulate with brushes larger than usual.

Practice, guided towards very definite objectives, such as learning how to apply the basic flat and graded washes, will build up your skill and confidence and help you to avoid reliance on the famous but rare "happy accidents", which happen mainly to the skilful.

Everyone who has made a success of watercolour has made mistakes in the early stages, they are a natural part of learning a difficult medium, so don't be discouraged.

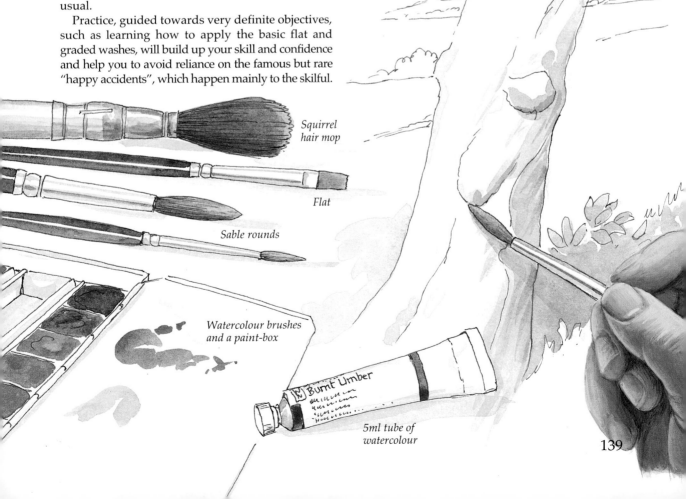

Squirrel hair mop

Flat

Sable rounds

Watercolour brushes and a paint-box

5ml tube of watercolour

139

Materials

Successful painting is much easier with good materials, and it is always worthwhile getting the best you can. It shows in watercolours more than in most other media.

PAPER

The best papers are made of cotton rag; there is some variety of whiteness and absorbency among them. Papers with a hard feel stand up better to repeated working-over than the more absorbent softer types. Most papers are mould made and do for all normal purposes. Hand made paper is occasionally obtainable and one or two firms specialise in it.

HAND-MADE AND MOULD-MADE

Paper is sold in four main forms:

1. Blocks: a stack of cut sheets, gummed together around the edges. They are most useful for smaller pictures where the surface doesn't get wet enough to cause uncontrollable buckling.

2. Books: the sheets are held at one edge only, otherwise they are similar to blocks.

3. Single sheets: usually measure about 56 × 76cm, which you can use full-size, or cut out whatever sizes you need.

4. Rolls: measuring about 152cm across and 10m long. Suppliers will cut off the length you require.

THICKNESS

Paper is made in different thicknesses, which are expressed in terms of weight. In the metric system 1 square metre of medium-thickness paper weighs 300 grams, abbreviated as 300gsm, – grams per square metre. This is equivalent to the old 140lb paper. A thickness of at least 300gsm (140lbs), is desirable to give a solid feel and body to the working surface.

190gsm

300gsm

600gsm

SURFACE

The paper surface, under strong magnification, is like an interwoven fibrous mat, and the size and scale of its texture is the basis of division into 3 surface types. Thicker paper has a more pronounced texture than a thinner paper of the same grade.

1. Rough has considerable texture and grain, providing an attractive and lively surface for larger subjects.

2. Not-, or Cold-Pressed has a medium grain, and is the most popular surface.

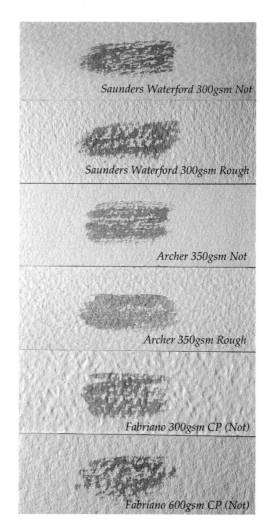

Saunders Waterford 300gsm Not

Saunders Waterford 300gsm Rough

Archer 350gsm Not

Archer 350gsm Rough

Fabriano 300gsm CP (Not)

Fabriano 600gsm CP (Not)

TINTED PAPER

Two Rivers and Bockingford supply lightly tinted paper in a range of colours specially for watercolour. Pastel paper can also be stretched and painted on.

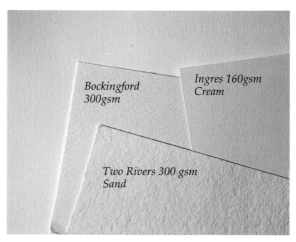

Bockingford 300gsm

Ingres 160gsm Cream

Two Rivers 300 gsm Sand

BUYING WATERCOLOUR PAPER

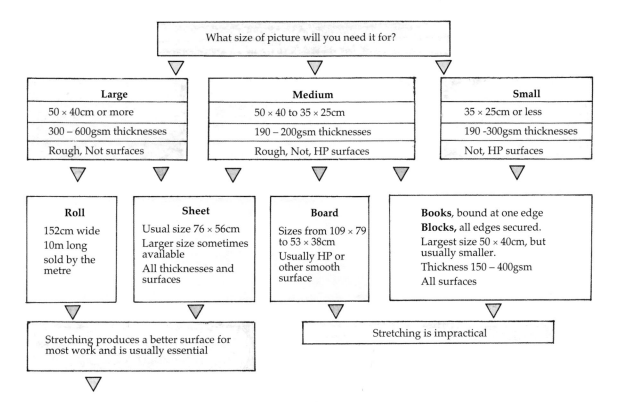

What size of picture will you need it for?

Large	**Medium**	**Small**
50 × 40cm or more	50 × 40 to 35 × 25cm	35 × 25cm or less
300 – 600gsm thicknesses	190 – 200gsm thicknesses	190 -300gsm thicknesses
Rough, Not surfaces	Rough, Not, HP surfaces	Not, HP surfaces

Roll
152cm wide
10m long
sold by the
metre

Sheet
Usual size 76 × 56cm
Larger size sometimes available
All thicknesses and surfaces

Board
Sizes from 109 × 79 to 53 × 38cm
Usually HP or other smooth surface

Books, bound at one edge
Blocks, all edges secured.
Largest size 50 × 40cm, but usually smaller.
Thickness 150 – 400gsm
All surfaces

Stretching produces a better surface for most work and is usually essential

Stretching is impractical

STRETCHING PAPER

For medium to larger pictures the paper has to be stretched on a strong board to maintain a perfectly flat surface at all times and prevent buckling when wet.

First wet the paper to make it expand, then stick it down. As it dries it contracts and tightens like a drum. If you regularly paint to a set size there are paper-stretchers available. These clamp the edges of the pre-wetted paper.

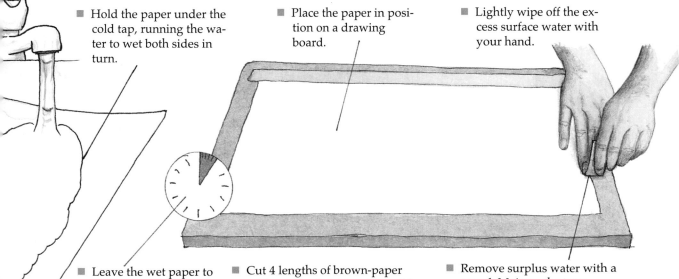

- Hold the paper under the cold tap, running the water to wet both sides in turn.

- Place the paper in position on a drawing board.

- Lightly wipe off the excess surface water with your hand.

- Leave the wet paper to expand and settle for about 5 minutes.

- Cut 4 lengths of brown-paper sticky tape, about 4 or 5cm wide. Masking tape isn't suitable as it doesn't stick to damp surfaces.

- Remove surplus water with a towel. Moisten the tape lengths and stick them firmly along the edges of the paper. Leave to dry.

BRUSHES

Watercolour paint isn't sticky enough to hold the brush in shape by itself, so the brush's own shape is transmitted directly to the paper, and its quality has a direct and clear influence on a painting. Brushes are relatively expensive items, especially in the smaller sizes where quality is most important, and at least one good quality brush in a small size is essential. The best guide in buying brushes is to pay as much as you can afford for sizes up to 4 or 5, then go for progressively cheaper types with increasing size. Before buying, test smaller brushes in water to check their points if you have any doubts about them.

For many purposes there are special brushes, cheaper and more effective than the equivalent larger sable, some with different shapes to the Round, and you may find these suit your needs better.

SABLE BRUSHES

Sable brushes are the best and most agreeable to use in terms of springiness, retaining their shape and paint-holding capacity, but price increases steeply with size. The top grades are hand-made with great care, and for the smaller sizes there is no real substitute.

The best hairs come from the middle of the bushy tails of minks that live in very cold climates. The individual hairs are narrowly spindle-shaped and have minute projections that hold the water, preventing it from running off too freely.

Size 3

Size 5

Size 7

SABLE AND SYNTHETIC BLENDS

Brushes made of a mixture of sable and synthetic hair are steadily improving in quality. Sable is available in various grades, so price is still a very good guide to what you will be getting.

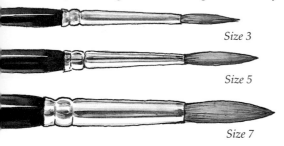

Size 16

Synthetic blends are a little less responsive than pure sables, and don't hold so much paint, but they are very practical in the larger sizes where they can cost less than half the price of a sable.

SQUIRREL HAIR MOPS

Squirrel mop, size 6

These are soft and floppy, but excellent for large washes. They hold a lot of wet paint, apply it very smoothly, and make the laying of a large wash unbelievably easy. They are carefully made and not as cheap as you might expect.

VARNISH AND FOAM BRUSHES

1" varnish brush

Varnish brushes work well for large unobstructed washes where there is room to manoeuvre. They hold plenty of paint, have a pleasant spring and are much cheaper than any other sort at this size, except for the foam mops. They apply the paint very smoothly and flat when well loaded, but don't hold all that much paint. Very cheap.

FLAT BRUSHES

½" flat

Side view

The lower brush illustrates the flat's ability to work in narrow spaces.

Their main use is in architectural work, for windows and doors, where the natural square edge keeps the crispness of shapes without having to work over them again. They are less good for washes as their flattened shape and synthetic hair cause them to hold less paint than the bulkier round brushes. Flat sables partially overcome this problem through their superior water-holding properties, but they are expensive, and most brushes are of the synthetic sort. Square brushes have a useful manoeuvrability.

WRITERS' QUILLS

Much longer than round sables and hold a lot of paint. Used for long strips of

Large duck (named after birds)

colour where the length of their hair helps to keep the edges parallel.

RIGGERS

Riggers are smaller and are employed to delineate long fine lines, such as the rigging of sailing ships.

Size 1

SPOTTER

Stubby brushes for spots. The small sizes are tiny, so buy the larger.

Size 2 spotter

THE CARE OF BRUSHES

After use, clean gently but firmly by pressing the hairs nearest the ferrule against the inside of the waterpot. Hold the pot so you don't push it over. Reshape the point when clean.

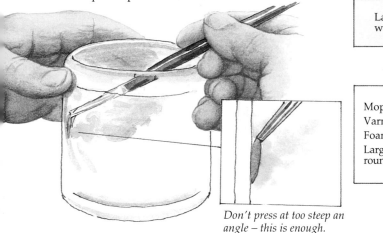

Don't press at too steep an angle – this is enough.

After shaping and drying, brushes are best kept in pots as shown, with the tips free.

For transporting brushes, attach them with an elastic band to a rod longer than the brushes to prevent the tips from touching the end of the container.

Dowel   *Elastic bands*

SELECTION OF BRUSHES

Depending on your needs, the smallest should be of the best quality you can afford. The large brushes solve many of the beginner's problems with washes. The chart below offers some suggestions.

Large washes	Medium washes General work	Fine detail Drybrush texture
	Blended rounds Flats	
Mops Varnish Foam Large blended rounds		Fine sables Spotters
	Quills, Riggers for lines	

Sable hair now comes from the mink, an animal that ranges across the north of Europe and Asia. The word "Kolinsky", used to describe some of the top quality hair, is a derivation of "Kola", the northern Russian peninsula bordered by the Arctic Ocean and the White Sea. The hair is at its best in spring, and is in short supply because of over-exploitation.

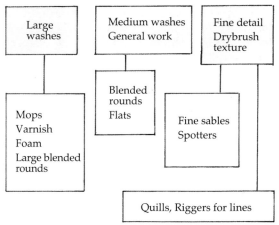

ACCESSORIES

PALETTES

Palettes made of china are the most pleasant and convenient if you are working at home; they stay white and are easy to clean, unlike plastic ones which stain and become oily so that the paint draws itself into blobs. This can also happen to the enamel palettes in paintboxes, in which case a wipe with a kitchen cleaner will remove the greasiness, and a harder rub will get rid of any stains as well. A nest of saucers is good for larger-scale pictures.

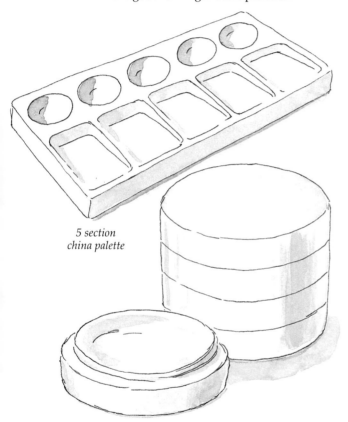

5 section china palette

Nests of saucers are made in two sizes, 9cm and 7cm diameter.

SPONGES

Sponges can be used as an extension to your brush set as a means of dabbing on textures or foliage, or for wiping out larger washes that are too strong or uneven – be careful not to abrade the wet paper. This operation should only be a last resort. Both the little natural sponges and the artificial sort can be useful to have around. When stretching paper (p. 141) use a sponge to wet the brown paper tape.

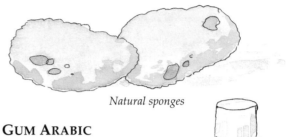

Natural sponges

GUM ARABIC

This is sold as watercolour medium, and can be added in small amounts to dark colours to increase their depth and intensity. It can also be diluted and painted over the top of previous washes.

Without gum   *With gum*

OX-GALL

Ox-gall comes in bottles and is a de-greaser. It will carry paint freely over previously invisible thumb-prints that your paint has just revealed, and assists the spread of paint on old paper that has developed a resistant surface tension. It is not so good in larger washes where it inhibits the spread of the paint so the wash could dry with traces of brushmarks.

Wooden ruler 30cm long

The brush's ferrule rests against top edge.

WOODEN RULER

A device you will have to make for yourself from a length of quadrant, a wine-cork, some glue and a hobby-knife to slice the cork. The construction and method of use are shown in the diagrams. Practise straight lines and edges on some spare paper, keeping your thumb and first two fingers touching the wood as you slide your hand along.

MASKING FLUID

Masking fluid is a rubber solution that can be applied over areas you want to protect from the surrounding washes. The paint will flow over the masked area without affecting the paper underneath. When the surrounding paper is *completely* dry the masking fluid can be rubbed off with a finger-tip or a soft rubber. If you put it on with a brush, use an old one.

HAIR DRIER

Used at a safe distance so it doesn't curl up the paper, a hair-drier can save a lot of time on wet pictures, as long as the paint is given time to settle itself first. Watch carefully so that the drying is reasonably even.

CLEANING

- ▪ White spirit will clean out the brush, although it takes time.

- ▪ The dry masking fluid can be rubbed off the nib.
- ▪ I have used the same set of nibs for years.

STUDIO LAYOUT

Anglepoise lamp with daylight 60W bulb

Sketch reference

Most people's studios are their dining or kitchen tables, but the painting arrangements, however portable and temporary, should be convenient, comfortable and well-lit. The level of brightness is especially important, as ordinary room electric light is too dim and can cause eye-strain. The solution is to use an anglepoise lamp on the table when the daylight is no longer sufficient. The subject matter, or anything to do with it, is placed straight ahead, just beyond the painting paper.

PAINTS

Watercolour is made of very finely ground pigment in a medium of gum arabic, sometimes with additions of glycerine and honey.

Tubes and pans are usually made to slightly different formulae, with a more liquid consistency in the tubes. Tubes and half-pans are generally identical in cost in the shop, but there is more paint in a tube. The choice between them depends on the size of your pictures, how often you paint, and personal preference. Tube paints are always fresh, so for strong colours or large areas they are the best choice.

They also keep better over a long period than pan colours because the tubes are air-tight.

The instant availability of pan colours is their great convenience, and they are more suited to small or medium-sized pictures. Pan colours come off strongly when new, but gradually harden as they dry in the paintbox, and after about 2 or 3 years, or sooner, the faster-drying ochres, umbers and blues should be replaced. Whole pans are a compromise, with a larger surface area for a bigger brush to work in.

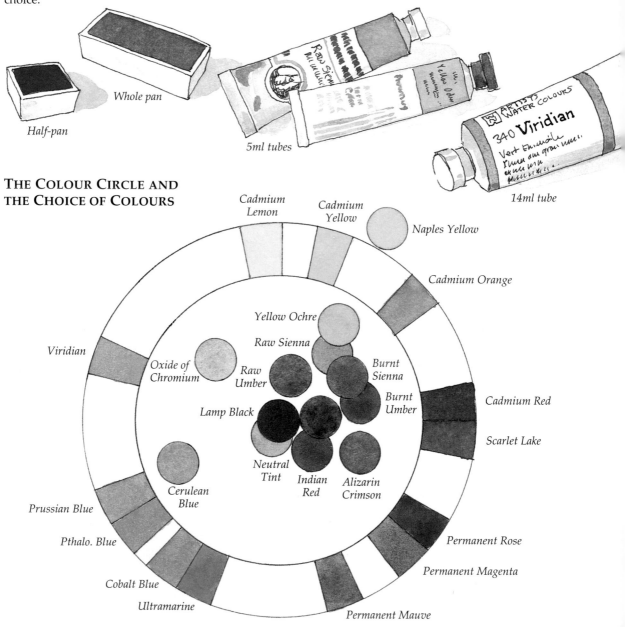

THE COLOUR CIRCLE AND THE CHOICE OF COLOURS

Some popular colours and their relationship to the colour circle.

COLOURS TO CHOOSE

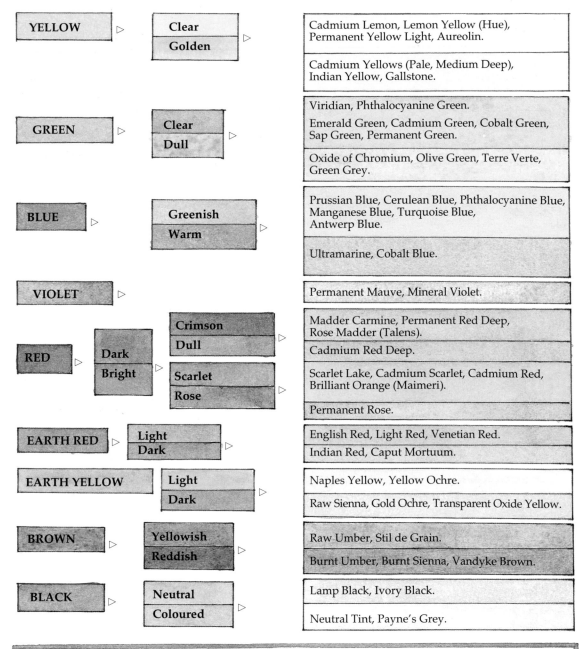

YELLOW	Clear	Cadmium Lemon, Lemon Yellow (Hue), Permanent Yellow Light, Aureolin.
	Golden	Cadmium Yellows (Pale, Medium Deep), Indian Yellow, Gallstone.
GREEN	Clear	Viridian, Phthalocyanine Green.
		Emerald Green, Cadmium Green, Cobalt Green, Sap Green, Permanent Green.
	Dull	Oxide of Chromium, Olive Green, Terre Verte, Green Grey.
BLUE	Greenish	Prussian Blue, Cerulean Blue, Phthalocyanine Blue, Manganese Blue, Turquoise Blue, Antwerp Blue.
	Warm	Ultramarine, Cobalt Blue.
VIOLET		Permanent Mauve, Mineral Violet.
RED Dark	Crimson	Madder Carmine, Permanent Red Deep, Rose Madder (Talens).
	Dull	Cadmium Red Deep.
Bright	Scarlet	Scarlet Lake, Cadmium Scarlet, Cadmium Red, Brilliant Orange (Maimeri).
	Rose	Permanent Rose.
EARTH RED	Light	English Red, Light Red, Venetian Red.
	Dark	Indian Red, Caput Mortuum.
EARTH YELLOW	Light	Naples Yellow, Yellow Ochre.
	Dark	Raw Sienna, Gold Ochre, Transparent Oxide Yellow.
BROWN	Yellowish	Raw Umber, Stil de Grain.
	Reddish	Burnt Umber, Burnt Sienna, Vandyke Brown.
BLACK	Neutral	Lamp Black, Ivory Black.
	Coloured	Neutral Tint, Payne's Grey.

CHOOSING THE COLOURS YOU WILL NEED

Choose some paints from each colour group – popular colours are listed above in the boxes on the right. The names in each box have been used by painters over the years, and, together with a few others, their names crop up repeatedly. There is no need to limit yourself to a few colours only, unless you are learning the basics of colour mixing. Most artists have between 12 and 20 colours in their boxes and others in reserve, although they only use about 9 or 10 in any one picture. Several yellows are useful in covering their extensive range, but two or three blues are often sufficient. A brilliant and a dark red are a basis for adding others. The earth colours, which include yellows, reds and browns, are important for softening the brilliance of other colours and save a lot of mixing time.

147

COLOUR MIXING

This is a mysterious subject for many, but some well-directed experiments of your own will start you on the road. The theory of colour mixing is based on the three "primary" colours; the theory's more useful extension to six primaries is explained on p. 37. Good judgement comes from knowing what the primary colours can do: the more you experiment the quicker you learn. When mixing, put out the weaker colour first, then add the stronger.

A few useful mixtures for common colours are described on the opposite page to show the practice and thinking behind colour mixing.

To match a colour, start with whichever colour in your box seems most like the one you are matching. How does it differ? – does it need more yellow, brown, red, or blue to make it closer in shade? Add a little of whatever it seems to need. You may need a third or even a fourth colour. Start again if you are getting nowhere.

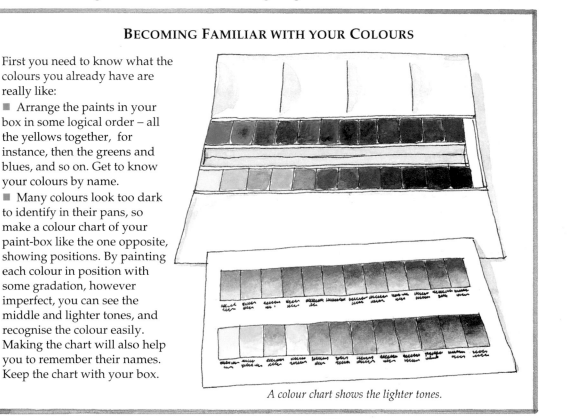

BECOMING FAMILIAR WITH YOUR COLOURS

First you need to know what the colours you already have are really like:

■ Arrange the paints in your box in some logical order – all the yellows together, for instance, then the greens and blues, and so on. Get to know your colours by name.

■ Many colours look too dark to identify in their pans, so make a colour chart of your paint-box like the one opposite, showing positions. By painting each colour in position with some gradation, however imperfect, you can see the middle and lighter tones, and recognise the colour easily. Making the chart will also help you to remember their names. Keep the chart with your box.

A colour chart shows the lighter tones.

SOME USEFUL MIXTURES

When mixing greys from brown and blue, choose the warm blues, Ultramarine or Cobalt, in preference to the greener and cooler blues, (Phthalocyanine or Prussian), which turn mixtures cold and greenish. The example opposite shows the difference.

■ Make the initial mixture fairly thick, then dilute some of it with water to the desired tone.

■ Colours are made paler by adding water, which retains the character of the pigment throughout its tone range.

■ White is not used in pure watercolour.

Water reflections: water is often blue-green, so here is the occasion to use the greener Prussian Blue, together with Burnt Sienna to tone it down towards a more neutral colour while retaining the greenness.

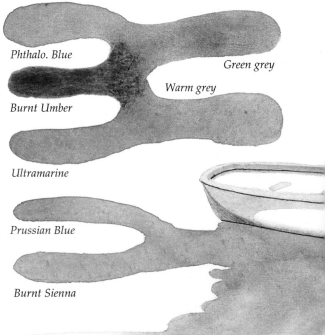

Phthalo. Blue

Green grey

Warm grey

Burnt Umber

Ultramarine

Prussian Blue

Burnt Sienna

Cloud shadows 1: these are more colourful than is often realised. A very small touch of Permanent Mauve added to Neutral Tint provides a useful small-scale cloud colour. Unless the wash is to be very pale, mix in small amounts of colourful additions to all blacks and strong greys. The varieties of Neutral Tint with a slight violet cast can otherwise almost be used on their own.

Cloud shadows 2: larger areas look good with a combination of Cobalt Blue and Venetian Red, a complex red that contains just enough yellow to prevent the mixture from becoming violet, but not enough to lose the warmth of the red and blue mixture. Any warm blue, like Cobalt or Ultramarine mixed with any earth reds, such as Light Red, English and Venetian Reds, will make attractive and natural warm greys.

Trees: Phthalocyanine Green, or the similar Viridian, is a powerful clear colour that can dominate mixtures, but by adding enough Raw Sienna, an almost brown yellow, the greenish colour becomes subtle and muted. Burnt Sienna, Raw or Burnt Umber, or some of the yellow-browns are alternatives to Raw Sienna. Keep the greens of your landscape trees warm and muted; clear natural greens can look out of place in a painting.

Landscape greens: the addition of Raw Umber to Prussian Blue produces a definite but subtle olive green. The Raw Umber acts as a very dark yellow, containing enough red to tone down the green. Prussian Blue always needs careful handling to prevent it dominating mixtures. Raw Umber can vary according to the maker; sometimes a little additional yellow may be needed to keep the mixture green.

Light greens: Phthalocyanine Blue with the addition of Naples Yellow gives a soft blue-green. There is little real yellow in Naples Yellow, so you can use it to control and harmonise colours and mixtures that may otherwise be too crude. It contains white and becomes opaque if applied heavily, so keep it thin. Only a little of the powerful Phthalocyanine Blue is needed in any mixture; use it with caution. The further addition of Aureolin turns the combination to a light soft green that is still quite bright.

Roofs: are very variable, but often a dull red. Indian Red, well diluted, is the basis of the roof shown here, with the addition of Raw Sienna to give some extra warmth and richness. Indian Red and the allied Caput Mortuum dilute to almost a reddish grey. Add brighter reds of any sort, and more yellow, if you need to liven up the colouring.

Brick: in its many varieties can be matched in the first instance with one of the brick-coloured red earths: English Red is used here, warmed in colour by the addition of Yellow Ochre, and reduced in intensity with plenty of water, or greyed with the addition of a warm blue.

Neutral Tint

Permanent Mauve

Cobalt Blue

Venetian Red

Phthalo. Green

Raw Sienna

Raw Umber

Prussian Blue

Phthalo. Blue

Naples Yellow

Aureolin

English Red

Raw Sienna

English Red

Yellow Ochre

Techniques

HOW TO LAY A FLAT WASH

Water not only carries, but distributes the paint. A sizeable wash uses a lot of paint: for a large wash it is advisable and safer to make up 3 or 4 times as much paint as you think you will need. The more water you put on the paper, the more evenly it will spread the colour, and the paint will dry with its maximum brilliance. Tilt the board slightly so the paint you are applying forms an elongated drop along the bottom side of the brush stroke. Use the largest brush you can manoeuvre within the area of the wash, and keep it fully charged.

■ Start at the top with a fully loaded brush, stroke on the paint without hurrying, keeping the brush moving.

■ At the end of the first stroke, return to just below the starting point and paint another band across the paper, continuing downwards. Each stroke just overlaps the previous one, which is still very wet.

■ Recharge the brush at the first hint that you may be pushing the paint across the paper – a lot of the paint that started in the brush has now transferred to the paper – and if you let it run short it will begin to dry out.

Two things to remember:

■ Mix enough paint. ■ Replenish the brush frequently.

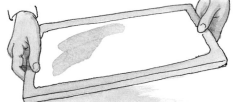

For a larger wash that is still shiny with wet paint, tilt the board back and forth to help the paint to run around and settle evenly. Lift off persistent drops with a clean, slightly damp brush.

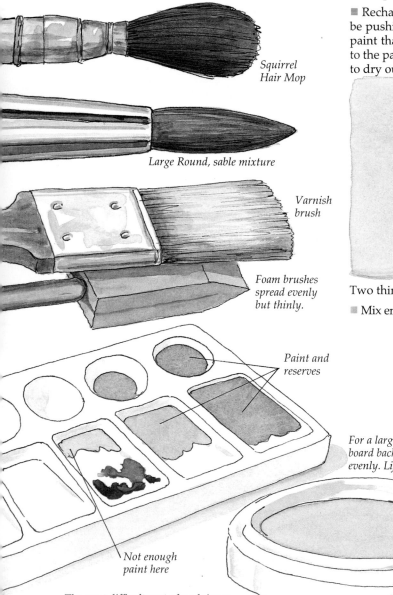

*Squirrel
Hair Mop*

Large Round, sable mixture

*Varnish
brush*

*Foam brushes
spread evenly
but thinly.*

*Paint and
reserves*

*Not enough
paint here*

*Mix up a great quantity
for a large wash. A china
plate will hold even more
than this saucer.*

*The most difficult part of applying a
large wash is to make up enough paint.*

HOW TO LAY A GRADED WASH

The success of a graded wash depends on preparing the paint in advance and keeping the paper wet until you have finished. The paper needs to be damp to slow the drying, so that successive applications of paint have time to mingle freely before drying

Mix up plenty of fluid paint to match the strongest part of the wash. Transfer some of this to another saucer and add water to make a weaker tone. Use some of this in turn for the next weaker tone, and so on.

For smaller areas add more water to the initial mixture: start with the strongest shade, add water to the mixture for each brush stroke.

Ready-mixed tones of paint. Make sure there is enough.

Use as large a brush as possible.

PREPARATION

Dampen the paper first. This is more important than with a flat wash because it keeps the first parts wet while you add new paint further down. The wetness of the new brushstrokes may even increase as more water is added to dilute the mixture. Try to avoid this. The dampening also helps to prolong the moist period during which the pigment distributes itself.

A sponge will damp the paper.

Wet the paper with a sponge or large brush. Don't press too hard with the sponge as the trailing edge will lift off most of the water you have just put on.

Tilt the board slightly towards you.

The method is the same as for a flat wash, (see opposite), except that the brush is recharged with progressively more diluted paint each time. It is most important not to let the wash dry out too soon.

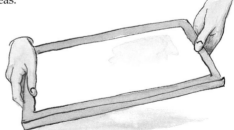

Lift off the excess paint with the tip of a brush that is just damp. The whole wash should still be wet and shiny, and if so, it will probably be useful to tilt the board in different directions so that the paint runs back and forth to make it blend and intermix evenly.

With a large wash, be prepared to take some time on this. When it is clearly drying evenly all over it can be left. Uneven drying can sometimes be prevented by directing a hair-drier onto the wetter areas.

Graded washes are more difficult and unpredictable than the flat ones, but are used more frequently. Trying some out on a dampened sheet of good paper is time well spent. Use a variety of mixtures, as pigments vary in their drying characteristics, some are smooth, others readily leave lines or brushmarks. Practise as much as you can, and you will soon build your confidence for the numerous occasions you will need to use graded washes.

VARIEGATED WASHES

Variegated washes are where one colour is smoothly graded into another.

Mix up plenty of the two colours separately, then use part of each to make two intermediate mixtures. All the mixtures should be of equivalent "wetness", as a thicker colour won't blend evenly with a more watery one. A thinner one will run back into the paint already on the paper.

Try various colour combinations to find out how the pigments behave.

HOW TO LAY A VARIEGATED WASH

Damp the paper first and then tilt the board slightly towards yourself.

With a large brush and plenty of the first colour, stroke on the paint horizontally without hurrying, keeping the brush moving.

At the end of the first stroke, return to just below the starting point and paint another band across the paper, continuing downwards. Each stroke just overlaps the previous one, which is still very wet.

As it becomes necessary, take your paint from the intermediate mixtures in turn.

Smaller washes need not be so wetly applied.

Recharge the brush whenever necessary, and keep the paper wet, but for smaller areas the wash need not be quite so wet, or the colours may mingle too freely and lose their identities as they run together.

If the variegated wash is not entirely satisfactory, it is sometimes possible to let it dry completely, re-wet the whole of it with plenty of clean water, and drop in colour to spread over parts of the underlying wash.

The whole area should still be wet or damp when you have finished applying the paint.

If it is still wet enough, you can then tilt the board at different angles by hand to make the paint run downwards in any direction you wish to help in blending the colours.

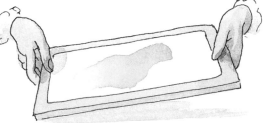

Use brushes as large as you can manage.

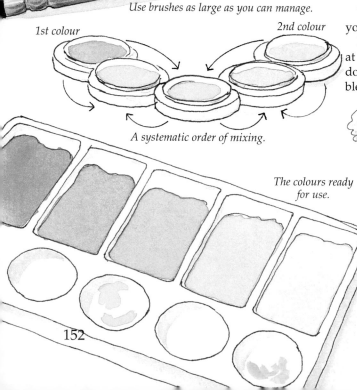

1st colour

2nd colour

A systematic order of mixing.

The colours ready for use.

Lift off excess paint with the tip of a brush that is just damp. As the paint begins to lose its shine and start to dry, lay the board flat to dry.

An Alternative Method in Two Stages

Where there is a contrast in strength of colour in a variegated wash, you can divide the operation into two separate parts:

1. Paint on a graded wash of the weaker colour and let it dry thoroughly. When it is dry, you can re-wet it with clean water and then brush it back and forth with a large damp brush; this process smooths out the gradation a little, removes some of the colour, and increases the luminosity of the remainder. Only work over pale colours, deeper-coloured washes may lift-off in patches.

2. When the underlayer is completely dry, paint on the stronger graded wash. This method, including the washing down of the first colour, is especially useful in achieving a luminous warm sky. The first wash is painted as a normal graded wash and left to dry. The second is painted over it starting from the opposite end. The two washes overlap to show their separate treatment. Put on the lighter, less important colour first.

Skies are especially suitable subjects for the more controlled type of variegated wash. Variegated washes are also used for much smaller areas, where a little colour variation brings life and interest; just drop in some blending shade as you apply the main colour.

WET-IN-WET

This is closely allied to the variegated washes, but here a second colour is added directly to a wet wash already on the paper, to mingle and spread within it. Make a few practice attempts until you can judge how much a colour is likely to spread. Try dropping colour into washes at different stages of drying to see how far the new colour diffuses into the wet paint, and also note the way some Ultramarines and Cerulean Blues become granulated as they dry.

PREPARATION

Prepare sufficient quantity of all the colours you are going to use. Then damp the whole area with a large brush to help the paint spread evenly. This makes the whole process more certain because the additional dampness in the paper prolongs the drying period, giving you more time to place the new colours. The wetter the wash on the paper the further the new paint will spread and the softer the gradation. This technique is often used in the earlier stages of a painting for larger areas, such as the dropping-in of soft-edged clouds into a background of sky.

STRETCHING THE PAPER

The paper needs to be well stretched so it remains flat while the washes are applied and while they are drying.

USE BIG BRUSHES

The larger the brushes the easier the large underlying washes become. The dropped-in wet paint will lose a lot of its effect if the initial wash is uneven or is developing drying marks. Wet really does mean very wet.

Squirrel Hair Mop

Foam brush

Natural sponge

MIX PLENTY OF COLOUR

Big brushes soak up the colour, and they need to be wet to work well. Mix up a large amount, bearing in mind that this stage usually comes at the beginning of a picture, and large areas are to be covered.

Saucers of ready-mixed

WET THE PAPER

A large brush well filled with water makes a start in building up the high level of wetness needed for this process. To be effective, the colours have to be able to run freely into each other. Alternatively, you could damp the paper initially with a sponge.

Colour the water with a drop of paint to show where the paper has been wetted.

APPLYING THE PAINT

Apply the basic colour wash, which should be as wet as you can reasonably make it, either flat, graded or variegated as you wish. Colour is then dropped-in where necessary and allowed to run into the existing wash. As the whole thing gradually dries, new drier colour can be placed more precisely, until the paper is dry again, when sharp strokes can be added.

Thicker colour flows and blends with a pale background.

DROPPING-IN FURTHER COLOURS

While the paper is wet, any number of colours can be dropped-in. Once it has dried it can be re-wetted and the process repeated, taking care not to accidentally lift or mark the first washes.

It is important to remember that as the wash on the paper has already begun to dry, the colour on your brush needs to be slightly drier than that on the paper to blend in evenly.

TILTING THE BOARD

When the paper is really wet the flow of new colour can be controlled to a surprising extent by tilting the board, and this can be used as the basis for reflections in water. Once everything is in position and drying evenly, lay the board flat to dry.

Very wet paint dropped into wet ground colour.

Paint mixture separating.

Wet paint dropped into damp ground.

Drier paint placed into damp wash.

The paper was tilted to make the paint run in this direction.

Green dropped into damp ground.

The drier red spreads attractively into the damp leaf colouring. After the paint is dry, further adjustments can be made with a small dry brush, with the methods described on the next page.

Red dropped in around edges.

Paint that is wetter than the wash already on the paper will spread out quickly in damp surroundings and push the existing drying pigment along before it, building up an edge that dries in a heavier patchy line. These are the common and unsightly drying marks.

DRYBRUSH

This is a way of using a brush from which most of the paint has been removed before it touches the picture. It is not dry, but damp rather than wet. By stroking the brush across absorbent paper most of the paint is drawn out and the tip becomes splayed out like the tip of a feather. This tip spreads the pigment lightly and with a soft edge; the paint will come off mainly on to the raised texture of the paper.

You can achieve very controlled modelling and gradation by keeping a light touch with the brush, and a high degree of finish and detail becomes possible. With a more rounded tip the paint is more concentrated and comes off with less of a soft edge. When the brush is too wet, the brushstrokes dry with a hard edge rather than soft. To control small scale modelling and achieve a realistic finish, a mastery of drybrush technique is essential.

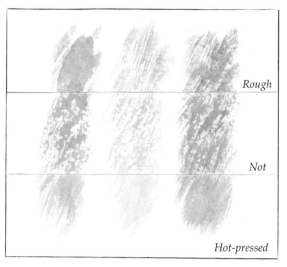

Rough

Not

Hot-pressed

Different surfaces react very differently as the grain is emphasised by drybrush work. Drybrush is generally more effective on the not- or hot-pressed papers.

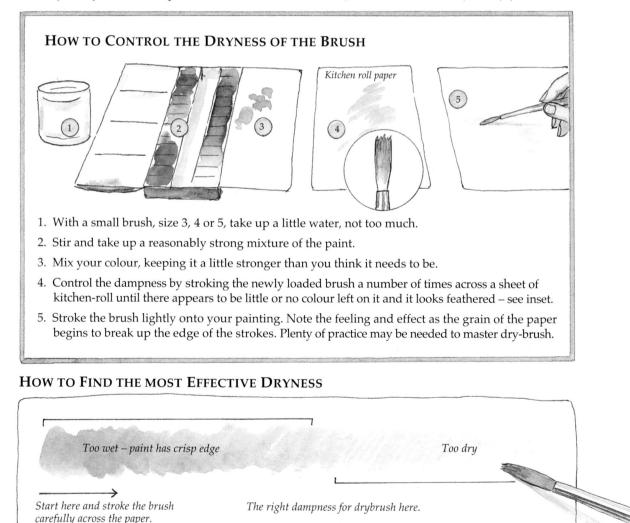

HOW TO CONTROL THE DRYNESS OF THE BRUSH

Kitchen roll paper

1. With a small brush, size 3, 4 or 5, take up a little water, not too much.

2. Stir and take up a reasonably strong mixture of the paint.

3. Mix your colour, keeping it a little stronger than you think it needs to be.

4. Control the dampness by stroking the newly loaded brush a number of times across a sheet of kitchen-roll until there appears to be little or no colour left on it and it looks feathered – see inset.

5. Stroke the brush lightly onto your painting. Note the feeling and effect as the grain of the paper begins to break up the edge of the strokes. Plenty of practice may be needed to master dry-brush.

HOW TO FIND THE MOST EFFECTIVE DRYNESS

Too wet – paint has crisp edge

Too dry

Start here and stroke the brush carefully across the paper.

The right dampness for drybrush here.

Work the brush slowly across the paper, remembering how it feels when the paint comes off softly.

HOW TO ADD DETAIL AND TEXTURE

A very high degree of finish and control can be achieved by a drybrush technique over a basis of washes. The initial washes build up the modelling and colour in the usual way and provide a pleasing foundation for the drier work that follows after the paper is dry again.

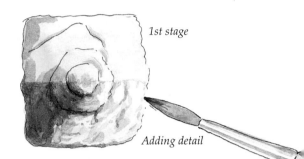

1st stage

Adding detail

In the painting detail above, the basic washes and shadows were laid in first, giving a good approximation of the finished picture. When it was dry, shapes were built up with small strokes and lines, and the three-dimensional effect grew as the darks and crisp details were added.

With a size 3 brush, using stronger and drier mixtures, find the right degree of dampness for the brush by following the method described on the previous page. When the brush has the right dampness, "draw" in detail and colour, blending them with the initial washes as you go. Wait for each stroke to dry. A build-up of dampness will prevent paint being added.

GRADATION

Graded washes are frequently uneven or incomplete in some way, but careful drybrush work can adjust and improve them. Once the wash is dry it can be scanned for unevenness, and the paler patches carefully worked over with a dry brush, building up the tones gradually. Only use very pale paint; it is hard to remove darker colour without it showing.

Accurate judgement of tone is needed to level up minor tonal differences, but you will be training your eye at the same time. The final effect of a lot of drybrushing over an area can be slightly gritty and dry looking, as the paint can build up on the paper grain. A final liquid wash, containing a trace of the colouring, and lightly painted across the surface will greatly improve the texture and restore its smoothness.

The varied and uneven washes, left, provide a good basis for the tone and textures added on top of them, right.

157

OCCASIONAL TECHNIQUES

Watercolours are rarely straightforward applications of a few washes, although the aim is often to make them look like that. Many effects cannot be achieved so simply, and sometimes require extensive drybrush work; minor mistakes often need adjusting, and the following techniques, carefully employed, extend the normal range of the basic washes.

LIFTING OUT

This refers to the removal of dry or nearly dry paint already on the paper. Because watercolour can always be dissolved, the paint can be re-wetted and worked on again. The difficulty is that the paper texture holds the paint firmly in place, once it is on the paper. The paint you remove is the thickness resting actually on the surface, so thicker colours and heavy applications come off more easily than thin layers. The fine stain-like colours work their way into the paper surface and are held there permanently.

■ Apply water and leave to soak in a little.

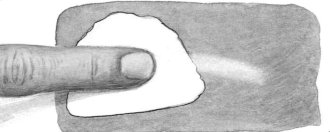

■ Press firmly with blotting paper to lift off the paint.

■ Wet again with the brush and blot again, repeating as often as necessary. Be careful not to scrub in any way with the brush, as it can damage the paper surface. It is much easier to lift paint from a smooth surface than a rough one.

SPONGING

Natural or artificial sponges can be used to apply paint. They are occasionally used for textures, and can sometimes be useful for foliage or rock if used with discretion and combined with normal brushwork and spattering. Small natural sponges provide the most natural textures.

Build up slowly so that the first layers have time to dry, otherwise they will smear, become formless, and require time-consuming rescue work.

△
Mix up a lot of paint, in two or three shades, in a rather thick mixture. Dip a small sponge into the lightest shade and apply the paint directly to the picture with a light touch.

Finish and complete with a brush, to blend in and incorporate with the rest of the painting.

LIFTING OUT FROM WET PAINT

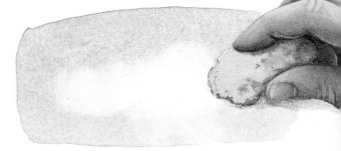

A damp sponge, screwed-up kitchen-roll paper or blotting paper can be used to lift off paint before it dries. This is sometimes useful for taking out cloud shapes from a blue sky.

SPATTERING

Useful textures on paths, beaches or walls are available through spattering, but the style of the rest of the picture has to accommodate it. After spattering, handwork is needed to remove some dots, add others, and blend in the effect with the rest of the picture. Mix up plenty of paint because spattering uses it up in quantity; each time you do it, try it out first on spare paper to see the effect you will getting.

SMALL SPOTS

Small spots are usually done with a toothbrush. Load the top with thicker paint and draw your index finger back along the brush to spray the paint.

MASKING

Masking fluid is a rubbery solution that can be applied to paper with a brush or pen to protect small areas of the painting from paint. Papers and smooth or hard surfaces are most suitable, because the solution grips the paper strongly and could tear the surface of a soft paper when rubbed off.

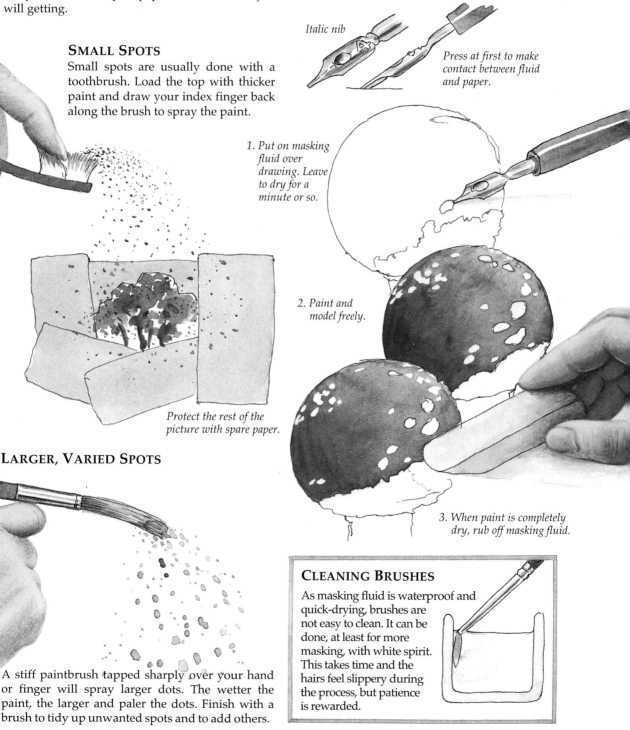

Italic nib

Press at first to make contact between fluid and paper.

1. Put on masking fluid over drawing. Leave to dry for a minute or so.

2. Paint and model freely.

Protect the rest of the picture with spare paper.

LARGER, VARIED SPOTS

A stiff paintbrush tapped sharply over your hand or finger will spray larger dots. The wetter the paint, the larger and paler the dots. Finish with a brush to tidy up unwanted spots and to add others.

3. When paint is completely dry, rub off masking fluid.

CLEANING BRUSHES

As masking fluid is waterproof and quick-drying, brushes are not easy to clean. It can be done, at least for more masking, with white spirit. This takes time and the hairs feel slippery during the process, but patience is rewarded.

SKETCHING

Although many artists work from photographs, sketching will keep you in touch with real life and train your powers of observation. The necessity for speed will also give you practice in selecting the essential parts of the scene to portray, and in recording them effectively.

Sketching is in some ways a summary of your technique. Difficulties in applying the paint can be a obstacle when everything needs to work smoothly to record the subject. It becomes much easier with experience, after you have learnt the basics at leisure at home.

You may well find it sensible to keep to monochrome until you are quite confident you can deal with outdoor colour-mixing efficiently.

MONOCHROME SKETCHING

Recording the tones of the scene before you is usually the fundamental reason for sketching, and this can be greatly simplified by using only one colour, such as black, grey or sepia. In the beginning, sketching in monochrome will be easier as well as satisfying. The freedom from having to match colours will liberate large amounts of time and energy which can be directed towards capturing the more important tones and the lighting.

If the sketch is just for reference for a more finished picture to be done at home, then colour notes can be written on in pencil at the scene.

Equipment is variable according to means and inclination. The essentials are:

■ **Paper** to paint on, usually a block. 600gsm paper is very stiff and will take any reasonable amount of wetness without buckling. Tinted paper is also satisfactory, especially when the colour is in sympathy with the scene or subject. Some types are thick enough for normal washes; the thinner papers with a larger colour range will need stretching beforehand. If the paper is heavily tinted, take some white paint with you.

EQUIPMENT

'Sit and sketch' easel   *Folding portable studio*

Paint brush tube

Pochette

Watercolour block

View-finder

■ **Paintbox** Tubes provide strong fresh colour and work best with a large tray or tin plate for mixing. Pans are handier than tubes, especially for smaller pictures, and hold all the colours in position. Check that all your pans are in good condition, so the paints come readily onto the brush. Most colours harden with age, and if they are too old can damage your brushes and waste time. Replace any that are mean with the colour. Special small boxes are sold for lightweight sketching, and the small pochettes incorporate a water bottle as well. All boxes include palettes.

■ **Brushes** need to be carried in a brush-tube to avoid damaging them. More than four brushes waste time.

■ **Water** A wide-necked plastic bottle from a camping shop is light and waterproof.

SKETCHING IN COLOUR

The addition of colour-mixing to drawing makes considerable demands on your skill, so be familiar with the colours you have. If you intend to base a finished picture on your sketch, then the best use of colour is to try to capture the light, atmosphere and feeling of your subject. You can do this with paint more easily and accurately than a photograph can. Memorise a few useful mixtures such as greys made from Light Red and Ultramarine, or greens from Raw Sienna and Phthalocyanine Blue, or Burnt Sienna and Prussian Blue. A good background repertoire of mixtures will free you to note and explore the unexpected colours you find in real life.

This is not the occasion to find you are without a number of your familiar paints, nor is it a good time to discover the considerable limitations of a restricted palette. Six colours are not enough, unless you really specialise in a limited palette, and a disproportionate amount of time can be spent in colour mixing.

A compromise is to select only a few duller colours to save mixing. This method is an elaboration of monochrome sketching; the colouring is approximate but can be very effective. Yellow Ochre, Light or English Red and Cobalt Blue work well together. If you have plenty of colours, use what you need but keep in mind an overall colour scheme as a control.

AVOID

- **Salt**. Sprinkling salt onto wet paint produces a pattern, but when the paint dries some salt is still there to attract moisture and eventually cause deterioration.

- **Candle wax** is greasy and never really dries, so in the long term the paper will suffer from its presence.

- **Scratching the paper** does it no harm, but the thin harshness of the scratches rarely blends with the surrounding brushwork.

CORRECTIONS

GETTING PAINT OFF AGAIN

If the paint has gone on too heavily, it is sometimes practical to remove some of it. Heavy areas come off much more easily than light ones. Wipe the dark parts gently back and forth with a large brush or wet sponge, and when the paint is softened it can be lifted off with blotting paper. Remember that the paper is soft and easily scuffed while wet. When it is dry again, it may need evening up a little with new paint, and a final glaze can sometimes restore the effect of a newly painted wash.

MUDDINESS

Muddiness is a result of tonal errors and of the way paint is put on. The most common reason for this is the drying of paint before the wash is complete. This is most often caused by using too small a brush, which holds so little paint that it starts to dry on the paper almost immediately. Lift off some paint if possible, then flood on a wash to restore the smoothness. Muddiness is rarely due to faulty paint mixing, and is not the same as a drab colour scheme.

COLOURS SEPARATING AS THEY DRY

Some mixtures, usually involving the red earth colours, blues and violets, separate out slightly as they dry. This cannot be rectified, but remember the colours involved and use their characteristics to deliberately create a texture in a future picture.

FLATTENING BUCKLED PAPER

If 300gsm paper is free at its edges while you paint on it, any buckling caused by the water usually disappears when it dries, but sometimes the buckling remains.

1. Lay the picture face down and wet the back with a clean sponge. Prevent any water from running underneath.

2. Hang the picture on a clothes line to dry. Repeat these two steps if necessary.

If there are still signs of buckling, lay the picture face down on a drawing-board, lay a damp cloth over it (a clean white handkerchief that has been held under the tap and thoroughly squeezed out), and iron firmly with a moderately hot iron. Try this out on a spare picture first.

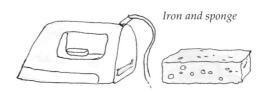

Iron and sponge

WATERCOLOUR STEP-BY-STEP

STREET SCENE, ALTEA

The aim here was to capture the warm and brilliant effect of Mediterranean sunlight by the use of strong clear-cut contrasts of tone and colour. Rough paper was used to achieve a lively textured surface, stretched to keep it flat while flooded with large washes.

The sketch

The sketch painted on the spot was a race against the clock because the shadows were changing all the time. Since the existing light and shade is part of the attraction of a scene, always try to fix their positions as early as possible. A pale grey wash over all the shadow areas as soon as the drawing was complete preserved their shapes.

The thin grey wash preserves the shadows without spoiling the heavy shadow washes painted on later.

The sketch matched the colours of the scene well and gave a good general impression. Two or three photographs provided any details missed in the sketch. Photographs are useful for checking detail and correcting drawing errors but are often misleading on colour; the sketch should convey the colouring you are aiming at and the feeling of the scene.

The sky colour

The sky had to be smooth, without any granulation, which eliminated Ultramarine, Cobalt and Cerulean Blues, leaving Phthalocyanine Blue or Prussian Blue. Phthalocyanine Blue is warmer and richer than Prussian, and the addition of a little Permanent Rose or Permanent Magenta made a very attractive sky blue.

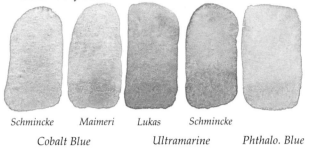

Schmincke   Maimeri   Lukas   Schmincke

Cobalt Blue   Ultramarine   Phthalo. Blue

The amount of granulation varies between makes of paint, and is increased by applying it with a lot of water. Test your own colours.

The graded sky

A large quantity of colour was made up, about three times as much as thought necessary. Unexpectedly running short of paint during a wash invariably leads to spoiling it with drying marks.

■ To pre-wet the sky a touch of the colour was mixed separately with a good quantity of water and painted all over the sky with a large brush. The slight tint helped to show any gaps that had been missed.

■ With the whole sky still damp, the sky colour was flooded on with a large brush, starting at the top. A more diluted wash was painted into its lower edge, and so on down to the roof-tops, going over the distant mountains and sea.

■ The wet sky wasn't entirely even, so the board was picked up and tilted in different directions to help the wet paint run into adjacent areas until it looked smooth and well graded. Where puddles collected in the corners or along the edges, a slightly damp brush lifted off the surplus. The sky was very wet and was left for a long time to dry.

Soak up the surplus with a brush that is just damp, if possible without the brush touching the paper.

The distance

The distance had to be kept soft so as not to compete with the strong foreground contrasts. The mountains were painted in thinly over the blue with a mixture of Cobalt Blue, Raw Sienna and a little Indian Red. The sea had thin washes of Ultramarine and Permanent Magenta laid over the existing blue. The bright roofs were put in with clean orange mixtures, with the detail added when dry.

The shadows

Before the shadows were applied, a very watery wash of Naples and Cadmium Yellows was applied to all the white walls to suggest the warmth of the sunlight.

Three separate mixtures of equal strength were used to give variety, and put on side by side to mingle and blend together. 1) Burnt Sienna and Cobalt Blue with a touch of Madder Carmine: 2) Burnt and Raw Siennas with Cobalt Blue: 3) Ultramarine and Madder Carmine with a little Burnt Sienna.

The main shadow tone was put on with a large brush in one liquid wash, which gave time for it to even itself out smoothly; it also dried cleanly with maximum luminosity.

Note that all the shadows in the scene are of the same strength, with only minor variations. A big range of shadow tones is unreal and destroys the whole shadow effect.

Wet   *Dry*

Watercolours dry lighter: if you are not worried that your wash may be too strong, then it is probably too light. To see their real effects, the shadow washes were tried out on spare paper first.

Overpainting

The road colour was washed on next, and when dry, the shadow crossing the road was darkened to adjust for the road's deeper colour.

The windows, doors and similar details were added with strong single washes where possible on top of the dried shadow wash.

Textures everywhere were put on with a drybrush technique (p. 156), making the most of the rough paper grain where possible. Finally some dark edges were strengthened carefully to increase the brilliance of the sunny surfaces, and the strongest darks intensified with Warm Sepia.

Street Scene, Altea.

Summary

The finished painting is noticeably crisper and more concentrated than the sketch. The extra shadow on the foreground adds depth and stability to the composition, but the palm leaves on the right-hand edge of the sketch would have distracted from the central contrasts, so were left out.

ACRYLICS

INTRODUCTION

Acrylic paint layers are tough, flexible and waterproof, and can be applied to almost any clean, non-oily painting surface. They are very versatile in their manner of application, from thin washes to thick impasto. Acrylics are generally used with a technique that is basically watercolour with the additional overpainting advantages of oils. Their possibilities of imitating other media are limited, as acrylics possess their own handling and surface characteristics which show up as especially different from oils.

As the medium is water-based, the paint dries quickly, and an important feature of acrylics is that once dry, the paint will in no circumstances dissolve again. While still wet, the acrylic binding medium has a milky colour that clears as it dries. This is why acrylic colours darken on drying.

Overpainting, without disturbing the lower layers, can be done as soon as the paint is dry, and effects similar to tempera and gouache as well as watercolours can be achieved if the paint is put on liquidly enough.

Acrylic paints are naturally thicker and less free-flowing than watercolours, even when considerably diluted, so larger washes are not so easy. Their consistency and stickiness is closer to oils, and in thick layers or impasto they are also structurally safer than oils. Acrylics are a popular choice with artists who aim at a realistic and lifelike finish.

Kentish Landscape.
The whites of the daisies have been left as white paper, which is distinctly brighter than any white paint. The golden fields are also fairly transparent, but the trees are painted opaquely as the lights had to be painted over the darks. Several coats of thin white were glazed over the sky and trees, to produce the feeling of space and distance.

Acrylic paints are pigments bound in a mixture of acrylic polymer emulsions, based on polymethyl acrylate, a suspension of large organic chain-like molecules in a water-based emulsion. Once the water has evaporated the residue sets as a flexible and slightly porous plastic which never entirely hardens, although like most plastics it can become brittle at low temperatures. Acrylic paintings are slightly porous and should finally be covered with glass to protect them from dirt and dust. Out-of-doors, paintings can be affected by a gradual dulling of the surface by ultra-violet light.

Acrylic binders originated in the 1950s, and so are a relatively recent invention. They have since passed accelerated ageing tests but have not been around long enough for the real test of time.

When used thinly and transparently, acrylics reveal their possibilities of brilliant colour.

	Drying time	Overpainting	Supports	Surface appearance
Acrylic	0-5 mins	Easy	Any	Matt or satin finish. Gloss varnish can be patchy.
Tempera	0-5 mins	Easy	Panel, thick paper	Satin finish, smooth
Gouache	0-5 mins	Easy in small amounts, difficult later.	Paper	Matt and smooth
Watercolour	0-5 mins	Easy over thin paint, harder over thicker.	Paper	As paper surface
Oils	4hrs-2 weeks	Easy	Canvas, panel	Shiny. As canvas or board surface, or textured.

A comparison of acrylics with the alternative media.

The greatest technical attraction is the quick-drying and water-proof nature of the acrylic surface, and the consequent ability to paint over it freely. The nearest medium in technique and final appearance is egg tempera, but the ready availability of acrylic materials in art shops compared to the need to send away for the pigments for tempera is a great practical advantage. Gouache is also similar, but overpainting can stir up and spoil the underlayers, whereas in acrylic they are completely resistant.

Acrylic tubes are large in size. Smaller tubes are made but rarely stocked in shops.

Wine bottle still life
The "watercolour with over-painting" technique of acrylics is ideally suited to the great variety of transparent and opaque textures – glass, cork, grapes, cloth, metal, wood and bread – in this still life.

Materials

Paints are generally sold in large tubes, although smaller tubes exist. Rowneys supply acrylics in two consistencies, and Liquitex supply both tubes and bottles. A number of liquid acrylic paints, or inks, have recently appeared. The quick-drying and waterproof nature of the paint has the practical effect of making acrylics detrimental to brushes, which need particular care in choice and cleaning. A number of special mediums are available to help in controlling the paint, notably a retarder to slow drying when using a fine brush. Others alter shine and consistency.

PAINTING SURFACES

Acrylic paints will adhere strongly to all non-greasy surfaces without causing any chemical reactions with them, and can match any ground for flexibility. Priming with acrylic gesso is only necessary on board if you need to change the absorbency or colour, but is needed on canvas to achieve a manageable painting surface. Commercial canvases are usually primed for either acrylic or oil paints unless specified as only for oils.

PAPER

Paper is best used in its thicker grades. It should be stretched like watercolour paper if it is likely to cockle during painting. A relatively smooth surface is the easiest to handle, as the grainy surface of rough paper breaks up the flow of paint which is naturally on the viscous side. Coloured paper nearly always needs stretching, but can then make an ideal background for painting on.

Bottles of acrylic ink

PANELS

Panels primed with either acrylic primer, or ordinary gesso as used for egg tempera, make good surfaces. Acrylic Primer can be bought ready to paint onto any clean surface. Leave to dry between each coat, and for at least an hour before painting on it. The surface may be exceptionally smooth on MDF panels (see also p. 204).

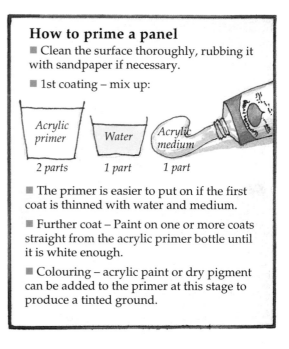

How to prime a panel

■ Clean the surface thoroughly, rubbing it with sandpaper if necessary.

■ 1st coating – mix up:

Acrylic primer	Water	Acrylic medium
2 parts	1 part	1 part

■ The primer is easier to put on if the first coat is thinned with water and medium.

■ Further coat – Paint on one or more coats straight from the acrylic primer bottle until it is white enough.

■ Colouring – acrylic paint or dry pigment can be added to the primer at this stage to produce a tinted ground.

CANVAS

Stretched canvases are sometimes used for larger acrylic paintings. Most commercial canvases are primed for both oil and acrylic. A fine grain canvas is most suitable for acrylic paint as a coarser grain invites unfavourable comparison with oils.

Raw unprimed canvas can be stuck to a panel with a mixture of 4 parts of primer diluted with 1 part of water, worked into the grain until saturated and pressed on until bubble-free before leaving it to dry overnight. The priming coats can then be applied in the normal way.

OTHER SURFACES

Acrylic paints will stick to almost anything, so can be used on walls, silk, leather, or any clean non-oily surface. Los Angeles is notable for its examples of giant acrylic murals painted on buildings. The walls are first thoroughly cleaned by scrubbing or sand-blasting before being sealed and primed with diluted acrylic resins, and finished off with a white surface.

BRUSHES

Acrylics can damage your brushes, so it is more economical to carry out most of the work using older brushes past their best. You will need at least one good quality brush, especially in the smaller sizes, to be able to put the paint on just where you want it; without this, control becomes impossible. When buying brushes, pay as much as you can afford for sizes up to 4 or 5, then go for progressively cheaper types for the larger size.

The paint is bulky, so for detail, the very small brush sizes are better as they retain their points more easily.

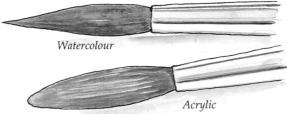

Watercolour

Acrylic

The bulky acrylic paint spreads the hairs of the brush, and works its way up to the ferrule where it can easily harden off.

SABLE

The best and most agreeable to use, but special acrylic brushes made of artificial fibres, or mixtures with sable, are now available and work well. There is no need to buy the very top quality.

HOG'S HAIR

Used by oil and some acrylic painters for large areas, they hold a lot of paint and will press it out evenly.

FLAT

Good for covering larger areas and also useful in architectural work where the natural square edge keeps the crispness of buildings and windows. They are surprisingly manoeuvrable.

Flat

RIGGERS

Useful for adding long even lines. Keep the paint thin and liquid so it flows off evenly.

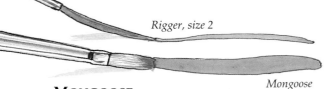

Rigger, size 2

Mongoose

MONGOOSE

Made in all the regular shapes; the hair is intermediate in stiffness between hog's hair and sable.

ACCESSORIES

Erasers, sponges and a hair-drier can be used as in watercolours. A sponge should be washed with soap and water after use with acrylic paint. To keep brushes wet while in use use a tin with a spring holder across the top which grips the brush handles so that the hairs are held in water (see overleaf).

PALETTES

China palettes are convenient if you are working at home; they stay white and are easy to clean because the dried paint peels off easily under the tap.

Storage

Mixing

A nest of saucers is good for mixing quantities for larger scale pictures and for covering and storing the squeezed-out tube colours while working. A large white china plate could also be used.

STAY-WET PALETTES

Stay-wet palettes prevent the paint from drying prematurely by maintaining a damp atmosphere inside.

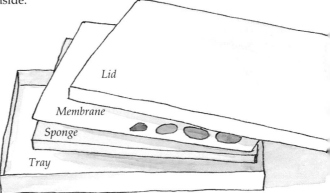

Lid

Membrane

Sponge

Tray

Mixed paint remains in workable condition for hours, and colour squeezed out from the tube for even longer. The palette consists of a plastic box with a tight-fitting lid; inside the box is a damp sponge, and on top of this is a sheet of special disposable paper to mix the paint on.

PLASTIC PALETTES

Avoid these. Although acrylic paint doesn't stick so well to plastic, it can still be difficult to remove without eventually damaging the surface.

ACRYLIC MEDIA

These improve handling for special purposes by altering the qualities of acrylics. The normal acrylic medium provides a little extra gloss and binding power to tube colours. Diluting the paint with a lot of water weakens its binding properties, so extra medium should be added to thin washes and to glazes.

RETARDER

A tube gel that slows up the drying rate of acrylic paints to give more time for manipulation. It is essential for detail and small scale work, where the paint could start to dry on the brush while you are working. Mix the retarder, one-to-one with water, before adding to the paint.

GLOSS MEDIUM

Gloss Medium adds a gloss to the normal very slight sheen of the tube paint. It can be mixed in and applied with the paint, or painted over in a thin layer afterwards. To achieve an even gloss, several thin coats should be applied to the finished painting.

MATTE MEDIUM

This has the opposite effect to gloss medium, and can be painted over the surface to remove unwanted shine.

GEL MEDIUM

Gel mediums include whitish pastes that thicken the paint for impasto effects. Mix well with the tube colours, or apply the moulding paste first and then paint over it when dry.

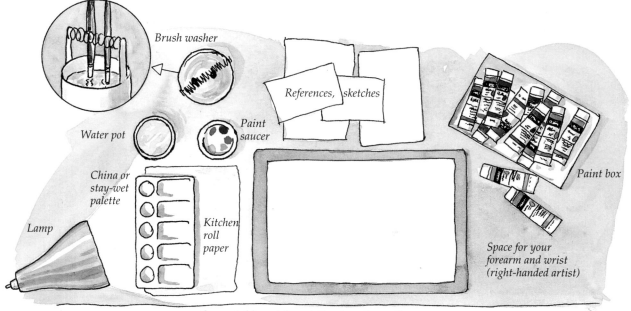

Suggested layout for painting in water mediums.

The illustration shows a sensible layout, with the waterpot, paints and palette making a group as close to each other as possible. Between the palette and the painting paper is a flat piece of kitchen-roll or blotting paper. The brush passes over it every time it leaves the palette with its load of paint; as it frequently holds more paint than you need, or is too wet; the absorbent paper will instantly remove the surplus before it reaches your painting. The lighting comes from the side, and shines onto the paper unobstructed by the hand. The subject matter, or anything to do with it, is placed straight ahead, just beyond the painting.

PAINTS

The paint makers produce smaller ranges of colours than for oils or watercolour, because certain pigments don't react well with acrylic medium.

Wet paint swells

Dry paint shrinks

TUBES

Acrylic paint is almost always sold in tubes because the paint has to be kept airtight when not in use. The tube size is quite large, about 60ml, from most manufacturers. The consistency is roughly similar to oil paint, but each maker has their own preferred consistency. Rowneys supply their colours in two consistencies, standard and "flow". The softer paint is easier to use in my experience, since the paint in any case has to be manipulated and diluted further in normal use. Golden acrylics are especially pleasant to use; they supply a very opaque Titanium White, full strength Umbers, and a wide range of intense colours.

60ml tube

JARS

Thinner paint is supplied in jars by Golden and Liquitex. This levels out more naturally than diluted tube paint, and works well for a more watercolour style of work, which generally suits acrylics best. Also good for airbrushing, where its greater liquidity is less likely to clog the airbrush nozzle.

Liquitex jar

INKS

A relatively new development. The colours are strong and effective and dry much more evenly in a wash than diluted tube colours. The colours are not true inks, as they settle out when unused, and need a good shake before use.

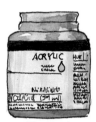

Rowney FW acrylic artist's ink

COLOUR SELECTION

The selection suggested below includes all the main colours and will enable you to create any reasonable colours for your pictures. They won't all be needed in any one picture.

The main colour areas (as well as the same neutrals and browns) should be represented in any selection.

Once you have grasped the essentials of colour-mixing and understand the colours you already own, there is no particular virtue in restricting your colour range; and much to gain from experimenting with new and interesting colours that you haven't tried before.

A colour always regarded as indispensable, Alizarin Crimson, has recently been shown to be less reliable than supposed, having failed the ASTM tests for light-fastness, so it should be replaced. A good substitute is Permanent Alizarin Crimson Hue from Liquitex; this is a mixture of permanent pigments.

Most of the alternative colours to Alizarin are usually a little brighter and not as dark, but as you will seldom need the exact Alizarin shade this should not present any problems.

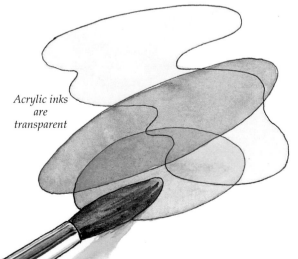

Acrylic inks are transparent

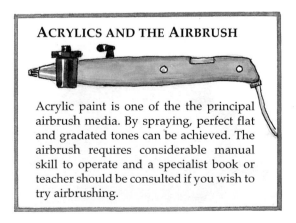

ACRYLICS AND THE AIRBRUSH

Acrylic paint is one of the the principal airbrush media. By spraying, perfect flat and gradated tones can be achieved. The airbrush requires considerable manual skill to operate and a specialist book or teacher should be consulted if you wish to try airbrushing.

Colour Selection (continued)

Cadmium Red serves for the brightest reds, and the less intense reds can be started with Burnt Sienna or Light Red.

Naples Yellow is a mixed colour, at its best in adding a softness and subtlety to other mixtures.

The Cadmium Yellows are the most useful bright yellows as they are intense and opaque, retaining their power in dilution or mixture.

The power of Phthalocyanine Blue makes it a difficult colour to manage, and the addition of Viridian to one of the other blues is usually enough to cope with occasional requirements for green-blues. Where this mixture fails in brightness, Brilliant Blue from Liquitex is a mixture of White and Phthalocyanine Blue, and their Brilliant Yellow-Green is good for light bright greens which are difficult to mix without becoming chalky through the over-use of White. Some natural browns are weak in acrylics.

A SELECTION

A representative selection of colours is shown below to serve as a starting point for your own choices. The earth reds are not well represented in some lists, but good substitutes are always offered, labelled as red oxides.

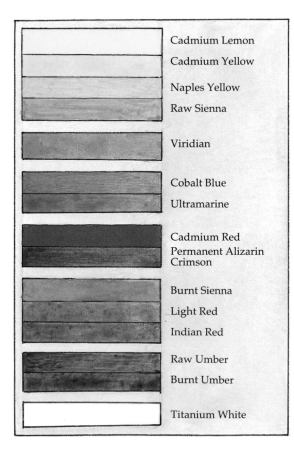

Cadmium Lemon

Cadmium Yellow

Naples Yellow

Raw Sienna

Viridian

Cobalt Blue

Ultramarine

Cadmium Red

Permanent Alizarin Crimson

Burnt Sienna

Light Red

Indian Red

Raw Umber

Burnt Umber

Titanium White

COLOUR MIXING

In the beginning, some experiments along the lines indicated below will give you a start and take the mystery out of colour mixing. The artificial red and brown oxides are more powerful than the natural earth colours. However, both Raw and Burnt Umber from Golden are strong and useful colours that make more natural-looking mixtures than those employing the darker oxides such as Indian Red.

■ Get to know your colours by name, and keep them in your box in a logical order – all the yellows together, then the greens, blues.

■ Make a Colour Chart showing some gradation of each colour, however imperfect, so you can see the middle and lighter tones which are most often used.

■ To match a colour, start with whichever colour seems closest. Ask yourself how your colour differs – does it need the addition of more yellow, or red, or brown or grey or blue? Often a third or even fourth colour has to be added. Either the addition of water or White will make a colour lighter in tone: try them both. Some examples are shown opposite, and described in more detail in the demonstration pictures throughout this book.

MIXING WITH WHITE

Colours are made paler by adding either water, or White which has a completely different effect. Water makes the colour paler in a logical and consistent way, whereas White acts as a colour in its own right and changes the nature of most colours it mixes with, usually making them colder.

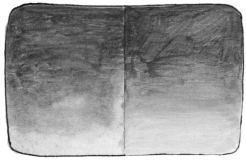

Thinned with medium   Mixed with white

When acrylic paint dries it darkens slightly and makes colour matching very difficult.

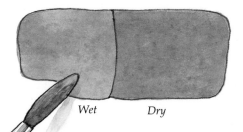

Wet   Dry

SOME USEFUL MIXTURES

A few common mixtures are illustrated to show the practice and thinking behind colour mixing.

CLOUD COLOURS

Naples Yellow, Yellow Ochre or Raw Sienna are the bases of warm creamy mixtures, with the addition of a red and sometimes a brighter warm yellow like Cadmium.

CLOUD SHADOWS

These are often more colourful than realised. It is important to avoid a cold greenish tinge. A natural looking combination is White, Cobalt Blue and Light Red, a complex red with just enough yellow to prevent the mixture from becoming violet, but not enough to lose the warmth of the red and blue.

BRICKS, ROOFS

Start with one of the red earth colours: Light Red, Red Oxide or Burnt Sienna. To tone the red down add Yellow Ochre or Naples Yellow, and a little Cobalt Blue if necessary.

HORIZON SKY COLOURS

Two colours seem superimposed, and can be painted this way. A creamy tone of Naples Yellow is overlaid when dry with a thin wash of Cobalt Blue or Ultramarine.

TREES

Phthalocyanine Blue and Cadmium Yellow make a rich bright green. By adding Burnt Sienna a proportion of red is introduced, so the greenish colour becomes muted and suitable for painting.

Naples Yellow

Burnt Sienna

Light Red

Cadmium Yellow

Burnt Sienna

Phthalocyanine Blue

Cobalt Blue

Indian Red

White

WARM GREYS

Mixing Ultramarine, a blue that has a red bias, with Burnt Umber, a reddish brown, produces a grey retaining a slight bias towards the red. This avoids the cold greenness that spoils many greys, caused by the mis-use of the strong greeny blues. Mixtures of Indian Red and Cobalt Blue also make warm greys.

Techniques

It is easiest to use acrylics with an essentially watercolour technique, starting with thin transparent washes or paint layers, reserving the introduction of white until it is needed for opaque overpainting. The traditional method of thin underpainting followed by a richer or thicker overpainting, (fat over lean), applies as well to acrylics as other media.

Approached in this way, there is no reason why acrylics should look crude either in colour or execution.

Acrylic tube paints are bulky in the brush compared to watercolour, so the brush holds less colour than it appears to, and is used up sooner than expected. The bulk also spreads the hairs and reduces the brush's ability to come to a point. Therefore the wetness of the paint needs to be carefully controlled. As the water evaporates, the paint dries and becomes insoluble. Keep the paint already squeezed out from the tubes in good condition by covering it with the lid of the nest of saucers, or with the lid if you are using a Stay-wet palette. If necessary, add a drop of water to the saucer to maintain a moist atmosphere within.

THE VERSATILITY OF ACRYLICS

The natural characteristics of acrylics are most closely related to tempera and gouache. The strengths of acrylics are similar to the other water-based media. With sufficient skill most of their effects can be duplicated.

■ The ability to paint over previous layers without disturbing them allows quick working, compared to oils, and the creation of colours and optical effects with semi-transparent overpainting.

■ Thicker painting in the style of some oil techniques is theoretically possible by using a retarder to slow drying and give more time to manipulate the paint. Even so, it is difficult to match the many qualities of oils and such methods can unfavourably emphasise the plastic sheen and the hard-edged nature of acrylics compared to oils.

APPLYING A FLAT TONE

The water-born media are most flexible and easy to use if they are applied thinly. Start your painting almost as if it were a watercolour, by applying transparent washes. For larger areas, moisten the paper surface with clean water first: the extra water will help the paint settle more smoothly and give you longer to apply it evenly. Unless just for a small area, this layer may not dry smoothly enough, so a second or even a third coat with the admixture of white will help to even it out.

TRANSPARENT PAINT LAYERS

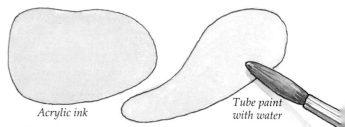

Acrylic ink   *Tube paint with water*

Acrylic inks run more freely and dry more evenly than tube colours, so if transparency is important inks have an advantage. Check the permanence of inks before incorporating them into your painting.

OPAQUE PAINT LAYERS

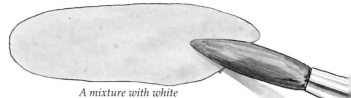

A mixture with white

The old rule of making lights opaque and shadows transparent, originating with the oil technique of the old masters, works very well with acrylics also.

Opaque colour is most satisfactory when introduced after the shadows are well established. It can then be painted over the lights and middle tones, and blended into the shadows by pressing the paint thinly on to the paper with a drier brush.

UNDERPAINTING

Acrylic is bulky, so the pigment is relatively dispersed in it and therefore less opaque than gouache. Underpainting will help to overcome this by building up an opaque layer in convenient stages.

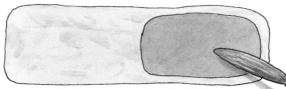

Opacity sometimes has to be built up.

A GRADED TONE

Because acrylic paint doesn't flow well and settle itself evenly like watercolour, and dries quickly, achieving a smooth gradation is difficult.

Keep the paper very wet, for while it is wet a certain amount of paint movement takes place, allowing manipulation for a short time. Once the surface is dry, add further light coats over the whole or parts as often as necessary to build up a smooth progression of tones.

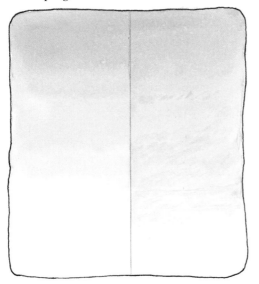

■ The first step is to put on a graded wash as carefully as possible, pre-wetting the paper or board.

■ The second step, when the paint has dried, is to add more of the same colour to any paler patches using a dry-brush technique. Continue to fill in and smooth the tones until you are satisfied it is as smooth as you can make it.

It may be practical to add some white mixed with the colour and paint this fairly thinly back over the initial colour, starting with the palest part and working upwards towards the medium and darker parts. The white has a surprising smoothing effect on the colours below, and it is much easier to grade tones this way than from dark to light. Grading can be done sometimes with a series of pre-mixed colours painted on and overlapped as you go.

DRYBRUSH

Remove most of the paint from a small brush, leaving only a little in it, and stroke it on carefully, building up a graded tone as smoothly as you can. This method is effective for smaller areas.

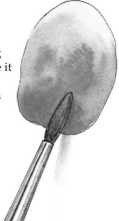

GLAZING

A transparent wash over a previous layer is a way of darkening a tone or altering a colour, and at the same time smooths away some of the signs of brushwork. The effect is to enrich the colouring and introduce variation. Add some medium to help bind paint that has been considerably diluted with water.

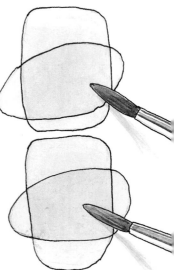

With water:

A diluted wash is floated over the under-colour. This works best when the paint is still thin and the paper grain can help hold and settle the glaze. Add medium if a lot of water is used.

With medium:

A more transparent effect is achieved by diluting with medium as well as water. The medium maintains some bulk as it dries, holding the pigment particles apart and increasing the effect of transparency. Gloss medium adds a sheen.

IMPASTO – THICK TEXTURED PAINT

The ability of acrylic paints and media to dry and hold their shape permanently makes impasto easy to achieve. Gel media can be used to add bulk, but they reduce opacity as well. Acrylic paint will hold its shape when applied thickly, whether from sable or hog's hair brushes, or from a painting knife. Allow plenty of extra drying time for thick paint to harden all through.

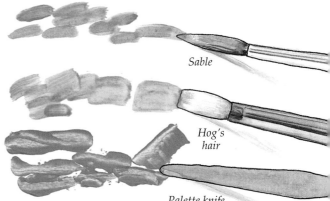

Sable

Hog's hair

Palette knife

Three varieties of impasto

> **Remember – acrylic is a form of plastic**
> Acrylic painting is often criticised for its "hard" and plastic look. Use impasto with care.

ACRYLICS STEP-BY-STEP

PUMPKIN FIELD

This is a composition made up of elements close together but disorganised in terms of composition. The photograph shows the general appearance of the scene including the chaotic middle distance, which was greatly reduced to make more of the pumpkins and the atmospheric background.

A watercolour sketch of the nearby pumpkins was painted on the spot and photographs of the general scene and some of the more complicated details were taken. Different parts of the scene were selected and brought together to make a composition. Most of the chaotic middle ground was either omitted or simplified.

Aims

Firstly, to contrast the texture and colour of the solid pumpkins with the silvery distant landscape. A "near and far" composition, accentuated by the colour contrast.

Secondly, to show the brightness and warmth of the day and the sunshine. Orange is a difficult colour to fit into a colour scheme, so it was kept towards the yellow to combine better with the

Drawing

A careful drawing was made with an HB pencil of the whole picture, taking the opportunity to improve the composition and shapes. Particular care was taken over the roundness of the pumpkins.

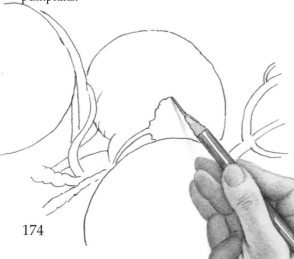

The pumpkins

The colour was made of Cadmiums, Yellow and Red, with a little Yellow Ochre to soften it. The highlights were left as paper rather than using White. The shadows were orange plus a mixture of Red Oxide with a little Cobalt Blue, to make a dark warm coppery colour.

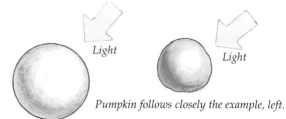

Light   Light

Pumpkin follows closely the example, left.

The lighting on the pumpkins follows the classic lighting of a sphere. For further description of this lighting see p. 24.

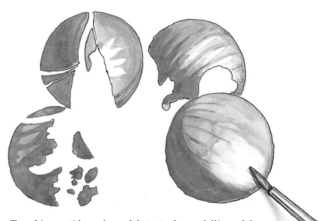

To achieve a tidy and careful start, the modelling of the pumpkins was worked up before any surrounding detail was begun.

Dead leaves

The dead leaf colour, White, Naples Yellow, Raw Umber and a little Red Oxide, was painted fairly transparently over all the foreground and the greens were painted over this. Using the drawing that

still showed through clearly, shadows were painted fairly strongly between the stems and leaves, using Burnt Umber and Cobalt Blue, with a little Alizarin Crimson Hue to keep a reddish cast.

Background

A creamy graded wash of Naples Yellow and Titanium White with plenty of water was applied to the sky, starting at the horizon, followed up with a stronger graded wash of blue started from the top. The sky was pre-wetted for smoothness.

The mountains were laid in with a flat medium tone wash of Cobalt Blue, White, with a little Alizarin Crimson Hue and Brilliant Yellow-Green to make a slightly violet blue.

When this was dry the trees covering the mountains were blobbed in on top. This had to be done repeatedly to build up an even tone and define the ridges. The nearer trees were given the same treatment.

Middle distance foliage

A medium to dark green, of Cadmium Yellow and Ultramarine with a little Burnt Sienna was painted all over the middle distance as a background for the detail.

The lighter greens were painted on top with a mixture of White, Cadmium Yellow and Brilliant Blue, and a spot of Yellow Ochre to tone down the sharpness of the blue. A film of whitish green was flooded over the distant hills to make them seem further away.

Foreground

Opaque greens were painted around the pumpkins where needed. The shadows on the pumpkins were reinforced with Red Oxide and Ultramarine with a little Crimson, followed by glazes of Alizarin Crimson Hue, Cadmium Yellow and Red Oxide over the shadow line near the lights, which made the reflections show up distinctly with a glow.

Finishing

The top half of the picture was pre-wetted, then the haze colour, mainly White, was flooded on. It smoothed the sky as the paint settled into the grain of the paper, and lightened the whole area.

The foreground shadows were evened up in tone and sunlit patches painted fairly heavily over them. Additional small pumpkins were added to the middle distance to join the two parts of the picture together.

Pumpkin Field.

Summary

The roughness of the paper, good for the pumpkin texture, turned out to be a disadvantage, as the stiffness of acrylics made it necessary to push the paint onto the paper firmly: some sharpness was lost as the grain of the paper broke up the brush strokes. The distant background is also heavier than intended but recedes well. The pumpkins with their foliage, on the other hand, stand out in the strong lighting and give the three-dimensional look that was one of picture's chief aims.

GOUACHE

INTRODUCTION

Gouache refers to a form of watercolour in which the artist incorporates white paint into the painting. You can either mix in white paint with normal watercolour materials on the palette or use ready-made opaque paints. A combination of opaque gouache for the medium and light tones, and transparent watercolour for the darks is most effective. In the early days of watercolour white was added quite naturally where it was thought necessary, and the distinction between pure watercolour and gouache is a relatively recent development. Even today there are many watercolours where small touches of white or body-colour pass undetected. The paint sold as gouache by the manufacturers is a body-colour paint containing white or a similar opaque ingredient. The term body-colour refers to the thicker texture and the natural opacity of the paint, in comparison with the thinner and more transparent true watercolour paints. The more opaque gouache shows to best effect on tinted paper.

There are two variations of gouache painting:

1. Titanium or Chinese White watercolour, or Permanent White gouache are added to ordinary watercolours, with the advantage of being able to use transparent paint in the darks and middle tones.

2. Gouache paints only are used, keeping the colours fairly opaque.

Gouache can seem to be an easy option, a watercolour with the recourse of covering up previous layers, and of working up the modelling freely, towards both lights and darks. However, new wet paint can re-dissolve the lower layers and the resulting mixture can prove difficult to manipulate. Keep the paint as thin as possible for as long as possible, and apply the thicker paint where necessary towards the end. It will seldom be necessary or desirable to use it at full strength.

The Governess Cart by Joseph Crawhall.
A small picture on linen. The paint has been applied very sparingly, highlighted with strong and clear-cut accents. A combination of opaque lights and transparent darks works well in all opaque media.

Materials

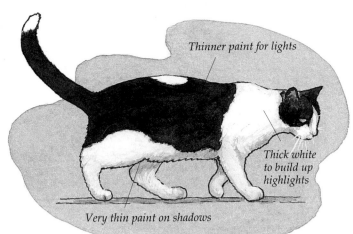

Thinner paint for lights

Thick white to build up highlights

Very thin paint on shadows

Different thicknesses of paint help to reinforce different effects. Dark tones work better when applied as thinly as possible, whereas whites look more real where opaque.

PAPER

The great range of tinted papers can be used; although made primarily for pastels, they are ideally coloured for gouache, many of whose advantages derive from using tinted paper. Canson Mi-Teintes make a range of 50 colours and white in a thickness of 160gsm. Ingres paper in 19 colours and Arte Media in 35 shades are of similar weight. Tiziano is thicker than the above, and all are available as sheets or in books of mixed colours.

All the pastel papers will need stretching as described on p. 141. Watercolour paper is better if tinted first, because the gouache paint's lack of genuine transparency dulls their effect.

	DIFFERENT WAYS OF USING GOUACHE	
	Advantages	**Disadvantages**
Thin paint	Allows considerable overpainting and reworking.	None, but thicker and stronger accents are also necessary.
Average thickness	Colour looks good on tinted grounds.	Overpainting becomes more difficult.
Thick paint	Good for accents, small areas.	Paint becomes unworkable, can crack.

Contrasting paint and paper

Light paint on dark paper

The paper provides the sky colour

The paper blends with the colours

Gouache is an easy medium as long as the paint is applied fairly thinly. It is seldom meant to be applied opaquely over much of the picture, as the paint surface can look too heavy and become subject to cracking. Small important areas can be painted opaquely and some of the larger parts treated semi-transparently; this method uses the colouring of the paper to blend everything together. The paper should naturally be chosen to set the key for the overall colour scheme.

The advantages of gouache show up best on coloured or tinted paper. Because of thinning with water, gouache paints are seldom entirely opaque, and so the paper tint nearly always shows through harmonising the colouring almost automatically.

All the pastel papers can be stretched and used for gouache.

A carefully chosen paper colour makes your picture look well advanced as soon as you start painting. ▷

177

CHOOSING PAPERS

Coloured papers work well where they supply some of the background colour for the picture, as well as contributing to a harmonious blending of colours by showing through the more transparently painted areas. For sketches and vignettes a contrasting colour paper can make a few washes and strokes into something exciting.

A few suitable pastel papers. Most shops keep a selection.
▽

BRUSHES

The brushes for gouache are the same as those for watercolour, bearing in mind that the thicker paint needs springy brushes, so that soft squirrel hair mops are unlikely to be needed. Round sables will serve for almost all painting, with the flats still being good for windows and other square architectural features, and the rigger is best in any medium for long even lines. For larger washes use as large a brush as possible. Very big areas are easier with a varnish brush, but the covering of large areas is not a strong point of gouache because of drying marks caused by varied drying times.

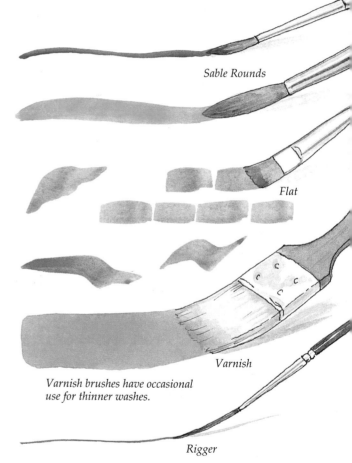

Sable Rounds

Flat

Varnish

Varnish brushes have occasional use for thinner washes.

Rigger

CLEANING BRUSHES

After finishing, wash your brushes under the tap to remove paint around the ferrules. Press your finger around the point where the hairs leave the ferrule.

Gouache paint is thicker than watercolour, so it builds up more solidly in the hairs around the ferrule. Because of this accumulation, the washing needs to be more lengthy and thorough.

ACCESSORIES

China palettes are the most pleasant to work with and easiest to clean. A nest of saucers keeps the paint moist. If you wish to overpaint substantially, a small addition of acrylic medium will fix the colour permanently, but wash out the brushes very carefully with soap and water straight away after use. Sponges can be used to apply paint where it helps the texture; foliage can be started thus and finished with a brush. Blotting paper and kitchen-roll paper are for the instant removal of excess water or paint from your brushes while you are painting.

Acrylic medium added to gouache paint makes it waterproof, to ease overpainting.

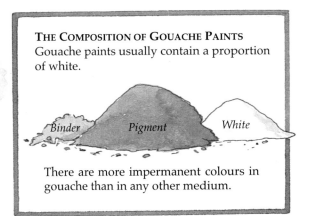

A nest of saucers keeps the tube paints and important mixtures fresh for long periods. Add a large drop of water if necessary to keep the air inside moist.

Nest of saucers

Eye sponges

STUDIO

Painting arrangements are identical to those for watercolour, which is sometimes used together with gouache

- Keep your water-pot, palette and absorbent paper together so the brush doesn't have to travel too far during and after mixing.

- Have all your colours out on the table where you can see them.

- Paint in a good light, and see that your hand does not cast a shadow over the work.

- Place any reference material, such as sketches or photographs, straight ahead in full view.

PAINTS

It is easier to paint with Permanent White (above) than the sometimes stringy Chinese White (right).

The composition of gouache paints usually includes white, but white can be added to watercolours by using Titanium White. Most gouache paints contain an opaque filler besides the coloured pigments; this is not to dilute or adulterate them, but to make them opaque. The binder is sometimes gum kordofan as used in watercolours, but dextrin is added by some makers to make the paint smoother and more opaque. Because of their popularity with commercial designers, most ranges include a number of bright and attractive, but impermanent colours, so make your selection with extra care if your picture is to be framed.

THE COMPOSITION OF GOUACHE PAINTS
Gouache paints usually contain a proportion of white.

Binder   *Pigment*   *White*

There are more impermanent colours in gouache than in any other medium.

Different makes of gouache

SELECTION OF COLOURS

WHITE WITH WATERCOLOUR

The normal selection of watercolours can be used with the addition of Titanium White or the gouache paint Permanent White. This is made of Titanium White also, and works smoothly as a watercolour. They are more opaque than Chinese White. White is not usually mixed with every colour but kept for highlights and bright overpainting. A good selection of bright light colours will give variety to your mixtures.

Because of the quantities of white that find their way into light-coloured mixtures there is a danger of their becoming too alike if you limit your palette. Buy several yellows to help you keep the colouring warm in the light colours.

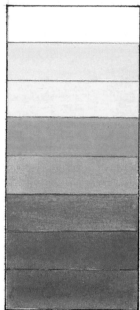

- Permanent White
- Naples Yellow
- Spectrum Yellow
- Cadmium Yellow Deep
- Yellow Ochre
- Raw Sienna
- Raw Umber
- Coral

The white, yellows, and red above provide a choice in making mixtures.

GOUACHE

The colouring and range of gouache paints are directed by a number of makers towards commercial artists and graphic designers, whose work is mainly for reproduction, where brilliance matters more than permanence. Take particular care in selecting gouache paints if the colour looks exceptionally bright or unusual to you. Colour charts will give guidance on permanence.

It is safer to keep to colours known to be permanent and avoid the unusual, unless the ingredients are printed on the label and found to be reliable (see the list of ingredients on p. 91). Schmincke use reliable artist's pigment in their gouache. The opaque surface of gouache favours the light bright colours, so a selection of dark browns is useful for creating the darker tones in conjunction with the stronger blues.

- Cadmium Red
- Magenta
- Burnt Sienna
- Burnt Umber
- Ultramarine
- Rowney Blue (Phthalocyanine)
- Oxide of Chromium
- Linden Green

The dark colours supply weight of tone. Choose a few brighter extras as well.

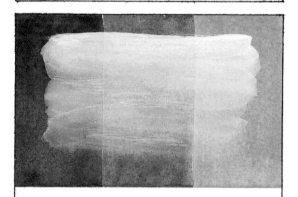

THE EFFECT OF WHITE OVER DARK TONES

A thin layer of white, or mixtures containing white, have the effect of making the under-colour colder: brown will become grey and grey will become blue-grey. This can be countered by adding a warm yellow like Naples Yellow or Raw Sienna to the mixture.

COLOUR MIXING

GREY PAPER

■ The unnaturally bright mixture of Permanent White and Ultramarine is tempered by the colour of the paper. The quantity and dilution of the white paint mainly determines how much the paper shows through. A little Jaune Brillant was added to the white of the cloud to keep it looking warm.

■ Jaune Brillant, a close relative of Naples Yellow, is toned down with a little Burnt Sienna, with the grey paper showing through.

TAN PAPER

■ A bright mixture of Cadmium Yellow Deep and Naples Yellow, thinned in places to let the paper tone it down.

■ Linden Green and Oxide of Chromium make a brilliant green, varied by the paper colour. Both colours are opaque.

OLIVE PAPER

■ A bright red, Coral, needs Cadmium Yellow Deep with it to help maintain its opacity and brightness over a strongly contrasting and complementary background.

■ Spectrum Yellow and Cadmium Red make an autumnal red-brown, modified by the paper colour. The yellow has to be fairly thick to remain opaque on the dark ground.

DARK PAPER

■ Rowney Blue makes cold colours. Only a touch was needed to colour the Permanent White.

■ Naples Yellow and Permanent White are painted thinly over the dark paper to give shades of stone and grey.

Mixing with white

Diluted   Mixed   Diluted   Mixed
           with white   with white

The coldness of white affects its mixtures in the same way that overpainting does, (see previous page).

Permanent White

Ultramarine

Jaune Brillant

Burnt Sienna

Grey paper

Tan paper

Cadmium Yellow Deep

Naples Yellow

Linden Green

Oxide of Chromium

Olive paper

Coral

Cadmium Yellow Deep

Spectrum Yellow

Cadmium Red

Rowney Blue

Permanent White

Dark paper

Naples Yellow

Permanent White

Techniques

CHOOSING THE PAPER

There is nothing to be gained over acrylics, watercolour or tempera in using gouache on white paper, where the semi-opacity of gouache will dull the colours and count against it, so tinted paper is the natural choice. The paper colour will influence the entire colour scheme, and the selection of a tint is an important factor in a gouache painting. It is easier, in general, to paint blues and cool colours over a warm ground than it is to warm up a blue ground. The yellows and reds are less able to overcome the ground colour, although Turner sketched successfully on a soft blue paper at times.

As far as possible, choose a colour that echoes the subject. This could be a general background colour, like green, blue or brown for landscape, or a colour to suggest the mood of the picture. It is seldom practical to depart very far from the paper colour in painting, except in smaller areas, because it takes too much unnaturally thick paint to cover up the colour on a large scale. As gouache is applied with water, it is used semi-transparently for much of the time; use the paper colour to modify and harmonise your colour scheme.

SHADING

Using thin dark paint, so that the paper shows through, the shadows and dark areas can be carefully built up in the manner of watercolour. The thinness of the washes makes overpainting safe as you add more tone to them. Start with the strong darks. No need to put them in at full strength, just by placing them you will immediately have a logical, simple, representation of your subject. If the middle or lighter tones were painted first, they would temporarily become stronger than the true darks, reversing parts of the tonal range. Use colouring sympathetic to the shadows, so there will be no need to change them much by adding opaque colour later. By doing the shadows first you create a suitable setting for the more opaque lighter tones that follow. With the darker tones done, the picture will already look well on the way to completion.

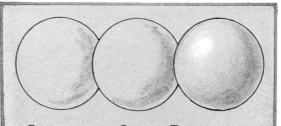

BUILDING UP THE SHADOW TONES
Thin paint allows a controlled and relaxed working out of the forms.

Opaque local colours

Transparent darks, watercolour or gouache

The darks of the figure were painted in first. The middle tone is provided by the paper, and the lights were painted opaquely, with gradations, over it. Because the lights are opaque, the paint is thicker, so is best put on at the end.

Opaque lights painted directly

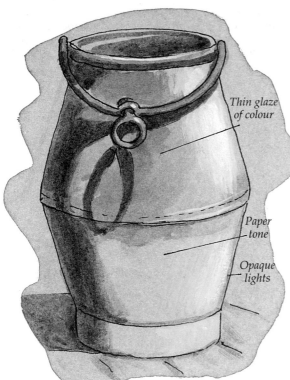

Thin glaze of colour

Paper tone

Opaque lights

The bucket looked almost complete even before the lights were finally added.

DRYBRUSH

Where the larger washes and areas have been applied reasonably thinly, detail can be added by dry-brush work. The brush, after picking up paint from the palette, should be wiped across some kitchen-roll paper to remove surplus paint and dampness, so there is just enough left on the brush to come off lightly and thinly.

The paper will show through at first and strongly influence the colour – allow for this by mixing colours that seem brighter than necessary. Keep the paint on the thin side and build up your shapes with overlapping brush-strokes. Continue modelling the brighter parts as if sculpting a three-dimensional form. Be careful to avoid spreading the thicker and brighter colour back into the half-tones – let the paper tone do as much as possible.

Detail and modelling can be built up to a high degree of finish once you have learnt to control the dampness of the brush. For more on drybrush technique, see p. 156.

For more on drybrush technique, see p. 156.

The paint was kept on the dry side all through. Most of the picture is detail built up on a few broad underlying washes.
▽

THE LIGHT TONES

The light colours and tones are the basis of gouache technique, for their opacity shows up well on tinted paper. To avoid the chalkiness that can appear in mixtures heavily laced with white, use your creams and yellows with, or instead of, White where possible, to give variety and naturalness. Paint the colours on fairly thinly so the paint remains manageable if you need to go over it again. Gouache is easy to manipulate at this stage because the paint dries fairly softly without the hard edges of wet watercolour. Remember that the paint first becomes more transparent as it dries, then lightens and becomes more opaque when dry. Once thick layers have been put on, they can become difficult to work over as the dampness and pressure of the brush will dissolve and stir them up; keep them to the end.

Naples Yellow   *Cadmium Yellow*   *Raw Sienna*

A selection of warm light paints increases your choice and range of colouring.

GOUACHE STEP-BY STEP

SMOKY MOUNTAINS, NORTH CAROLINA

The opaque paint surface has a light bright character not unlike pastels, the most similar medium. Colour matching can be very difficult once your original mixture is used up, as the paint dries much lighter than may be expected, so paint each part as completely as possible while the paint is there. Detail blends in easily afterwards and small tonal adjustments can also be made later.

Aims

The mountains of North Carolina have a characteristic blue haze, accentuated here by the contrast of a root crop's yellowing leaves. The aim was to record and remember this feature of the Carolina countryside. The close-up trees emphasise the open spaces and provide texture and depth.

The sketch

A full colour sketch was painted in watercolour and white on the spot. The yellow came out brightly – the colour was more effective on the green paper than expected. The trees on the left were simplified and some hedgerow trees obscuring the field were left out.

Choice of paper

The paper has to accommodate the brightness of the yellow and the contrasting blues. Pale green paper, made by Two Rivers, suited the sketch so was used again. Buff paper was a good alternative to help the warm colours, and the blues would have shown up well on it, but changing from green would have altered the colour balance unpredictably.

The drawing

The main positions and shapes were very lightly indicated with a graphite pencil; there are very few shapes to draw as the trees are best done freehand with paint. Additional information on detail came from photographs taken at the time.

The sky

The sky mixture was tried out first on spare paper and allowed to dry, to see its dry colour which is much lighter. Ultramarine and Permanent White with a little Rowney Blue, (Phthalocyanine Blue), make a warm sky blue.

Paper – to be painted white

Creating soft edges by blending wet paint.

While the blue was still damp, the grey of the clouds, which had also been tested to match the blue in tone, was blended in at the edges. Gouache blends naturally as the paint is fairly slow drying and is too thick to run out of control into the neighbouring colours. White was blended into the grey at the bottom of the clouds and then painted more thickly on the sunlit clouds, up to a definite edge at the top.

Dry

Wet   *Gouache dries lighter.*

Mountains

The dark and light colours were put in side by side and blended while wet. The colour was continued behind the left-hand trees.

Blending the edges before they dry.

Yellow field

Spectrum Yellow needed some White to soften its sharpness and add opacity, and a golden glow came from adding a little Burnt Sienna. The grain of the paper provides texture as the paint was applied with the side of the brush rather than the point.

Cross section of paper surface

Using the side of the brush gives texture as the paint can only touch the raised grain. ▷

Hedges and road

The hedges were painted over the top of the field and mountains, then the road and grass was put in. The near grass has an open texture in the foreground made by dragging the paint on with the side of the brush. Light bright green was painted over the darks to suggest the clumps of leaves in sunlight.

The left-hand part of the scene, a picture within a picture, is nearly done. Further detail was added at the end.

Foreground trees

Strong shadows on the smaller trunk were put in with Ultramarine and Burnt Umber, and then the dark green background of the pine branches was laid in thinly. It was made up of Ultramarine and Spectrum Yellow, darkened with Burnt Umber and a spot of Red Earth. These colours, in differing proportions, were used for nearly all the medium and dark greens.

When dry, a light bright green, made of Linden Green and White, with a little Spectrum Yellow and Rowney Blue, was used with a small brush to draw in the pine needles and the deciduous leaves further down. The lights only show up well if the background is dark enough. The larger spaces between them needed darkening afterwards: surprisingly dark paint was needed to make them show up, as new paint tends to sink into, or disappear into, the lower layers.

Summary

The picture is closer to the sketch than expected, but has a softer and airier appearance, in spite of containing more detail. With the sketch, one is looking more at the paint itself rather than what the paint is meant to convey, which is the open air, and the colour and feeling of the scene.

Smoky Mountains, North Carolina.

Large tree trunk

The shadow was painted on liquidly with Burnt Umber and Ultramarine, but on the sunlit side the colour was dragged across lightly with the side of the brush, just skimming the top of the grain. A little tidying up with a small sable brush improved the texture. This completed the trunk, which is otherwise untouched green paper.

Brush just touching the surface

Wet paint applied normally

Foreground grasses

The corner below the trunk was darkened with an olive green mixture in preparation for the lighter detail to go over it. The grass, made mainly of White and Linden Green, was put on with a Large Duck brush, a brush rather like a large rigger. A few darks were added between the grasses afterwards with a sable.

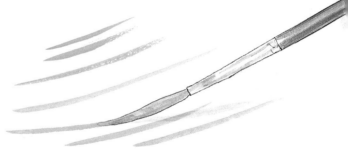

The Large Duck is ideal for lines, keeping a constant width. The brush is pulled along with the hairs trailing behind like a fox's tail. The even thickness of line needed for grass and plant stems is much easier to achieve with the long-haired riggers and quill brushes than with the standard sables.

EGG TEMPERA

INTRODUCTION

Tempera is the oldest of the media described in this book, and has enjoyed a revival in recent years. When dry, the binding medium is so invisible that the pigments show their individualities with singular clarity, leading to a luminous, high-key finish which lends itself well to representing everyday textures and surfaces. Tempera is a word denoting any substance that binds pigment into a paint, but the term is now confined to a range of water-based emulsions such as egg, casien and gum. Of these, egg has come to be the most important. A number of egg and oil mixtures can also be made up, and have their adherents, but they are complicated to make and use, and will not be considered here.

It is a most permanent medium because of the unique properties of egg-yolk, a water-based emulsion which dries to a thin colourless film that lasts almost unchanged for hundreds of years. After the initial drying, which happens within a few minutes, the film gradually hardens for a day or two, becoming more insoluble, and then toughens more slowly for several months.

One of the chief obstacles in the past, besides a lack of knowledge of the medium, has been the difficulty of obtaining the artists' pigments in their dry powder form. A very considerable range of colours can now be ordered from shops who will post them promptly. A list of suppliers is given on p. 252. Storage jars are usually available also.

At the time of its early flourishing in the Renaissance at the hands of Giotto, egg tempera was a slow and strict discipline, where the work was divided into separate steps of drawing, tracing and cross-hatch shading in ink; colour was then applied from a range of pre-mixed tones rather than from mixtures made on the spot. This method has features that seem inflexible and tedious to the modern mind, although it was well-suited to the needs of its time. By the time of Botticelli, oil paint was used in conjunction with it, and by about 1600 tempera was largely abandoned in favour of oils by painters who were looking for more flexibility and richness.

Cats' Journey to the Letterbox
Tempera paint dries as quickly as gouache or acrylic, so the textures of fur, wood, leather and asphalt are easily developed by overpainting, and the smooth panel surface is good for detail. Tempera blacks, and dark tones generally, are less intense than those of oils, but they are sufficient and there is ample compensation in tempera's light and airy tonal range, which is well suited to outdoor subjects.

A number of modern painters have taken advantage of the benefits of tempera without sacrificing their freedom, and there is no technical reason why you shouldn't be able to do the same. The most difficult part can be assembling the materials, which are not available in the average art shop, but can be obtained by mail order.

The simple materials of egg tempera

The simplest medium, egg-yolk and water, is also the easiest to manipulate. Alternative mixtures include linseed oil, an ingredient of tube tempera colours, which are not treated here. Once oil is introduced, the nature and feel of tempera immediately changes, not necessarily for the better, although some artists prefer it. Using the whole egg, the white as well as the yolk, causes the paint to dry too quickly, leaving no time for manipulation; egg-white by itself is too brittle to use.

EGG TEMPERA COMPARED WITH ACRYLICS AND GOUACHE

	Appearance	Application
Egg Tempera	A rather light and airy look. The surface dries with a silky sheen, very flat, without texture. Darks are a little less intense than in other media, and tempera is not well suited to dark subjects.	The paint is put on thinly. Layers are built up slowly in the beginning until an opaque surface is achieved. Much easier after that.
Acrylics	Can be flat or textured. A light sheen, seldom glossy. Capable of a rich appearance with good handling, but through frequent misuse has undeserved reputation for hard garish effects.	Applied in the manner of tempera, gouache or watercolour. If applied more texturally it becomes difficult to manage.
Gouache	Matt surface resembling pastels where the paint is thick enough. There is a generally light and bright effect as gouache darks are not very intense.	Paint on thinly as far as possible, building up to thicker paint as the picture nears completion.

Eggs last perfectly well if kept in the refrigerator, and there is no reason why the mixture should smell. The medium becomes difficult to use long before it starts to go off.

Textures and muted colours suit tempera

The providers of the materials

Materials

PAINTING SURFACES

Tempera paint films are not very flexible in the long term, so panels made of medium density fibreboard, hardboard, chipboard or plywood are the most common supports. Plywood is best covered with fine canvas, which can be glued over it, otherwise the grain will show through the paint film and distract from the picture. Egg yolk sticks strongly, but to ensure adhesion to the support a partially absorbent white priming is applied before starting to paint. The first paint layers fill this and attach the paint film firmly. Thick paper, 600 gsm, can also be used, and there is no need to prime it.

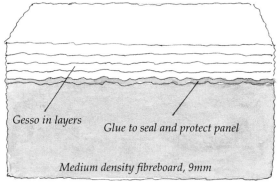

Gesso in layers　*Glue to seal and protect panel*

Medium density fibreboard, 9mm

The panel surface is prepared for painting by several layers of a bright white priming mixture called gesso. The glue in the gesso eventually becomes brittle, so the support has to be rigid.

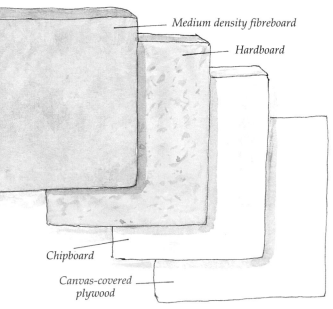

Medium density fibreboard

Hardboard

Chipboard

Canvas-covered plywood

SIZING

A glue and water mixture called size is used to seal the panel, which would otherwise absorb too much glue from the next layer and weaken it. It is then painted over with several coats of an opaque white mixture of glue and whiting, called gesso, to give a slightly absorbent painting surface.

HOW TO MAKE THE SIZE

Quantities

Rabbitskin glue or gelatine　25gm

Water　400ml

1. Put the glue into tepid or cold water and leave the granules to swell up.

Water

Glue granules

Melting the glue solution over hot water.

2. Heat the bowl in a saucepan of water, stirring the glue mixture until it all dissolves. When steam appears from the surface it is hot enough – don't let it boil, which will weaken the glue.

3. Apply a single coat with a broad brush. The heat will help it flow readily from the brush and penetrate the surface. It sets as soon as it cools, so do a large board in squares or sections.

4. If the board is thin, do both sides to equalize the tension and prevent warping.

5. Put the board aside to dry thoroughly. Leave it overnight if possible. The remaining size can be kept in a cool place, to be used later as an ingredient for the gesso.

PRIMING – MAKING THE GESSO

Gesso is a mixture of size and whiting, to which may be added some 10% of Titanium White pigment to make it whiter. Gesso is easy to make and keeps for a some time. Because of the glue content, it dries to a very hard surface which is difficult to sand down.

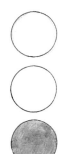

Whiting is a form of chalk, calcium carbonate, which covers opaquely in water mixtures and is fairly absorbent. The best type is Gilder's Whiting.

Titanium White is much more expensive, but a proportion brightens the whiting.

Rabbitskin glue is the usual glue, but cooking gelatine, which is a purer but weaker glue can also be used.

1. Thoroughly mix some whiting with up to 10% Titanium White pigment. The pigment makes the gesso whiter but is not an essential ingredient.

2. Gently stir in some water to make a smooth paste, and leave for a few hours. This will minimize the chance of pinholes appearing in the final surface. Cover to keep out dust.

3. The size will have cooled to the consistency of a jelly. Reheat it in a saucepan half filled with water.

Re-melting the size

4. Gradually add the whiting to the glue solution, stirring very gently to avoid air bubbles. 600cc of size will take up about 400gm of whiting, to equal the consistency of a thin cream.

The water in the saucepan moderates the heat

Use immediately. If it cools it will set to a jelly, which can be melted again over gentle heat.

HOW TO APPLY THE GESSO

Keep the gesso warm in its saucepan, and paint it on quickly. As soon as it dries to a matt finish, which is very quickly, put on the next coat. All the coats must be applied one after the other in the same session so they blend and dry together, or cracks could appear. Prepare several boards at the same time.

1. With a large brush, quickly stroke the gesso onto the board in parallel strokes. Dip the brush back into the gesso carefully to avoid making air bubbles.

Keep the gesso mixture warm in a saucepan of hot water.

2. When dry, apply a second coat at right angles to the first, and further coats in alternate directions, until the surface is as white and even as you want. With skill, 6 or more thin coats can be put on.

3. If you think the panel could warp, paint at least one coat onto the back.

4. Leave to dry thoroughly for a day. Each coat you apply takes longer to dry than the previous one, as a residual dampness builds up.

If the fine grain of the surface is to your liking, the boards are ready to use, but if you would prefer a smoother surface, wrap some medium-fine garnet-paper around a flat block and rub down until the grain is smooth enough. Ordinary glass-paper is too slow. The traditional surface is very smooth, like ivory, and at first will show every brush-stroke. It is naturally suitable for very fine detail.

Painting Surfaces (continued)

CANVAS MOUNTED ON BOARDS

The tooth of a fine canvas can provide a very sympathetic surface for tempera. Canvas can be mounted by coating the board with size, pressing the canvas onto it, then painting more size over the canvas and pressing out any air bubbles. Fold the edges over onto the back and glue them down in the same way. As long as the gesso doesn't fill the grain, a very agreeable tooth is preserved.

HOW TO ATTACH THE CANVAS

■ Seal both sides of the board with size.

■ Paint on a generous layer of size, and press the raw canvas flat on to it.

■ Press out any air-bubbles, then paint over another layer of size. Make sure the canvas lies completely flat. Fold the corners underneath and glue them with the size

■ When the size is completely dry (after at least 24 hours), paint several thin layers of gesso over the canvas, taking care not to lose the grain by filling it in.

■ Paint the underside with gesso as well to prevent the panel from warping.

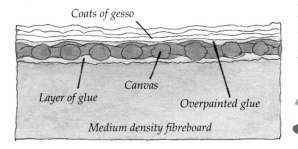

Coats of gesso

Layer of glue

Canvas

Overpainted glue

Medium density fibreboard

USING PAPER TO PAINT ON

Extra thick watercolour paper (600 gsm) will also serve as a support, and the surface doesn't need any preparation. A smooth or fine-grained surface is the easiest to paint on and closest to the traditional panel surface. Once the painting is finished, ensure that it is kept as flat as possible because tempera gradually loses its flexibility. Frame it behind glass for additional protection. Dampness working through the paper from the back is the chief danger, so seal the back if possible.

BRUSHES

Watercolour brushes serve very well for tempera, which is a moderately thick medium but soft in texture. The bulk tends to spread the hairs, so good watercolour brushes are desirable because they keep their shapes and points under these conditions. The softness of wet tempera needs a soft brush because a stiff brush will scrape the paint off with the same stroke that puts it on.

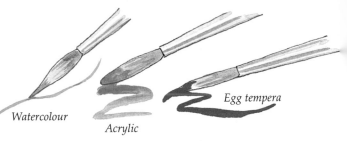

Watercolour

Acrylic

Egg tempera

The way different media spread the hairs of the brush.

Because tempera washes out well, it is safe to use your best watercolour brushes for it. While the egg-yolk mixture is wet it stays soft, and though it works its way up to the ferrule, it can be removed with soap and water. The round sable brushes are the most useful, especially for the fine detail which suits tempera so well. Small sizes are helpful as the paint spreads the points slightly. For sizes 5 or 6 upwards, good mixed sable and synthetic brushes are satisfactory. There is no substitute for riggers for thin lines, but they are not firm enough for general detail. Larger areas of paint can be applied with the flat brushes with longer hairs, such as a varnish brush or even a small house-painter's brush.

Sable rounds

Small house-painter's brush

The flat brushes are good for applying glazes over large areas.

Varnish brush

HOW TO CLEAN THE BRUSHES

The egg in the brush will have begun to dry, so at the end of the painting session it needs more than water to remove it. After rinsing out as much paint as possible under the cold tap, squiddle the brush into some soap and gently but thoroughly work the soap through it, finally rinsing under the tap. Use cold or tepid water. Hot water can set the egg and damage the sable.

ACCESSORIES

The tempera paint is made up as you paint, so a few accessories are necessary to manage the paint. The dry pigments can be kept in jars, with smaller watertight ones for storing pigments already ground with water.

If you use tempera regularly, grind a quantity of each pigment (except Ultramarine), with water and store in small wide-necked jars, ready for use. Add water to cover the surfaces to prevent them drying out.

Jars for storing the egg-yolk and pigments

■ A china palette is preferable to a plastic one, which will soon be scratched and stained through mixing the pigments with the tip of a palette knife.

■ A palette knife is the most versatile tool for picking up the pigment powder from the jars, and for any small-scale mixing where grinding isn't necessary.

■ A nest of saucers keeps the moisture in so that paint can be kept in good condition for a while.

■ An eye-dropper will control the small amounts of water that go into the egg-yolk, and the initial mixture of water with the pigment.

■ A mortar and pestle or a ground-glass square and muller can be used for mixing larger quantities of paint. Larger quantities should be stored in tightly-closed jars. A few colours won't keep under these conditions.

THE STUDIO OR WORKSPACE

All the waterborn media have basically the same arrangement which centres on a worktable. The panel is surrounded by your paints and any references leaving free space under your wrist and forearm so you don't rest them on the palette and its paints. If you prefer to work at an angle on an easel, then a side table can hold the paints and palette.

If you have pigments ready-ground with water in bottles, remove some with the tip of a palette knife and place in the circular palette wells. If you are starting with dry pigments, mix them directly with water in the wells. Keep them damp by adding drops of water whenever you see them starting to dry out.

Roll of kitchen paper

Mortar and pestle

Eye-dropper

Nest of saucers

China palette

191

PAINTS

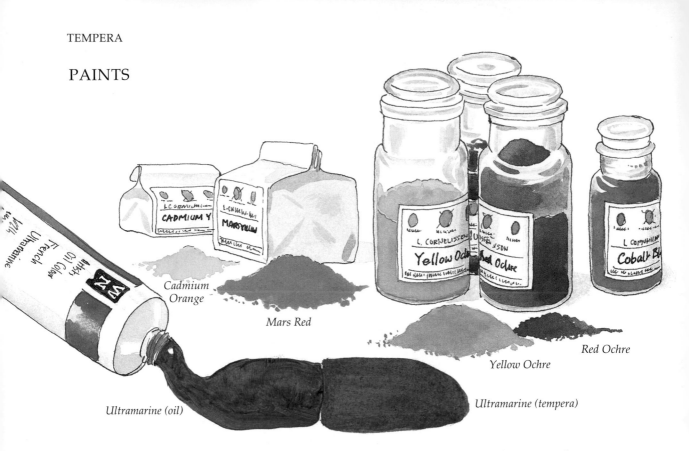

Cadmium Orange

Mars Red

Yellow Ochre

Red Ochre

Ultramarine (oil)

Ultramarine (tempera)

The paints are made up from dry pigments by the artist, either in quantity for storage in jars or directly on the palette for immediate use. A number of pigments are toxic if breathed in or eaten in sufficient amounts, so be careful to wash your hands after handling them. The list of toxic colours, included in the colour selection pages, shows where care needs to be exercised, but in normal artistic use, if reasonable precautions are taken and you avoid licking the brushes, there are no real dangers.

Opaque pigments form the basis of the tempera palette, as the most practical of the painting methods rely on the semi-opacity of the paint layers. The alternation between translucence and transparency is one of the strengths of the medium. Mixture with White adds opacity, but as all colours are put on thinly, they are necessarily more transparent than in other media. The truly transparent colours are useful for glazing and modifying colours already applied.

HOW TO MAKE UP TEMPERA PAINTS

To mix a quantity of colour:

■ Put out a heap of pigment on a hard surface, ideally a square of ground-glass with bevelled edges, or a marble working-top.

■ Shape a hollow in the centre with a palette knife and add a little water with an eye-dropper, so you can control the amount you are putting on.

■ Stir the water in and around with the knife until it is mainly mixed

■ Scrape it all into the centre, then press down on it with a muller and grind it around. This grinding action will force the water into better contact with the pigment and improve the texture of the paint.

■ When the paint is spread too thinly, scrape it back into the centre.

■ When you are satisfied that the consistency is right, so that paint stands up and holds its shape, scrape it up and put it into a small jar. Add water to cover.

Mixing paint directly on the palette.
▽

Paint stored in jars, the surface protected by water.
▽

Grinding paint thoroughly for storage, using a muller and ground glass. ▷

SELECTION OF COLOURS

Dry pigments have more individual character than tube paints; a generous selection of pigments will enable you to take full advantage of their distinctive characters and reduce unnecessary mixing.

WHITES

Titanium White is a satisfactory and very pleasant white to use, it sticks to anything of its own accord, almost without the need for a binder, and is entirely non-toxic. Titanium White is the most opaque of all the Whites. (Flake White is very poisonous as a dry pigment and should be avoided in this form. It should only be used as a ready-made oil colour).

YELLOWS

Mars Yellow is lighter and brighter than Yellow Ochre, and can be the first choice for a yellow. Many shades of Yellow Ochre are available. Yellows are bright in tempera, and brighter yellows than the above are seldom needed, but when they are, Cadmium Yellow is the most suitable – strong in colour, opaque, and brushes out very pleasantly. Raw Sienna is noticeably darker than Yellow Ochre and has many uses. Cadmium Lemon is a sharp yellow, and Aureolin is also satisfactory, although transparent.

READY-MADE TUBE COLOURS

Rowney's ready-made tempera contains an emulsion of egg and a little linseed oil. The addition of oil changes the handling character of the paints, making them a little more like oils, which some artists find to be an advantage compared to natural egg tempera. Because of the oil in the tube colours it is best to avoid their occasional use in paintings of pure egg tempera as the overlapping of different media can create instability and cracking in the paint film. Sennelier's tube colour is leaner, more like gouache or watercolour in appearance and use. The same firm also supply an egg tempera medium.

Tempera tubes

Yellow Ochre   *Mars Yellow*

REDS

Cadmium Red is a brilliant opaque red, available in a number of shades. Winsor & Newton's Scarlet Lake is a good substitute. Naphthol Crimson is a light-fast improvement for Alizarin Crimson, although all crimsons are very reluctant to mix with water. Start them with a drop of methylated spirits.

Naphthol Crimson   *Alizarin Crimson*

BLUES

Cobalt Blue is the most useful blue, but dries very quickly on the palette, so add drops of water to it often. Ultramarine also works well, but make it up on the palette as you need it because it is said to set solid in storage jars. Phthalocyanine Blue or Prussian Blue can be over powerful, but there are alternatives in the brilliant ready-mixed blues in which Phthalocyanine Blue is combined with a White. Cerulean and Manganese Blues are fine cool blues.

Cerulean   *Phthalocyanine*   *Cobalt*

BLACKS

The slight differences between Blacks show up in tempera, and they mix well to make clean greys. Ivory Black is the warmest in colour, Spinel Black is the darkest.

EARTH COLOURS

The yellow, red and brown earth colours and their Mars equivalents (p. 100), are all satisfactory and present no problems except that Raw Umber and Burnt Umber are both toxic and dry quickly on the palette. The differences between colours are more noticeable in tempera than in any other medium, so it is worth trying a selection of fine ochres and umbers, available as pigments in an wide range from Old Holland.

The deep iron oxides, Indian Red and Mars Violet, are intense and opaque; both are useful for making strong darks in combination with Ultramarine.

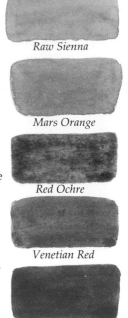

Raw Sienna

Mars Orange

Red Ochre

Venetian Red

Indian Red

GREENS

Viridian is a useful occasional colour for brightening greens or cooling blues, and saves the need for the over-powerful green-blues. Bright greens look out of place in tempera unless the colour scheme is planned around them. Terre Verte and Oxide of Chromium are more useful.

Terre Verte

Oxide of Chromium

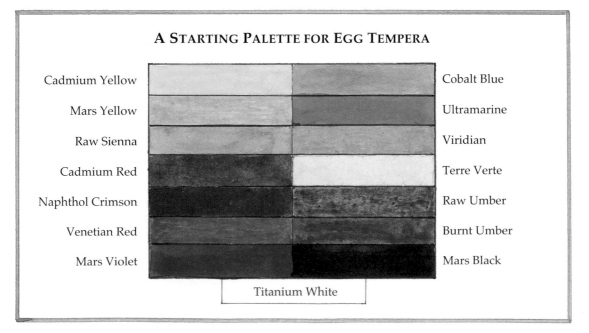

A STARTING PALETTE FOR EGG TEMPERA

Cadmium Yellow		Cobalt Blue
Mars Yellow		Ultramarine
Raw Sienna		Viridian
Cadmium Red		Terre Verte
Naphthol Crimson		Raw Umber
Venetian Red		Burnt Umber
Mars Violet		Mars Black
	Titanium White	

COLOUR MIXING

Whatever colours you mix, they are combined visually with the previous layer. The translucence of the paint film means that every pigment or mixture is influenced by the colour beneath it. Naturally opaque colours are the basis of most mixtures. Transparent pigments such as Burnt Sienna, Viridian and Aureolin exert their influence most effectively as glazes.

The addition of the egg medium has little effect on the appearance of a colour, compared to its aspect as a dry pigment, so variations between colours are distinct in tempera; the earth colours such as ochres, umbers, siennas and red oxides frequently vary from one batch to another. The early painters didn't mix colours to the same extent as modern artists, so there is a tradition of using wider range of pigments than in other media.

Cobalt Blue and Titanium White over a graded tone.

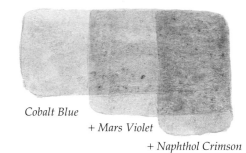

The semi-transparent nature of tempera alters the usual colour mixing systems as the colour underneath influences the one above.

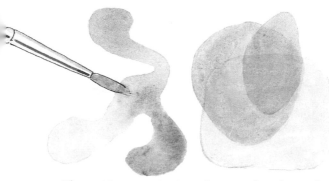

Cobalt Blue

+ Mars Violet

+ Naphthol Crimson

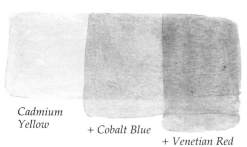

Cadmium Yellow

+ Cobalt Blue

+ Venetian Red

Two examples of building up a colour through overpainting rather than by direct mixing.

To paint a solid opaque area, apply the same mixture over and over to the same part until the colour is consistent and flat. Modelling could be added on top of this, but creating a smooth gradation is difficult. An easier way is to paint the modelling and detail as an undercoat, in a complementary colour, and then cover it with the true colour.

In the diagram above an undercoat of grey, made of Titanium White and Peach Black, was painted on, with medium grey at the top and white at the bottom. When this was graded evenly, a mixture of Cobalt Blue and White was used to paint over it. Starting with a mixture that was mainly blue with a little white at the top, the paint was stroked onto the top third, reducing in thickness all the time. Then a medium sky mixture was introduced and painted over the central parts, thinner at the top so it blended with the darker blue. The lightest blue mixture was blended into the medium colour and then continued down to the bottom.

Flesh colour used to be painted with an undercoat of soft green, usually Green Earth. Here the hand has been painted in Green and then coloured afterwards.

195

MAKING THE EGG-YOLK MIXTURE

The medium with which the pigment is bound, or tempered, is just egg-yolk and water. This is the simplest and most common way of painting with tempera.

One egg should be enough for several hours work, and can safely be stored in a refrigerator for two or three days. The sign that you need to change to a fresh egg is when it starts to become stickier, when a thread of it follows the brush when lifting it from the medium.

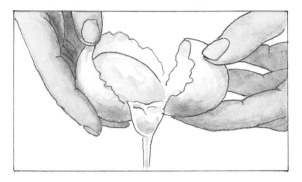

1. Crack an egg as nearly into equal halves as you can, and slide the contents back and forward from one half to the other to drain away the white. Or use an egg-separator.

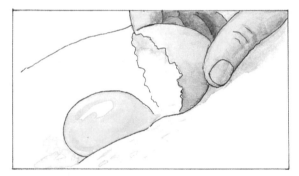

2. Hold a sheet of kitchen-roll paper in the open palm of one hand and carefully slide the egg-yolk into the centre.

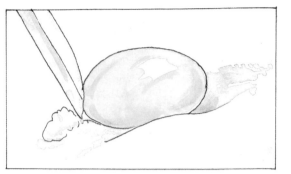

3. By tilting your hand, slowly roll the yolk around to dry it. When the white has been soaked up, cut off any jelly appendage with the tip of a sharp knife if necessary.

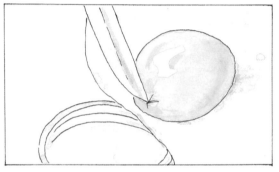

4. Manoeuvre the yolk to the edge, so it is poised over a small wide-necked glass jar. Pierce the yolk-sac with a knife point so the yolk can run out.

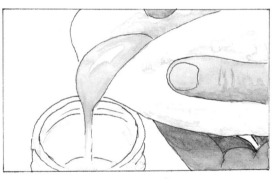

5. Guide and carefully squeeze the liquid yolk into the jar, retaining the yolk sac on the kitchen-roll paper.

6. Add a small amount of water with an eye-dropper, a quarter or a third of the amount of egg, and stir thoroughly. The medium is now ready for use.

If the yolk breaks before you are ready, you could add a little water to the mixture and filter it all through a cheesecloth, or better still, give it to your cat who will love it, and start again.

Techniques

HANDLING THE PAINT

■ First grind or mix the dry pigment with water into a paste. The tip of a palette knife can be used for stirring.

■ Take some of the paste onto your palette.

■ Add the egg medium to the paste and mix thoroughly with a brush – the addition of medium to the pigments is called tempering.

■ Then dilute the paint as necessary with water in the same way as for any other water-based medium

ADDING WATER TO THE PIGMENT

If you are adding water to the dry pigment in one of the palette wells, only add one drop a a time, because pigments vary in their take-up of water. Start any colour that repels water with alcohol or methylated spirits.

Add a drop at a time

ADDING THE EGG

The pigment-and-water paste has about the same consistency as the softer tube paints. Add some of the egg-yolk medium to this paste and mix. This is the binder that will stick your paint to the panel.

Stir the egg in with a brush

HOW TO TEST THE PAINT

There should be enough egg in the tempered paint to dry with a slight but distinct sheen. A matt finish shows there is not enough egg in the paint. Some dark colours need a surprisingly large amount of egg to bind them, White needs very little, so keep an eye on the shine as you paint.

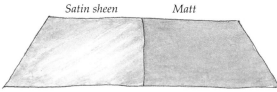

Satin sheen   *Matt*

If insufficient binder is added, some of the dark colours will dry with a matt finish (right).

LIQUIDITY OF THE PAINT

To retain the luminosity of colour that is characteristic of tempera, the colour should slip easily off the brush. The brush should have much of the paint squeezed out of it before applying it to the picture, so that a blob of wet paint doesn't remain at the end of the stroke where the brush is lifted off. The paint should be neither too viscous, so that it has to be pushed around, nor so sparse that it has to be forcibly spread. It needs to come off the brush without excess liquid. Practise this.

The layers are built up with many adjacent and overlapping strokes, thin enough to dry quickly and so permit overpainting without delay. Large scale liquid washes in the manner of watercolour are most suitable at the beginning, to seal and tone the gesso if desired, and in the later or final stages as glazes. Even with plenty of water, the paint doesn't run or spread in the same way as watercolour, but stays where you put it.

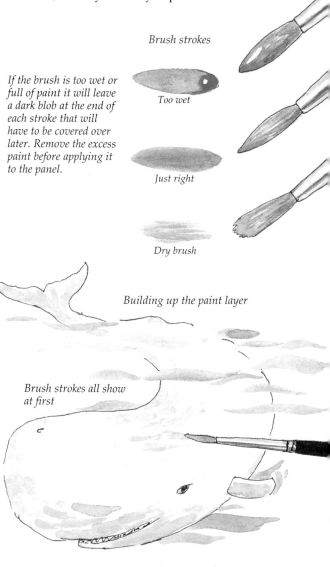

Brush strokes

If the brush is too wet or full of paint it will leave a dark blob at the end of each stroke that will have to be covered over later. Remove the excess paint before applying it to the panel.

Too wet

Just right

Dry brush

Building up the paint layer

Brush strokes all show at first

BASIC PRINCIPLES

Tempera paint has to be applied thinly as the egg-yolk mixture is too runny to allow more than the slightest impasto. Even opaque pigments become semi-transparent when thinned, so any one paint layer has an opalescence somewhere between transparency and opacity.

■ White is used in most mixtures, and opaque pigments are the basis of tempera painting.

■ Dark paint glazed over a lighter layer will seem transparent.

■ Lighter paint over darker will produce an opalescent effect.

■ Tones and colours are developed in glazes and scumbles rather than in repeated layers of the same colour. Repeated layers of the same paint will give an even and opaque colour when you need it.

MONOCHROME AND SHADING

When the drawing is complete, the traditional method is to begin by shading and modelling in monochrome; in this way, the forms will emerge from the beginning. Ink can be used for this as well as Raw or Burnt Umber, or a mixed olive-brown made from Black and any Earth colour you wish, called "verdaccio". Apply the paint to build up the modelling as if you were shading with a pencil or charcoal, and continue until the weight of tone is nearly as dark as the intended finished picture. When the undercoat is painted over it, the effect will still show through in a softer form, and becomes the foundation of the ensuing development of form and colour in the final picture. The use of warm colours produces an inner glow over which bluer mixtures, if required, look very well; avoid using a blue colour for the shading as it leads to an unnatural coldness that is difficult to dispel.

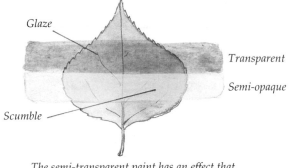

The semi-transparent paint has an effect that depends on the colour and tone under it.

After the initial drawing and shading, the first essential is to build up a fairly opaque surface free of visible brushmarks. Begin painting over the drawing, as far as possible selecting the opaque colours to use in mixtures containing some white. In the early stages all the overlapping translucent brushmarks show up individually until the accumulation of brush-strokes and paint layers eventually produces a fairly opaque underpainting. Colours can be used adventurously in the knowledge that succeeding paint layers can tone them down if necessary, while leaving them still able to influence and enliven the final effect. Painted over the basic modelling, the paint will suddenly begin to look solid and real, and the hardest part of Tempera, when you may have wondered why you ever started, is over. Over this foundation you will be able to develop your colouring and refine the forms.

The light and shade is fully developed in a mixture of Raw and Burnt Umber.

The shading (top), is made with Peach Black and Titanium White. The colour is established by being painted over it, allowing the shading to show through, (middle band), and the whole is developed and modelled until complete, (bottom band).

Local colours have been painted over each part, retaining the forms below.

198

THE CONTROL OF FORM

Once a solid effect has been achieved it can be modelled towards both light and dark. Nearly all mixtures contain some Titanium White, which not only maintains the slightly opalescent quality of tempera, but also improves the consistency of the colours so they brush out more pleasantly.

Over opalescent middle tones that are neither entirely opaque nor transparent, the modelling of the lights is achieved by the application of relatively opaque light colours, usually containing white. Each layer is still influenced by the underlying colour. The darks and shadows are developed in the opposite direction with glazes which add transparency and depth. Only the final darks or glazes are usually free of White, and this is enough to produce a transparent effect where it is wanted.

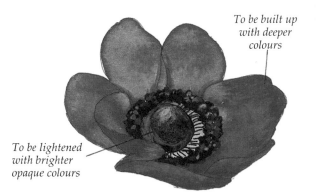

To be built up with deeper colours

To be lightened with brighter opaque colours

The rich colouring is achieved by keeping the shading to a minimum and not allowing it to spread into the lights.

△
The whole range of colours is available to develop and improve lights, shadows, colours and detail.

HOW TO CREATE TEXTURE

A number of textures are possible even using thin paint, but most texture is worked up by dry-brush work as you paint. A small painting-knife tip makes a texture as deep as is practical, and a small sponge will put on paint in a characteristic pattern, which is occasionally useful for foliage. Thicker textures are not really appropriate for such smooth paint.

Light texture made with the tip of a palette knife

Splattering makes overlapping dots and blobs that work well for some rocks and hard outdoor surfaces. Lay the picture at a fairly flat angle. Cut out and position paper shapes to cover any parts of the picture you wish to protect. Take up plenty of paint with a large brush and, deciding which direction you want the splattering to go in, bring down the brush ferrule sharply across your fingers. The paint will fly off onto the picture; the wetter the paint, the larger the dots.

A large varnish brush is practical for splattering paint.

Try it out first on a piece of plain paper to give yourself an idea of the effect. Have a brush ready to modify or remove any badly placed ones before they dry if possible, but there will always be additional work to blend in the effect with the rest of the painting.

CORRECTIONS

Egg hardens in stages, so at first the paint can be almost completely removed by re-wetting it and lifting off with a brush and kitchen-roll paper. During the first 24 hours the paint can still be carefully scrubbed off. After a day, paint can be scraped off carefully with a curved-edge scalpel or with a razor blade. If necessary, garnet paper can be used to smooth out small scratches before repainting.

TEMPERA STEP-BY-STEP

CICADA TREE

Aims

1: to record the way the light catches the tree trunk and wooden palette in contrast to the surrounding shadows. 2: to capture the warmth of the weather and the view of the distant peninsula. 3: to paint a faithful reminder of the tree which was home to a noisy and continuously chirping population of cicadas.

The photograph exaggerates the contrast and concentrates on the foreground, besides containing extraneous detail. Although the painting is very realistic, there are big differences in interpretation from the photograph, which didn't give the balance I wanted between the foreground tree and the seascape behind.

The sketch

This was a fairly elaborate watercolour on warm oatmeal-coloured paper. I had a comfortable place to sit, out of the sun and with plenty of time, although the moving sun always puts a limit on how long the lighting will last. The warmth of the paper had a big influence that was difficult to reproduce on the painting. Individual parts of the scene were photographed to supply detail for the final version. The dry foreground textures and crisp detail immediately suggested tempera.

The drawing was done lightly with a hard pencil, because the gesso surface takes the pencil strongly, so rubbing out is hard work, even with a putty rubber. The first solid paint was the cream of the sky and sea, to give a glow of warmth which the sketch automatically possessed from its coloured paper. Over this was painted a layer of sky blue made from Cobalt Blue, Titanium White and a little Yellow Ochre. The sea was a stronger version of the same mixture. A preliminary green layer was painted over the tree foliage.

Some more solid building up on the wood and the tree trunk came next. Special attention was paid to getting the golden brown colour of the tree trunk, and the crisp detail of the shadows of the lifting bark. The earth colours, Yellow Ochre, Red Ochre and Raw Umber were used, modified and darkened where necessary with Cobalt Blue. Some more Cobalt was mixed with Yellow Ochre to give a dull dark green for the pine foliage.

200

The sky and sea were built up with layers of Cobalt Blue and White with a little Hansa Golden to turn the sea greenish. The brushmark effect of these coats was reduced by scumbles of yellowish white. White always has a smoothing effect, and increases the opacity so that the paint layer becomes more solid. and easy to work.

The foliage was developed with a bright green containing White to give it opacity, and the darks were built up with Ultramarine, Aureolin and Indian Red. Modelling on the trunk was done with warmer colours, while the lights were emphasised with mixtures including White. It needed more of the feeling of warmth which was one of the objects of the painting, so a transparent fiery orange mixture of Aureolin and Cadmium Orange was carefully applied over the prepared modelling.

A mixture of White, Mars Yellow, Red Ochre and Ultramarine was painted back and forth over the road, aiming for a warm pink to blend in with the fallen pine needles. A dark background of warm brown was built up, over which to paint the dead grasses. These were flicked in with a finely pointed brush, using a strong opaque cream made of White and Cadmium Yellow. Glazes were painted over every so often to tone them down before continuing with the near, lighter, stalks.

Darker green was needed to intensify the shadows and increase the contrast range, so a mixture of the darkest blue, Ultramarine, and the strongest yellow, Cadmium Yellow, with Burnt Umber to darken it further, was painted into the shadows and darks.

Summary
Some of the aims have been accomplished well enough. Tempera is ideal for the textures, owing to its sharpness and ability to overpaint quickly. The painting hasn't been so successful in capturing the feeling of warm hazy distance. A thin milky glaze of White with a spot of Mars Yellow might correct this.

OILS

INTRODUCTION

Oil paints provide the most complete and flexible means of expression available to artists, and lend themselves readily to a wide range of effects: the paintings are not limited in size, the paint can be directly mixed or overlaid in glazes, applied thinly or thickly, it can be opaque or transparent, possess any degree of gloss or otherwise, allow a greater depth of colour and tone than can be achieved in any other medium, and at the same time gives ample time for the manipulation of the paint.

The convenience of oils led to their being adopted in the 1400s as a replacement for tempera, and oils have been the major medium for most large scale art ever since. The early technique, based on paint made on the spot and applied thinly, quickly reached a high degree of technical perfection.

Pigments were few in number and except for genuine Ultramarine, a specially prepared and ground semi-precious stone, more expensive than gold, all the old yellows, reds and blues have been superseded by more brilliant and permanent pigments. Lead White (Flake or Cremnitz White today), the ochres, earths and umbers, together with Black, were their working colours, augmented by the brighter chemical pigments. Some of these have since faded considerably.

Research into the media used by the Old Masters suggest that an oil, either walnut or linseed, cooked with lead driers and known as "black" oil, was the basis of paints and the medium. The medium used to apply the paint also contained a thick mastic solution, and sometimes wax, the resulting mixture taking the form of a jelly that held its shape, but liquefied when worked with a brush; the paint dried quickly and would be ready to work on again within a day or two. Its versatility and advantages for artists are clear to see in their paintings in the great public galleries

The consistency of commercially manufactured paints introduced after 1850 has remained stiffer than the earlier hand-made paints, and influenced the change in the popular painting style during the time of the Impressionists. The necessary adjustments of technique have helped bring about a new orthodoxy, which sometimes limits the scope of many artists to a style where there is little place for detail.

Modern media that approach the ideal of ease of handling and quick drying are recommended in the section on Media, p. 218, and in the demonstration pictures at the end of this section.

River Landscape with horseman and peasants, by Albert Cuyp.
A very large painting, with magical golden light in the distance and strong contrasts of sunlight and shade in the foreground. A showpiece of what oil paints can do.

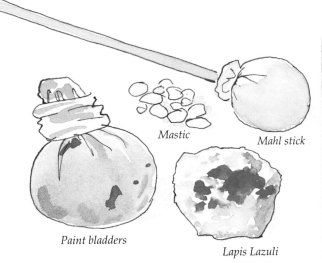

Mastic

Mahl stick

Paint bladders

Lapis Lazuli

Some traditional oil painting aids and materials. A mahl-stick supports and steadies the wrist, preventing it from resting on wet paint. Pig's bladders were once used to store ready-made paints. The resin, mastic, originates in the form of tear-shaped crystals. Lapis lazuli, from which genuine ultramarine is still extracted.

Man with a Blue Sleeve, by Titian.
Soft blending and sharp detail are both present in this portrait, and the solid and opaque lights stand out effectively from the insubstantial shadows. This painting is now thought to be a self portrait.

The full scope of oils can only be realised by a method that includes painting in more than one layer. The choice of medium is crucial in modifying the behaviour of the paint, and to gain the most from oils, remember two especially useful points:

■ Paint thinly, especially the initial coats.

■ Use a modern painting medium, such as Liquin, or one of the other fast-drying media.

The medium of oil paints has much the widest range of materials available, reflecting its popularity and versatility. One high quality paintmaker supplies a range of over 160 colours. Others concentrate on smaller but still extensive ranges.

Materials

Modern materials are generally more permanent, purer, and varied than in the past. The achievements of the Old Masters' technique, like that of the Stradivarius violins, have often been attributed to secret formulae and materials, but research has shown it to be unlikely that they had access to superior basic materials, rather that they used them in different ways with consummate care, knowledge and artistry.

Many of their problems, such as the incompatibility of some paints with others, have been overcome by the replacement of such pigments with safer substitutes, so that almost any colour can now be mixed with any other. Their painting media were almost certainly different, thick, but fluid and quick-drying. The loss of these together with the use of raw linseed oil as a replacement has coincided with a clear decline in technique. Some commercial media represent a return to better things.

PAINTING SURFACES

Canvas is the traditional surface for oil painting, which benefits from a surface with a tooth to grip the paint as it comes off the brush. Panels are sometimes used for smaller pictures with fine detail, and canvas can be stretched over panels covered to gain rigidity.

The surface of all materials is first covered with a "priming", consisting of layers of glue and paint that:

- Protect the material of the support from chemical attack by the oils.
- Provide a white or coloured tone to work on.
- Control the absorbency of the surface.

PANELS

The most popular panel materials are reconstituted wood pressed together with glue, such as Medium Density Fibreboard (MDF), hardboard and chipboard. These materials, especially MDF, are stable and grain-free, and will not warp. MDF, although heavy, is the most satisfactory of these.

Medium Density Fibreboard (MDF)

Chipboard

HOW TO PREPARE A PANEL

A good clean surface still needs sealing and priming to protect it and make it ready to accept the paint without change or deterioration. The surface colour and absorbency is regulated by the priming.

SIZING

Size is the name given to the glue and water solution that seals the surface of the panel. Sprinkle the glue or gelatine granules into warm water, and leave to swell.

1.5 litres of water

100gm of glue or gelatine

After two or more hours, warm it up, stir until the glue has entirely dissolved, and paint it immediately onto the panel.

PRIMING

Priming is the covering of the sized panel with a white and suitably absorbent painting surface.

- **Acrylic** primer can be bought in bottles and painted on. It dries quickly and is soon ready to paint over with acrylics or oils.

- **Gesso** is more absorbent, for rigid surfaces only, and is mainly used for tempera but will take oils. See p. 189.

- **White Lead** is the most suitable, as it is an oil ground, but takes times to mature. It needs to stabilise for many weeks.

- **White Lead over gesso** has the advantage, if required, of the whiteness of the gesso which brightens it.

TONING

A ground is often tinted, which can be done with a thin layer of colour, or the colour can be added to the priming.

CANVAS

Canvas can be chosen according to surface texture and appearance. The best is unbleached linen, made from flax, the most durable natural fibre. Unbleached cotton is cheaper and has a less interesting grain, but can make a satisfactory support.

Linen is a more stable material than cotton, not so affected by changes in humidity, and gives a richer looking surface to the painting. Both linen and cotton are sold in several grades, either ready-primed or unprimed. Use the best canvas you can afford, to add to the quality of your work.

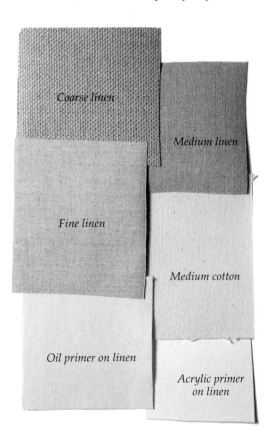

From very fine to very coarse, there is an extensive range of canvases available, cut from a roll or ready-stretched.

COMMERCIALLY PREPARED CANVAS

These often already have a universal primer, suitable for acrylics as well as oils. The oil-primed canvases are very reliable and there is no need to prime your own except to save money for quantities.

To make them less absorbent, give them an extra coat of White oil paint, toned if you wish by the addition of one of the umbers or ochres.

HOW TO PRIME A CANVAS

Linen canvas is made from the flax plant whose seeds produce linseed oil, and its fibres contain a small percentage of oil which acts as a preservative. Any oil beyond this small amount will attack the fibres, for it becomes acid as it dries. A glue size is applied to seal the cloth against both oil and other pollutants. Cotton contains no oil but needs the same protection. Priming should not be too thick.

SIZING

As with a panel, size is used to seal the canvas fibres and prevent their penetration by oil. It should be brushed in firmly but thinly, without filling the grain or any pinholes; the priming will do that, and if the sizing is too thick it will crack.

1 litre of water   75gm of glue or gelatine

Sprinkle the glue or gelatine granules into warm water, and leave to swell. After two or more hours, warm it up, stir until the glue has entirely dissolved, and paint it onto the panel while warm.

THE OIL GROUND

The traditional ground contains White Lead, (Flake White), ground up with linseed oil. White Lead primer can be bought ready-made in tins.

Apply it to the sized canvas with a palette knife and work it well into the grain to fill up the weave. A "Wavy Mottler" brush, below, is good for spreading the primer evenly. A second coat gives a whiter finish but fractionally reduces flexibility.

Drying seems quick, but an oil ground needs at least two weeks, preferably a few months, to mature and stabilise.

205

MAKING A STRETCHED CANVAS

It is easier to make a smooth and tightly stretched canvas if you use raw canvas and then size and prime it afterwards. Cut out a piece of raw canvas 12cm larger in each direction than the frame, to allow for shrinkage and folding.

Wet the canvas first in a bath and dry it on a line. This will pre-shrink it and stop it stretching too tightly on the frame. If it is creased, iron it.

STRETCHERS

The pieces are bought separately and assembled at home; a mallet will drive the corner joints together.

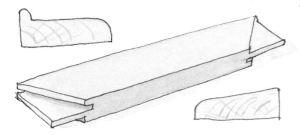

The bevelled or shaped side is under the canvas, the flat side faces the back. Canvases longer than 76cm need a cross-piece. Use thicker pieces for large canvases.

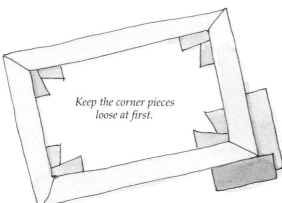

Keep the corner pieces loose at first.

1. Use a set square to check the corners.

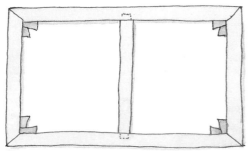

A cross-bar support is used for sizes of 76cm upwards.

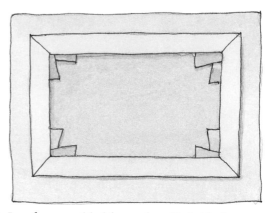

2. Lay the assembled frame, bevelled side down, centrally on the canvas. Keep the canvas weave square to the frame.

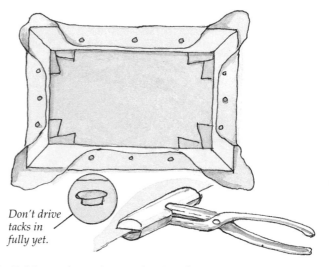

Don't drive tacks in fully yet.

3. Fold over first edges and tack lightly. Pull opposite edge and then other edges with canvas pliers and tack. Check the corners are square

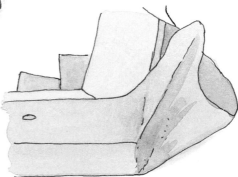

4. Fold the corner as shown.

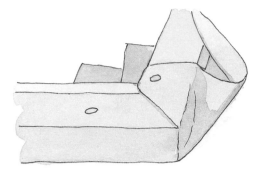

5. Continue folding and tack. Avoid putting tacks through corner joints, which would stop them moving.

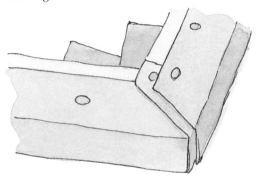

6. Finish the fold and tack again. The canvas is now ready for sizing.

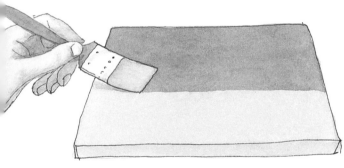

7. Size the canvas thoroughly. As it dries it will shrink and tighten. If necessary, tighten the corners by lightly tapping in the wedges.

PRIMING

When it is dry the canvas can be primed as described above, or with an acrylic primer which dries ready for use in 24 hours.

Oil primer is better for intended oil paintings, but ideally needs a long maturing period before use. An over absorbent priming makes the early stages of painting hard work as the brush drags across a surface that is pulling the fluid out of it. The undercoat can look dry and harsh as a result. A thin coat of Flake White or a toning colour will cure this.

CANVAS MOUNTED ON A PANEL

The hard surface of canvas glued onto a strong panel is preferred by some artists, as it allows the image to be traced on without denting the canvas, and the firmness of the surface is no disadvantage. The strength of the glue holds the canvas but staples can also be used on the back if the panel is thick enough.

1 litre of water

75gm of glue or gelatine

▪ Paint the warm glue onto the panel, including the edges and the overlap at the back

▪ Lay the canvas over the glued surface, with the weave square to the edges.

▪ Paint the warm glue firmly all over the canvas, pressing out any air-bubbles.

▪ Fold the edges over onto the back and glue them as flat as you can.

▪ Coat all of the back with glue to prevent warping.

▪ Leave to dry for 12 hours, then prime as above.

CANVAS BOARDS

These are made of cotton canvas stretched over a cardboard mount. They are not as permanent as the previous supports because the cardboard will eventually deteriorate, but they are very much cheaper than regular canvases and much slimmer to store. They are often rather absorbent, making the surface unsympathetic at first; an extra coat of White oil paint, or White with one of the umbers or ochres, will seal them and improve the feel as you paint.

PAPER

Strong watercolour paper or board can be used as a support, provided the paper is protected from the acid attack of the dried oil. Acrylic primer will protect the paper sufficiently. A spot of coloured watercolour or acrylic paint mixed in with the primer will make it easier to see if you have missed covering anywhere. Retouching varnish has also been used to protect the paper.

The oil coated paper used for sketching is very suitable for this purpose.

BRUSHES

Oil paintings require more brushes than the water media because they take notably longer to clean as you change from one colour to another. The normal practice is to keep a brush for its own colours throughout a session and clean them all afterwards. A good range of well-cleaned brushes makes oil painting much easier.

HOG'S HAIR

The white-bristled hog's hair brushes are the work-horses of oil painting. The best have interlocked hairs that hold their shape well, the others tend to spread. Long haired brushes are the most sympathetic to use, and the hairs should tend to curve inwards. They are most useful when pressing the paint into the weave of the canvas over sizeable areas, but are not suitable for detail. Hog's hair brushes vary in quality but are very much cheaper than sables so buy the best you can.

LONG FLAT

General spreading brushes. Those with interlocked bristles keep their shape.

SHORT FLAT

Often called Brights. They are about one-third shorter than the long flats and so are much stiffer. They scrape the paint along leaving a raised ridge on either side, a sort of texture rarely needed.

FILBERT

These are like the long flats but the edges are shaped to curve inwards. They are generally useful for spreading paint smoothly without leaving any pronounced texture. A brush collection can usefully start with these and the round varieties of hog and sable.

ROUND

All-purpose brushes for spreading paint. They are most useful when they retain their tapered points, so interlocked bristle is important. The medium to large sizes are the most useful. The small ones are better replaced with sables.

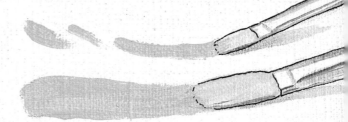

SYNTHETIC HAIR

Some of the new synthetic brushes have proved to work well with oils. Interlon hair brushes are like dense springy sables, and the smaller sizes are much more controllable for detail than hog's hair, and last longer than sable. The larger sizes don't hold as much paint or control it as well as hog's hair.

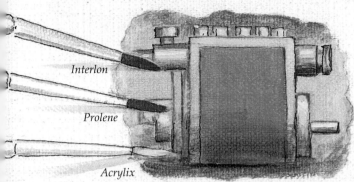

Interlon

Prolene

Acrylix

Prolene and Acrylix are rather similar, and like the Interlon, are made for acrylics. The brush hairs are densely packed, and so leave less paint-holding space than a sable. They will paint all but the smaller details. These types of brush are improving steadily, so are well worth trying.

SABLE

For the finest detail, sables are still necessary, as they have a flexibility that no other hair can match; the small synthetics are short and relatively stubby and so quickly run out of paint.

MONGOOSE

The hair is just a little stiffer than sable, without such good points. The filbert shapes are useful for blending tones into each other. They are most useful as small-scale fan brushes for blending.

FAN

These are not for applying paint, but for very light stroking across the paint surface, blending adjacent areas of colour and smoothing out brushmarks. Once they have picked up paint during blending, they need cleaning and drying before they are ready for use again, so more than one is needed.

Fan brushes

RIGGER

Riggers are for drawing long even lines, such as ships' rigging, or cats' whiskers. They should be pulled along like a fox's tail, not manoeuvred back and forth like an ordinary brush.

HOW TO LOOK AFTER YOUR BRUSHES		
1	Remove the paint	Squeeze the hairs between folded kitchen-roll paper to remove surplus paint; dip into white spirit and repeat until no more comes off on the paper.
2	Rinse with white spirit	Rinse out by squeezing the hairs against the side of the container until no more paint comes out. Replace the White Spirit as necessary.
3	Wash with washing-up liquid	Squeeze some liquid into your palm and press the brush hairs carefully into it and work up a froth. If any colour comes out, repeat with fresh liquid.
4	Rinse	Rinse the hairs out thoroughly under a cold tap and reshape the tips. Leave to dry.

PAINTS

There is a tremendous range of good quality oil colours available, with some makers offering over 160 colours, and others specialising in smaller ranges of about 50. There is no need to restrict yourself to a small handful of colours, your colouring range will be extended and improved by experimenting with colours new to you. The greater your knowledge of the materials you work with, the greater the likelihood of producing worthwhile work.

Additions to the pigment and oil are sometimes made. Stabilisers prevent some paints separating out into oil and pigment while in the tube, and in some cases improve the paint's consistency. Extenders, or fillers, reduce the cost of expensive paints, or the strength of over-powerful paints by replacing a percentage of pigment without affecting the colour too noticeably, although the brightness will inevitably be slightly reduced. Driers speed the drying of slow-drying pigments.

The paints should have as high a proportion of pigment to the binder as possible, and some makers emphasise their quality in this respect.

Although the price is higher when a tube contains only genuine Cobalt or Cerulean Blue, the colour is more intense, goes further and mixes more brightly. The cheaper makes contain less pigment in a tube of equivalent size, but the strength of colour remains satisfactory. Your choice can safely depend on your own preferences, bearing in mind that there are still a few colours around that are not lightproof.

OIL PAINT

The majority of makers supply straight oil paint, made of pigment ground with refined, or better still, cold-pressed linseed oil. The oil, which holds the grains of pigment together, is called the binder. The best paints incorporate as much pigment as possible with the minimum amount of cold-pressed linseed oil. The paints are also hand-ground with stone rollers rather than steel, and cost noticeably more than the standard factory-made types. The whites and some of the blues are ground with lighter coloured poppy or safflower oils to keep their colours as clear as possible. These oils dry more slowly than linseed. All the oils have a protective function against atmospheric pollution and damp, and for this reason pigments in oil are generally more permanent than in watercolour.

Many less familiar colours are mixtures, sometimes of three or four pigments, but their quality is in no way lowered by this. All of the standard makes can be used with confidence and any of the different brands may be safely mixed together.

RESIN-OIL PAINT

Schmincke's range of Mussini oil paints incorporates about 10% of mastic and dammar resins with the oil. This improves the lustre and brilliance of the paints, and is based on an old Florentine formula. They are compatible with standard oil paints.

ALKYD RESIN-OIL PAINT

Alkyd colours are ground with oil-modified alkyd resin. They have the advantage of drying overnight and are less prone to yellowing with age. The bulk of the alkyd resin makes the paint slightly more transparent than normal oil paints and weakens some colours, especially Flake White, which loses much of its opacity. The alkyd colours are compatible with all other oil colours. Liquin, or Alkyd Medium (Rowney), are the recommended media, and their use with normal oil paints imparts many of the alkyd properties to them.

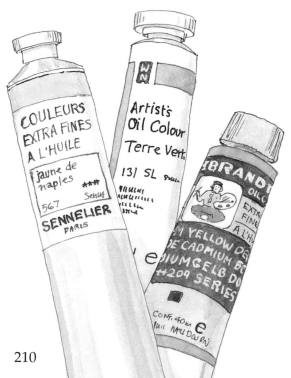

MAKING YOUR OWN OIL PAINTS

The Old Masters' paint was made in the studio, and some artists still consider that a brighter or purer colour can be made this way. It is likely that the earlier paints were of a softer consistency than present day tube colours.

INGREDIENTS

■ Artists' pigments. (Flake White is too poisonous to work with as a powder, so is the rare genuine Naples Yellow).

■ Cold-pressed linseed oil. This is superior to refined linseed oil, although this could be used.

and

■ A ground-glass slab, about 30cm square, for grinding the paint on.

■ A palette knife for initial mixing and manipulating the paint.

■ A muller for the grinding together of oil and pigment.

■ Empty tubes, if you wish to store the paint.

1. Put out some pigment in a mound, hollow out the centre, and carefully add linseed oil, drop by drop. The aim is to use as little oil as possible. You can add more later if necessary.

2. Mix the oil into the pigment with a palette knife, and scrape into a heap.

3. Grind the paint thoroughly with the muller, adding more pigment as the mixture become softer, or oil if it stiffens too much. When it feels really smooth it is ready for use. The pressure ensures the thorough coating of the pigment with oil.

4. Some colours become softer after standing for a while. Add more pigment and re-grind.

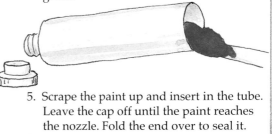

5. Scrape the paint up and insert in the tube. Leave the cap off until the paint reaches the nozzle. Fold the end over to seal it.

Grind the paint thoroughly so that every grain is evenly coated with oil, which protects the colour against atmospheric pollution, as well as holding it in place. Notice how much darker the pigments become when wetted with oil; for this reason I try to obtain the lighter shades of Ultramarine and Cobalt Blue. Some manufacturers use poppy oil for making Ultramarine, as it is clearer, but it is said to eventually yellow as much as linseed oil.

Making your own paint will give you valuable insights into the ways of pigments, and provide good paint free from additives, which are mainly for maintaining the long-term condition of paint in a tube. However, the manufactured paints are of a high standard, and some makers do not use additives. If some separation has occurred in a tube and the oil comes out first, soak up the excess oil with blotting paper before using the paint.

THE RANGE OF COLOURS

This is enormous and can be confusing. There are certain basic colours that are the foundation of nearly everyone's palettes: the familiar names like Cobalt Blue, Burnt Umber or Cadmium Yellow. Once you have selected a basic palette representing the main colours, feel free to try any others that seem useful or interesting. They will add to your enjoyment and improve the colouring of your paintings, but in any one picture you are not likely to feel the need for more than about ten colours, however many you have. The austere disciplines of a "limited palate", using only about five or six colours, is only for a minority, and needs experience to avoid repetitiveness.

YELLOWS

Cadmium Yellows are the most suitable as they are bright, opaque and dense. Naples Yellow is a very useful creamy yellow, and the Old Holland Indian Yellows provide an interesting transparent addition.

EARTH COLOURS

A range is useful, from Raw Sienna, the Mars Yellow, Orange, and Red and Gold and Brown Ochres. These colours add warmth and solidity to a colour scheme. Indian Red is good for lending a touch of violet to blue mixtures.

GREENS

Viridian, or one of its mixtures (see Greens, p. 106-7), is good for the occasional brilliant green or blue-green. Roberson's Olive Green is especially good as a basis for darker greens. Golden Green is another useful mixed colour.

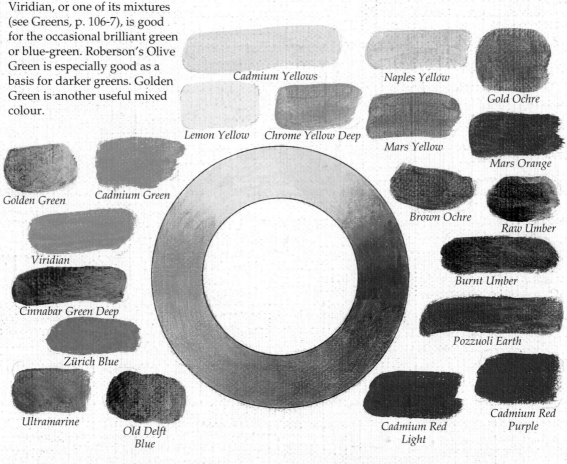

Cadmium Yellows

Naples Yellow

Gold Ochre

Lemon Yellow

Chrome Yellow Deep

Mars Yellow

Mars Orange

Golden Green

Cadmium Green

Brown Ochre

Raw Umber

Viridian

Burnt Umber

Cinnabar Green Deep

Pozzuoli Earth

Zürich Blue

Ultramarine

Old Delft Blue

Cadmium Red Light

Cadmium Red Purple

BLUES

Cerulean Blue is excellent for skies; some mixtures containing white resemble this colour. Cobalt Blue Light is useful in every picture, and Ultramarine provides the beautiful deep blues. Prussian Blue is rather fierce in oils and seldom necessary.

REDS

Cadmium Red Light is a fine all-purpose bright red. The darker reds can be chosen from the permanent alternatives to Alizarin Crimson (p. 102). The rose colours may not be needed, but Permanent Rose and the crimson replacements give clear colours.

WHITES AND BLACKS

Flake White is a solid quick-drying white used since the beginning of oil painting. Some makers add a proportion of Zinc White to it. Titanium White is slightly more opaque and distinctly whiter in colour; it is to be preferred for the Alkyd colours where it is noticeably more opaque than Flake White.

Ivory Black gives neutral greys with white and is the most popular black.

COLOUR SELECTION GUIDE

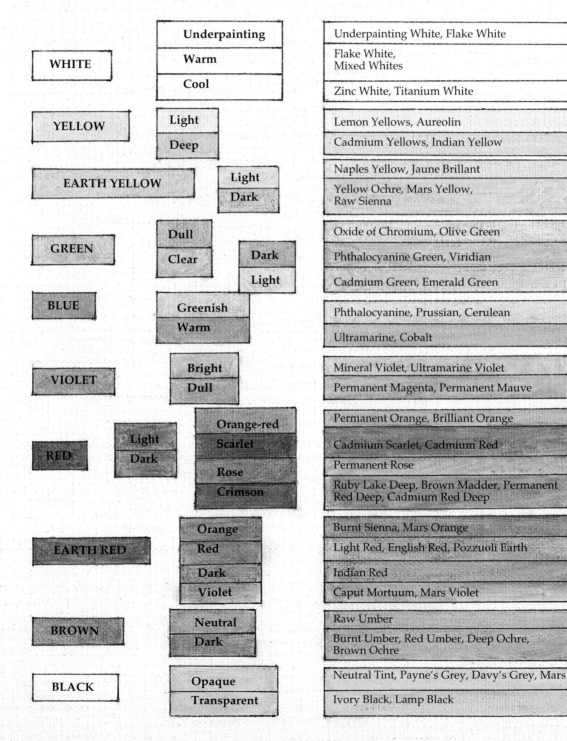

WHITE	**Underpainting**		Underpainting White, Flake White
	Warm		Flake White, Mixed Whites
	Cool		Zinc White, Titanium White
YELLOW	**Light**		Lemon Yellows, Aureolin
	Deep		Cadmium Yellows, Indian Yellow
EARTH YELLOW	**Light**		Naples Yellow, Jaune Brillant
	Dark		Yellow Ochre, Mars Yellow, Raw Sienna
GREEN	**Dull**		Oxide of Chromium, Olive Green
	Clear	**Dark**	Phthalocyanine Green, Viridian
		Light	Cadmium Green, Emerald Green
BLUE	**Greenish**		Phthalocyanine, Prussian, Cerulean
	Warm		Ultramarine, Cobalt
VIOLET	**Bright**		Mineral Violet, Ultramarine Violet
	Dull		Permanent Magenta, Permanent Mauve
RED	**Light**	**Orange-red**	Permanent Orange, Brilliant Orange
		Scarlet	Cadmium Scarlet, Cadmium Red
	Dark	**Rose**	Permanent Rose
		Crimson	Ruby Lake Deep, Brown Madder, Permanent Red Deep, Cadmium Red Deep
EARTH RED	**Orange**		Burnt Sienna, Mars Orange
	Red		Light Red, English Red, Pozzuoli Earth
	Dark		Indian Red
	Violet		Caput Mortuum, Mars Violet
BROWN	**Neutral**		Raw Umber
	Dark		Burnt Umber, Red Umber, Deep Ochre, Brown Ochre
BLACK	**Opaque**		Neutral Tint, Payne's Grey, Davy's Grey, Mars
	Transparent		Ivory Black, Lamp Black

213

COLOUR MIXING

White is the foundation of oil painting, and makes up a large percentage of the paint on the canvas. Add the more powerful colour gradually to the weaker when mixing to avoid waste, and mix quantities with a palette knife. Colour mixing is influenced by the method of painting. The Old Masters, who painted on coloured grounds, seldom needed to do much mixing; the colour of the ground in combination with underpainting enabled them to use their colours singly or in very simple combinations. The practice of painting directly onto a white ground leads to the need to cover it up before being able to assess the overall effect of the picture. The need to assess the effects of the colours against the brightness of a white ground can make colour mixing more difficult.

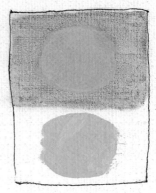

The effect of coloured and white grounds.

Glazing offers another form of mixing, in which simple colours are thinly spread over a coloured or white ground; the transparent colour is held in a resinous medium and colours and modifies the light coming from the paint below.

THE EFFECT OF WHITE IN MIXTURES

White acts as a cold colour in mixtures, lessening the effect of yellows and browns. To counter this, extra yellow has to be added to some light-coloured mixtures to preserve the balance, particularly of greens. Pink and violets remain clear and bright with White.

THE LAYOUT OF THE PALETTE

It helps to have a consistent layout, so you know where to find each colour, but this is not as important in oils as watercolour, where sometimes speed is essential. Put the pale and other yellows next to the White, and put out more than one lot of White so there is always a clean supply for new mixtures.

If you are concentrating on a particular colouring, for instance the greens of trees, always include a complementary colour to the main colours. The yellows, greens and blues by themselves easily become too sharply green, so put out some red or brown, such as Burnt Sienna, as a readily available counterweight to soften and modify the over-bright mixtures.

Diluted   with White
Raw Umber

Thinners   with White
Cadmium Yellow

Diluted   with White
Pozzuoli Earth

Thinners   with White
Mars Violet

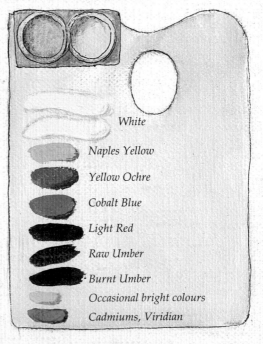

White
Naples Yellow
Yellow Ochre
Cobalt Blue
Light Red
Raw Umber
Burnt Umber
Occasional bright colours
Cadmiums, Viridian

A typical layout

SOME USEFUL MIXTURES

Naples Yellow, Cerulean Blue

Naples Yellow loses some of its yellowness in mixture with White, so that there is no more than a hint of green in the transition from cream to blue. These useful sky colours don't have to be mixed directly with each other: the mixture is more brilliant and controllable if the blue is glazed (see p. 227) over the yellow.

Cadmium Yellow, Ultramarine

These two colours make a rich and variable green, suitable for bright greens, but needing a red-brown to tone them down for most landscapes. The addition of White progressively cools the mixture until the pale green becomes chalky and unnatural. Increasing the Cadmium Yellow doesn't entirely cure this, and the addition of a powerful transparent yellow or mixed golden green can be more successful.

Viridian, Mars Yellow

For bright greens, the relative warmth of Mars Yellow is just enough to cope with the sharpness and intensity of Viridian, a clear transparent green. Viridian, or the even stronger Phthalocyanine Green, should be used with caution, preferably as a glaze to adjust an already painted area. White plays an influential part in avoiding an over-bright colour.

Cerulean Blue, Raw Umber

A cool grey is the result of a cool brown and a greenish blue. The Raw Umber goes towards grey as soon as White is added to it., and is one of the colours most changed by White. Cold greys are seldom necessary, and Cerulean predominates here in the formation of a range of subtle light blues.

Raw Sienna, Burnt Umber

Raw Sienna is one of the most golden of the yellows, and Burnt Umber adds redness and depth. The White cools the mixture to a bright warm grey-brown. These three colours in different proportions will make a good selection of browns, and the Sienna and Umber are both good for glazing, where their effects are quite different from their mixtures.

Cadmium Red, Yellow Ochre

With White, these two colours make a sound basis for a clean flesh colour. Most makers produce a ready-made flesh colour which can be modified with additional colours in the same way as this mixture. Flesh often needs additional colouring to achieve the subtlety of real life or to match your imagination, but is often most successful when the flesh colour is applied as a veil or glaze over a tonal underpainting.

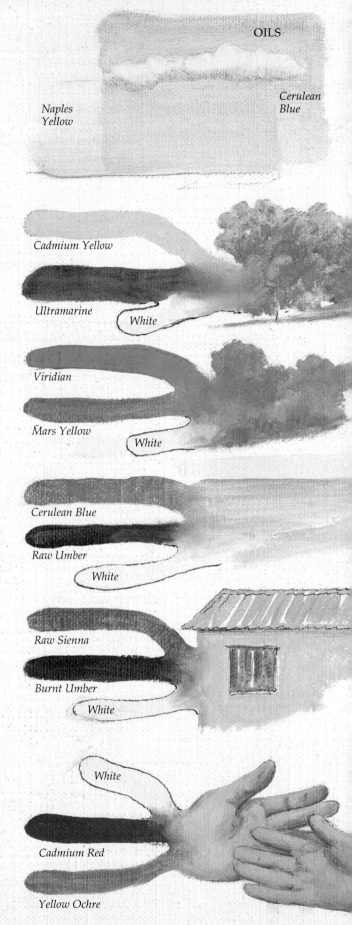

Naples Yellow

Cerulean Blue

Cadmium Yellow

Ultramarine

White

Viridian

Mars Yellow

White

Cerulean Blue

Raw Umber

White

Raw Sienna

Burnt Umber

White

White

Cadmium Red

Yellow Ochre

215

OILS, RESINS and DRIERS

The drying oils, linseed, poppy and safflower, are the basis of oil painting and colour grinding. These raw oils are used for grinding the pigments, but there is evidence that cooked oils, similar to the quick drying oils listed in the chart below, were used for grinding paint by some of the Old Masters. Their secrets unfortunately died with them and much research has been done to re-create the mixtures of cooked and raw oils, resins (p. 217) and waxes that proved so versatile in their handling. Resins are clearer than oils, dry with a greater shine, and at the same time maintain their structure, minimising movement in the drying paint film and so making overpainting safer. Drying speed is influenced by the pigments themselves, so many of the makers add driers to slow drying colours such as Ivory Black.

OILS

Paints are ground with oil (p. 211), and linseed is preferred for nearly all colours as it dries well to a tough film, although it has a tendency to yellow with time. Linseed oil comes in a variety of forms. Poppy or Safflower oils are used by some makers for grinding their Whites and Ultramarine; they are slower drying, but paler.

LINSEED OIL

THIN	**Cold-pressed**		This is the highest grade and costs twice as much as refined. It dries to a flexible and durable film, and the best oil paints are ground with it. It is not necessarily paler than refined oil.
	Refined		The oil is extracted from the seeds with heat and pressure, and then chemically refined to clean it and lighten the colour.
THICK	**Thickened oils**	**Sun-thickened oil**	Treacly oil in which the drying process has already started. Dries more quickly than refined oil to a strong elastic film that resists yellowing. Driers are often incorporated in this oil.
		Stand oil	Slower drying than sun-thickened oil, it can take a week. Good for glazing and as a constituent of glazing media. Ages well, and yellowing is minimal.
DRYING	**Quick drying oils**	**Light drying oil**	Much darker than refined oil, which has been heated and had driers added. Megilp, the painting medium, is made by adding an equal quantity of mastic varnish. Similar to the following.
		Black oil	This has been heated with lead driers. It speeds drying and does not yellow further. Difficult to obtain. Lefranc & Bourgeois make a black oil based on walnut oil.

Light drying oil   *Stand oil*   *Thickened oil*   *Black oil*   *Boiled oil*   *Refined linseed oil*

POPPY OIL

Poppy oil yellows less than linseed, but dries slowly and not so well, so it is more likely to eventually crack. Its clarity leads some makers to use it for White and Ultramarine. Drying poppy oil contains cobalt driers and is faster drying but darker in colour. It can be added to liquid media to retard drying.

WALNUT OIL

Walnut oil is a thin oil intermediate in character between linseed and poppy oil, but its drying time is closer to linseed's. Rarely used as it does not store well, but Black Oil from Lefranc & Bourgeois is made from walnut oil cooked with lead driers.

SAFFLOWER OIL

A pale oil used for grinding White by some makers. It dries faster than poppy oil, and more satisfactorily, but not so quickly or well as linseed. It is not generally available in shops.

RESINS

Resins are hard crystalline substances supplied already dissolved in turpentine, so when it evaporates the resin hardens and holds the paint film in place while the oil dries. This allows overpainting to be started much sooner.

MASTIC

Mastic is a very fast drier with a high gloss, but has a tendency to yellow with time. An important constituent in media.

DAMMAR

Slightly slower drying than mastic, softer, and yellows less. It is a popular constituent of media as it holds the paint film, to allow quick overpainting, and dries with a rich gloss. Makes a good final varnish.

COPAL

A hard resin with a bad reputation for yellowing. In small amounts it behaves well in applying glazes and is sometimes used in media. Best avoided.

SYNTHETIC RESIN

Alkyd resins are synthetic substances with minimal yellowing and are thixotropic – a gel on the palette that becomes liquid while being manipulated. It is the basis of the quick-drying Alkyd paints.

DRIERS – Siccatifs

LEAD

Lead, a constituent of Flake White, accelerates drying. Oils heated with lead in the form of Litharge dry faster than natural oils. White Siccatif de Courtrai is a lead drier.

MANGANESE

The manganese in Raw and Burnt Umber makes them dry very quickly. Brown Siccatif de Courtrai contains lead as well as manganese.

COBALT

Cobalt drier is one of the safest and is used in Roberson's Siccatif.

HOW TO USE DRIERS

Use a drop or two in your medium, and only in thinly painted pictures. Driers should be used as little as possible as they can be the cause of eventual cracking or yellowing. Fast-drying coats of paint should not be applied over slower-drying layers.

VENICE TURPENTINE

A very thick liquid that gives clarity and brilliance to the paint, but slow drying. Good for glaze media with stand oil and a drier. Very expensive. It is very viscous, and benefits from gentle warming before adding to a medium.

CANADA BALSAM

Similar to Venice turpentine, but dries in a few hours, is not so viscous, and is even more expensive.

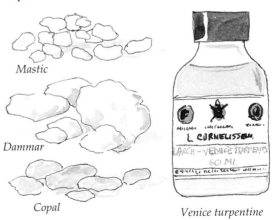

Mastic

Dammar

Copal

Venice turpentine

OIL PAINTING MEDIA

A painting medium is a combination of oils, resins and other substances designed to improve the handling of the paints. A medium will influence:

- the fluidity of the paint
- "setting-up" (the time it takes to become sticky)
- drying speed
- surface gloss
- flow and levelling
- permanence
- bulk

Throughout the history of oil painting artists have striven to find a combination of ingredients that gives maximum control of the paint, together with quick drying. Your own enjoyment of oil painting, and the success you achieve, will largely be determined by the medium with which you apply the paint.

Avoid using either refined or cold-pressed linseed oil by itself as a medium, there is already sufficient linseed oil in the paint itself. Some of the many dependable commercial media are listed below, and a few simple formulae for making your own are described on p. 220.

WHICH MEDIUM TO USE

Quick drying	Liquid	Colourless (L & B) Flemish Siccative Medium Duroziez Harlem (L & B) Kremer Oil Paint Medium-fast	Liquid media containing mastic or other resins and drying oil, drying quickly to a rich brilliant finish.
	Gel	Roberson's Medium Liquin (W & N) Alkyd Medium (Rowney) Siccative (L & B) Win-Gel (W & N) Rapid Malmittel (Schmincke) Flemish (L & B) Venetian (L & B) Maroger Medium (Roberson) Parris Marble Medium	Thixotropic media are gels which behave as a liquid when touched. Some of these contain synthetic resins. The alkyd media dry quickly and set-up, or start to become firm, even during the painting session, permitting continuous modelling without stirring up the colours on which they are laid. Liquin and Venetian media dry with a medium gloss and Parris's has a matt finish. Rowney's Alkyd Medium is fast drying. The Maroger Medium has to be diluted with linseed oil rather than thinners, but still dries quickly.
Impasto	Oleo-pasto Malbutter Impasto (L & B)		These lend a stiff quality to the paint so that it remains just as it comes off the brush, with no tendency to level itself. Their bulk effectively dilutes the strength and opacity of the paint.
Slow drying	J-G. Vibert Painting Medium Winton		The paint remains workable for long periods, so that wet-in-wet painting can be superimposed Once drying is under way, avoid overpainting.
Glazing	Roberson Lacquer (L & B) Cristal (L & B)		Very transparent, based on resins and stand oil. Cristal is a poppy oil and colloidal silica mixture that gives body as well as transparency.

W & N = Winsor & Newton; L & B = Lefranc & Bourgeois

Every maker produces media along with their paints, and it is worth trying any that are not just linseed oil/turpentine mixtures. The paint already contains linseed oil, and the paint-maker uses as little as possible, so adding more to it merely makes the paint slippery and over-oiled, with poor drying and ageing properties. This has led many to regard a medium as an enemy rather than a valued helper.

Likewise, solvents by themselves can over-thin the paint, washing away much of the binder, leaving an unprotected and lifeless matt surface when dry. Because the first layers should be thin, many artists dilute their colours with turpentine only, and apply the paint almost like watercolour. Although most paints contain enough oil to cope with this dilution, the paint layer is impoverished. It will in turn deplete the top coats by absorbing oil from them. The answer is to use diluted painting medium for the undercoat. There will be enough to penetrate and seal the absorbent ground and sufficient will remain to provide a non-absorbent surface for further coats.

More than one medium can be used in a painting, keeping to the rule of fat over lean (paint richer in oil over paint with less oil). In particular, glaze media need a viscous quality, and usually contain a thick resin or stand oil to hold the paint and stop it from running down into the grain of the canvas. It is worth experimenting with media until you find one that suits you. Start with a quick-drying medium if possible.

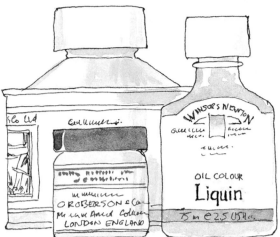

*Use a medium to improve the handling.
qualities and appearance of your paints.*

RETOUCHING VARNISH

During the course of a painting, some areas may dry with a matt surface. The protective oil and painting medium will have been absorbed by the ground or undercoat, a process called "sinking in". Brush some retouching varnish thinly over these areas to seal the paint layer, restore the sheen and improve the feel of the painting surface. It will also help to lock the next layer to it. Retouching Varnishes consist of a resin dissolved in a solvent, and dry very quickly.

SOLVENTS

RECTIFIED TURPENTINE

This the best grade of turpentine, which should be used for making up media or diluting them. Although it is double distilled to remove all traces of stickiness, it doesn't keep very well in the presence of air and eventually becomes sticky again. Not to be confused with the viscous resin, Venice Turpentine.

WHITE SPIRIT

Good grades are recommended for use with Alkyd paints and media. Cheaper and keeps better than turpentine, but is not a substitute for it in a medium. Use it freely for cleaning brushes.

PETROLEUM DISTILLATE

This can be used as a thinner for most media. Dries more slowly than white spirit and keeps well.

OIL OF SPIKE LAVENDER

A slow-drying solvent that can be used instead of turpentine, but at many times the price. It retains the desirable smell of lavender.

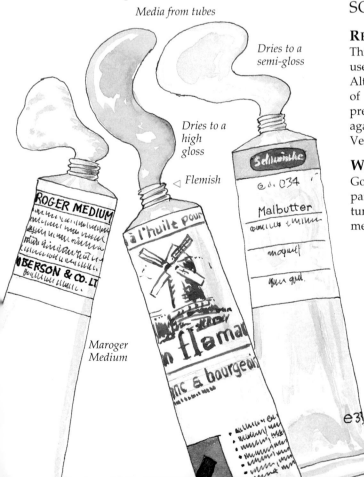

Media from tubes

Dries to a semi-gloss

Dries to a high gloss

◁ Flemish

Maroger Medium

Malbutter

MAKING YOUR OWN MEDIUM

Commercial media are quite satisfactory for most needs, but there are times when they are not to hand and you need to carry on painting. Some processes, like glazing, may not warrant a specially bought medium. Many painters have developed particular combinations which ideally suit their methods.

Media are simple to make up at home if you use resins that are already dissolved, in the form of varnishes. The usual ingredients are an oil, a thinner, a resin, and sometimes driers or wax. The best thinner is rectified turpentine, because it is the only satisfactory solvent of mastic and damar. The staple constituents of a medium are listed below.

■ Thicker oils are most often used for their drying powers or viscosity, increasing gloss and levelling out brush-strokes to give an enamel-like finish. Thickened oil has already begun the drying process, so hastens drying. Stand oil slows it.

■ Mastic or Damar are the most suitable of the natural varnishes. They dry quickly, increase transparency and regulate the flow and stickiness of the paint. Synthetic varnishes are best avoided in home-made media. Copal Varnish has a reputation for yellowing and cracking.

■ Turpentine is already present if you use Mastic or Damar varnishes.

■ Beeswax can be melted in moderate heat. It sets-up quickly and dries with a matt finish.

A SIMPLE MEDIUM

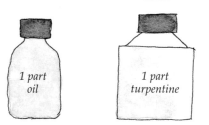

Thickened oil is a faster drier than refined linseed oil, so it can be made into a medium with rectified turpentine. Use sparingly, especially in the undercoats, or the top layers won't stick to the high-gloss surface. This is simple to make up, difficult to use. The addition of a resin would speed the drying and make the paint more workable.

QUICK-DRYING MEDIUM

Thickened or drying oils may already contain some driers. Mastic or Damar will speed up the drying, and help control the paint when painting detail. Various combinations can be tried based on the three main ingredients, oil, resin and turpentine.

Damar varnish: 1 part.
Thickened oil: 1 part.
Rect. Turpentine: 2-4 parts, (less in each succeeding paint layer).
Drier (optional): 1 or 2 drops.

SLOW-DRYING MEDIUM

Poppy and stand oils are slow driers and can be used as the basis of a slower drying medium instead of sun-thickened oil or one of the prepared drying oils.

GEL MEDIUM

A gel medium forms from the combination of cooked oil and varnish. Rowney's Light Drying Oil can be combined with equal parts of mastic varnish. The resulting medium is Megilp. Megilp has had a controversial history, but there is no way of finding out whether its dubious reputation was due to faulty materials or other causes.

There seems no reason why they should not make a medium with lasting properties. Schmincke supply a ready-made megilp in a tube. Black oil combined with mastic varnish has been proposed as the gel medium employed by the Old Masters, and their effects have been successfully reproduced by Jacques Maroger in France and Joseph Sheppard in America.

GLAZING MEDIUM

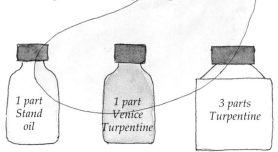

A thick transparent medium, which levels away brushmarks but stops the paint running liquidly into depressions, is necessary for glazing. Both stand oil and Venice Turpentine are very viscous, and need gentle warming to help mix them.

1 part Stand oil

1 part Venice Turpentine

3 parts Turpentine

Stand oil: 1 part

Venice Turpentine: 1 part

Rect. Turpentine: 3 parts approximately

IMPASTO MEDIUM

Beeswax is one of the safest providers of bulk, but even so, it never dries as well as linseed oil and impasto is best when it is nearly all pigment. Warm the turpentine in a double saucepan and stir in the wax.

Beeswax: 1 part

Rect. Turpentine: 3 parts

The Doge of Venice by Bellini.
Impasto on the clothes contrasts with transparent shadows in this early oil painting.

THE FINAL VARNISH

Linseed oil takes a long time to mature after the initial drying, and the presence of oxygen is necessary for this process. When a resin varnish is applied to it, the paint layer is sealed off from the air and the process of drying stops, so for this reason varnish should not be applied for six months to a year after finishing the painting.

The varnish is a protective layer, not a part of the painting, although it does provide a unifying surface of gloss or matt-ness that the artist requires. As the years go by and the surface deteriorates through the effects of dusting and atmospheric pollution, the varnish should come off easily without affecting the paint below.

Damar Varnish is the most popular natural resin, giving a glossy finish which brings out the richness of the colours, with minimal yellowing, but synthetic varnishes are now also very reliable and are non-yellowing.

Matt varnish contains beeswax, so care is needed in wiping it clean later on as it will gradually polish up like furniture polish.

Varnish can be painted on with any large brush, and dries very quickly.

Damar and mastic varnish can be removed by dissolving them with turpentine.

ACCESSORIES

Besides the essential palettes, dippers and palette knives, assorted hand-rests such as the mahl stick are useful in steadying your hand while keeping your wrist or hand off the wet paint.

You will also need some clean rags for wiping surplus or used paint from the brushes and a bottle of white spirit for cleaning. If the paint has a way of straying too far from the picture and palette, then a smock would be useful.

PALETTES

The old wooden palette was the right colour for the darker grounds of the past, so the colours appeared the same on the canvas as they did on the palette. A paler wood than mahogany is more suited to the lighter colouring of modern paintings. Plastic palettes are also available in white or wood grain colour.

Clean palettes by carefully scraping off the bulk of the paint with a palette knife, without scratching the surface if possible. After cleaning with white spirit, wipe over with a paint-free cloth. An attractive patina gradually builds up with use. Where cleaning isn't practical, pads of disposable paper palettes are an alternative.

Dark palette for dark tones

White palette for high-key work

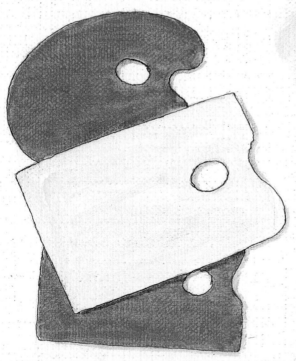

The shape and size of your palette can be entirely a matter of personal preference.

DIPPERS

Dippers often come in pairs, one for the medium and the other for a solvent. The non-spill dippers are good for out of doors but hard to clean.

Oil cup is another name for a dipper, and suggests all sorts of other possibilities holders for your medium. Small china jars, rounded inside, are excellent and easy to clean. A lid is useful if you are keeping a mixture for longer than a day, and also for the solvent, to minimise the odour.

Non-spill dippers with screw-caps

Open dippers

MAHL STICK

A stick with a pad on one end. The pad rests on the frame of the canvas while your free hand supports the other end; you rest your brush-hand on the rod to steady it. A "bridge" is a piece of wood, with feet at each end, that straddles the picture and supports your hand. This is most convenient when you are working flat on a table.

PAINTING KNIFE

These are shorter than palette knives and have a bend in the neck to offset the blade from the handle. They come in a range of sizes and shapes.

The longer bladed knives can double as palette knives, and are among the most useful for spreading paint on the canvas in knife painting. For this specialised technique you will need a selection of different sizes.

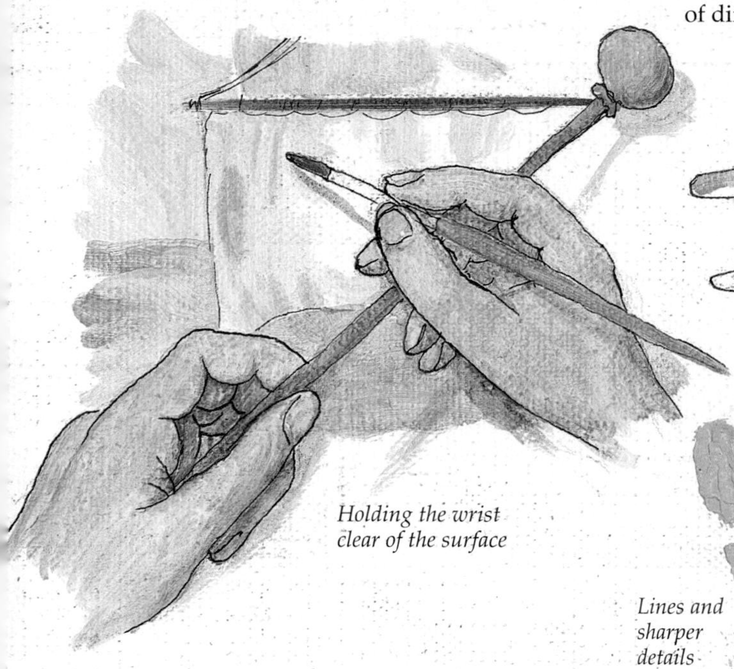

Painting knives

Holding the wrist clear of the surface

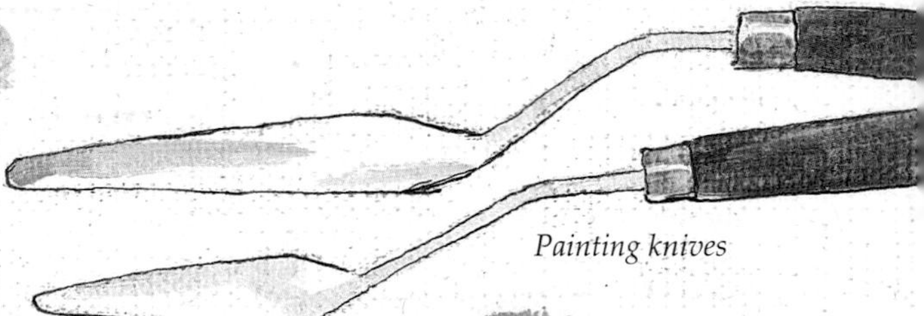

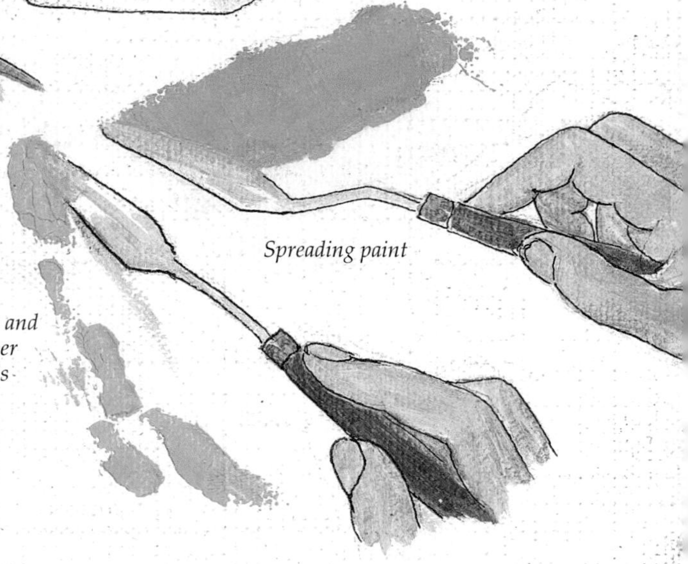

Spreading paint

Lines and sharper details

PALETTE KNIFE

This knife is used for large scale mixing on the palette, also for scraping off the surplus at the end. It is characterised by a long blade.

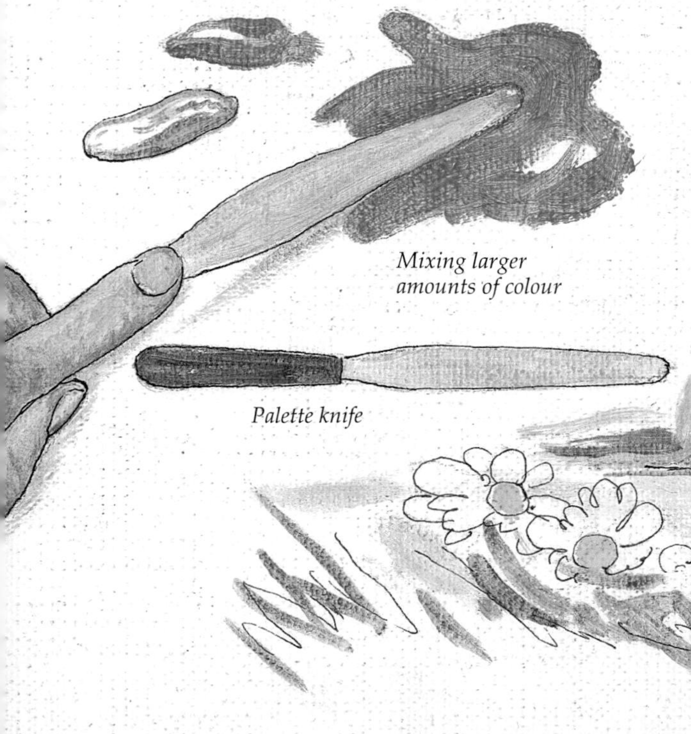

Mixing larger amounts of colour

Palette knife

Adding detail with a small knife

223

Techniques

By observing the basic principles while you paint, the technique of oil painting becomes easier, and the results more permanent. The purpose of technique is to keep the paint manageable and under control; when the paint is easier to manage, you become more able to bring your vision into reality. Without the technical means, no amount of creativity will achieve very much. On the other hand, the more you know and understand your materials the more you will be able to achieve. In this, the choice of a good medium is crucial.

Modern tube paint consists of a pigment ground in the minimum practical amount of oil; it therefore has a stiff consistency which is not suitable for use straight from the tube. The stiff paint needs combining with a medium, which will regulate its handling qualities, setting-up and drying times.

The absorbency of the canvas also plays a part. The cheaper commercial canvases absorb so much oil that the brush seems to drag drily, as if painting over blotting paper. After the canvas has been sealed and rendered non-absorbent, preferably by an overall thin preliminary coat of paint, the painting surface will feel much more sympathetic.

DIFFERING STYLES OF OIL PAINTING

A wide range of styles is possible and technical knowledge and practice will make them available to you. Find a painting, or reproduction of one you really like and keep it in view while you paint; you will gradually absorb the style and some of the technique. As you improve, your own style will evolve and grow.

■ **Realistic** painting is always popular with artists and the public. It requires the greatest level of skill as success or failure is immediately apparent. Careful painting in two or more layers will offer the opportunity to exploit all the advantages of oil painting.

■ A **coloured ground** provides immediate modelling effects and harmonious colour.

■ A **white ground** gives maximum brilliance to the colours in outdoor or light-toned pictures.

■ **Impressionist** styles have held sway for many years. Stiff paint, stiff brushes and a refined linseed oil medium almost guarantee an impressionist style. Accurate placing of each brush stroke is called for in a technique that generally avoids smooth effects or lengthy manipulations.

PRINCIPLES OF OIL TECHNIQUE

The paint needs the protection of the binder, the oil it is ground with, and a medium. This dries with a sheen. If the paint dries with a dull and matt finish, paint over with retouching varnish or painting medium before continuing.

■ Apply the paint in thin layers.

■ Each layer should contain relatively more oil/medium than the previous layer – the rule of fat over lean.

■ Earlier layers should be quicker-drying than succeeding layers.

■ Keep impasto (thick textured paint), till the end.

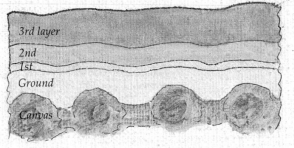

The cross-section of a painted canvas shows the greater thickness of the upper layers of paint compared to the lower. Some of the extra bulk will be the medium.

PROPORTIONS OF MEDIUM AND SOLVENT IN SUCCESSIVE PAINT LAYERS

On a ground that is not too absorbent, that will not soak all the oil away from the pigment, the paint for the initial layer can be put on with turpentine. The next can be applied with the medium diluted with its solvent. After that, use the medium at its normal strength for the rest of the painting. In the last stages, other slower-drying media can be used.

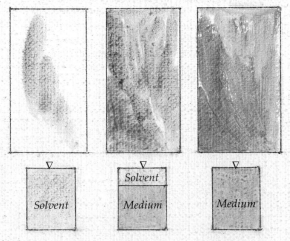

HOW TO APPLY THE PAINT

A hog's hair brush is the most efficient spreader of paint across the canvas grain, but for detail and blending of tone and colour, sable, synthetic, and fan brushes are necessary as well. There are no rules about how to spread the paint or whether the brush-marks should show or not; there are only passing fashions. Every way has been employed with success. Use the brush and medium of your choice according to your aims. Palette and painting knives produce special effects, but are mostly used for working paint on the palette.

Murder Inc. (1979) by Claude Yvel.
This shows the unlimited possibilities of oils in the hands of a master, whose penetrating observation and technique is able to distinguish and render all the numerous tones of the jacket. Sable brushes are needed to manipulate the paint on a fine-grained canvas to bring out the varied textures of the jacket and badges, wood, book and glasses. Trompe l'oeil paintings are often painted life-size, and the close-up background has to be as detailed as the main subject.

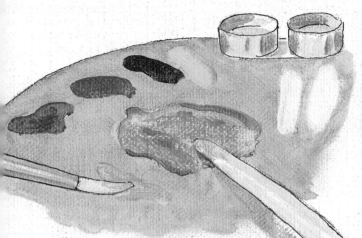

Palette knives will mix quantities more quickly and efficiently than a brush.

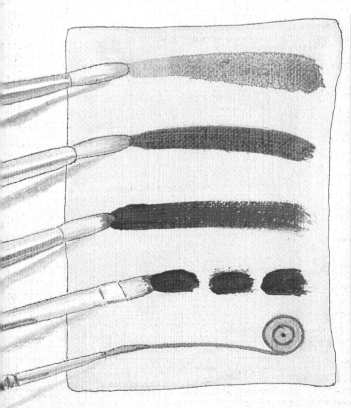

Van Gogh's Chair by Van Gogh.
A painting characterised by thick paint and vigorous brush-strokes. Any underpainting would be thin, reserving the texture for the final stage.

225

SOME WAYS OF APPLYING PAINT

Modern paint is stiff and packed into tubes. Before paint was sold in tubes painters made their own on the spot, and this was necessarily of a softer and more liquid consistency, and long-haired brushes were used to put it on. This combination still gives the greatest freedom of manipulation when painting. Starting from thick paint, by adding media, and with the aid of a variety of brushes, you can obtain all degrees of opacity, transparency and texture.

OPAQUE BRUSHSTROKES

The foundation of a painting is opaque paint applied with a hog's hair brush. The higher the quality of paint the denser and more opaque it will be, because it will be packed with pigment.

Long-haired hog brushes give more control over the paint than short stiff brushes; they hold much more paint, are more manoeuvrable, and do not impose their own texture. Thick paint should be kept for the later stages.

▽

SCUMBLING

This is a two-stage process in which thicker paint is dragged across a more thinly painted undercoat. The scumbled layer is usually lighter in tone than the underlayer; this need not be dry as long as it has set enough to take the scumble without mixing with it. Scumbling is a useful way of showing rough texture.

Initial tone

Scumble

■ Paint on a thinly applied tone that is darker than finally intended. Leave to dry.

■ With rather dry paint, and not too much on the brush, drag the paint across the undercoating so that the top of the grain picks up the paint, leaving the undercoat to show through between. The light paint can be applied in a more solid and continuous manner in places, to show changing light and texture.

Ways of applying the paint, showing the variety of texture and appearance.

▽

Thinner opaque paint

The lighter scumble produces a grainy and varied texture suggesting the material of the rock.

Initial tone

Scumble

Thick opaque paint

APPLYING A VEIL

A veil is a semi-opaque mist of colour, like a more liquid version of a scumble with a continuous film; it has a wider range of uses because it doesn't impose a particular texture on the underlayer. On a toned ground, veils are immensely useful for modelling the light tones.

GLAZING

A glaze is a transparent layer of colour over previous work. Apply the paint and medium thinly, either by rubbing it in with a stiff brush, or if it is the last coat, with a larger proportion of glazing medium. It is usual to reinforce highlights or detail while the glaze is still wet.

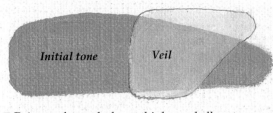

Initial tone   *Veil*

Initial tone   *Glaze*   *2nd glaze*

■ Paint on the underlayer thinly, and allow to dry or set.

■ Paint over a lighter semi-opaque colour and model it as required. The thickness of the veil can vary as much as you like. Another name for this layer is a frottie.

■ Paint as usual with opaque colour. Keep it lighter than the intended effect.

■ Mix some colour with a glaze medium and apply it fairly thinly; glazes should not resemble a watercolour wash in which a little colour floats in a quantity of medium. Use a soft blending brush to even the glaze as much as you need to.

Veils and glazes are used to improve modelling or to increase depth and colour. The thickness and opacity can be varied continuously.

▽

Glazes eat light and air, so use them discreetly, especially in outdoor scenes.

▽

Initial tone

Modelling and colour can be continuously altered by veils in a variety of thicknesses and colour. They all contain white – a transparent layer is a glaze.

Veil

Glaze

Initial tone

Initial tone

Glaze with sponge

Glazing (continued)

Glazes with transparent colours, can accomplish nearly all the shading in the same manner as in watercolours, although there is a practical limit to the amount of medium put on the canvas, as too much will dry badly and deteriorate with time.

Before glazing

After glazing

Before

After blending

The glaze can be varied in depth, with very little on the lights, which are restored by having the highlights reinforced with new paint, added as the glaze layer begins to set and become sticky. Dark paint to strengthen the shadows can also be introduced into the wet glaze.

Glazing media tend to be viscous and contain thickened oil, so the rule of fat over lean implies that they are the last layer. Intermediate glazes should be scrubbed on with the painting medium used for the picture.

To equalise the tensions in the paint films and reduce the chances of cracks eventually appearing, add just a very small amount of white. The transparency will not be noticeably affected by such a small addition.

Glazes can be as varied from place to place on the picture in the same way as veils and scumbles. For a large graded area such as a sky, mix up two or three tones first, then apply them in position and blend them together. It is not always practical to have just one tone and try to vary its thickness by pressing it out more and more thinly with the brush.

It was noted earlier that a semi-opaque layer mainly consisting of white had a considerably cooling effect on the colour below, turning browns into greys; a glaze, on the other hand, warms colours slightly, so that a glaze of Ivory Black, for instance, inclines towards the brown.

BLENDING

Adjacent colours and tones can be painted in side by side and blended at any stage before the paint becomes too stiff. Paint that has begun to set is the easiest to blend, as it moves slowly and not too far; new wet paint can move too freely with the brush into the adjoining colours and the process can come to resemble ordinary mixing on the palette. It is easier to blend lights into darks than the reverse.

A painted area can be blended as soon as it begins to set. With alkyd paints, this can be about 10-15 minutes after application.

Draw a fan brush across the brushmark lines to remove them. The brush should be dry: as soon as it has picked up any quantity of paint, it stops blending and becomes another brush putting on paint. Clean and rinse immediately, then dry it for further use.

IMPASTO – THICKLY TEXTURED PAINT

Thick paint is inherently less sound than thin, but if carefully applied adds a new dimension to your pictures. Impasto media, (p. 218), add bulk and structural support to impasto, but reduce its opacity.

KNIFE PAINTING

Whole paintings can be done using a variety of painting knives instead of brushes. The long knives scrape the broader areas into the canvas and smaller blades place detail. The pressure of the knife forces excess medium to the surface, so less medium should be added to the mixtures. A normal brushed undercoat can be employed.

THE EFFECTS OF MEDIA

Media need as much care in their choice as the paints, brushes and canvases, but although their influence is considerable, they will not make up for a lack of dexterity in applying and manipulating the paint, which only comes with practice.

A gel medium becomes liquid under pressure from the brush. Gels are among the most desirable media. See p. 218 for a list.

When returning to a painting that has dried, Retouching varnish can be painted onto areas that have sunk in and become flat; this will not only restore the shine but make a sympathetic surface for the new paint.

Throughout the entire history of oil painting the medium has dominated the technique of the time more than anything else. No other material has changed so often or so much. Now there is an improved selection, try out some of them.

When drawing thin lines with a rigger, the paint comes off more smoothly and evenly if a thin coat of medium is first rubbed into the surface.

The palette knife picture on the left is executed over a thinly painted undercoat; this provides an immediately favourable base for the knife-work but avoids a build-up of paint too early and fills the gaps between the knifework that follows. The thick paint should be put on with the knife, which makes its own textures and detail.

DIRECT PAINTING ON A WHITE GROUND

MORAIRA BEACH

The ground is left white to achieve a light-toned effect of brilliance. The colour of the water could be painted in directly without having to neutralise an existing tone.

Aims

■ To bring back the memory of the warmth and sunlight of the day and place.

■ To capture the green-blue colour of the Mediterranean Sea.

■ To recapture the feeling of the wetness of the swirling water round the rocks.

■ The shine, texture and richness of the oil paint surface should be of great assistance in achieving this.

There was no time to do a sketch, but the overall atmosphere made a strong and lasting impression. The general outlines of the scene are very simple, and it is the colour and moving detail that counts, and this is where the camera scores. The painting was done from three photographs.

Preparation

The drawing was done directly with a brush using Raw Umber diluted with a little Flemish Medium and plenty of turpentine to make the paint liquid. Corrections were made with turpentine and a rag.

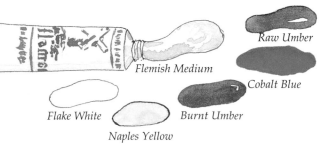

Raw Umber

Flemish Medium

Cobalt Blue

Flake White

Burnt Umber

Naples Yellow

The colours of the scene were put on the palette, Cerulean and Cobalt Blues, with Naples Yellow and Titanium White. The rocks were started with Raw and Burnt Umber.

Colouring-in

A mixture of Flake White and Naples Yellow was painted across the sky, yellower towards the horizon. This colour will show through the pale blue to go on later, giving the sky a warm glow. Raw Umber darkened the rock shadows.

The distant rock

Mixed warm greys were painted thinly over the rock, which was modelled as far as possible with lighter and darker tones.

Building up the rock with mixed greys

Naples Yellow and white were used for the lights. The rock shadows were strengthened with Burnt Umber and Cobalt Blue and then skimmed over with some of the medium brown colour to lighten them a little.

Cerulean Blue

Flake White

Cobalt Blue

Naples Yellow

Painting the sea

A hazy light blue was painted over the sky. The water was put in with White, Cerulean Blue and a touch of Naples Yellow, which was mixed with the rock colour where the water covered them and altered their colours. The more distant waves were darkened a little, and the bluer shapes near the centre and right were strengthened and improved in shape with Ultramarine with a small addition of Burnt Umber to give a warmer blue.

Foreground rocks

These were prepared with varying proportions of Burnt Umber, Cobalt Blue and Naples Yellow with plenty of Flake White. The detail of the water was painted over it when dry.

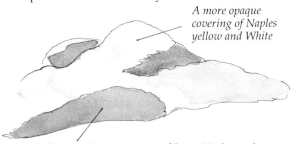

A more opaque covering of Naples yellow and White

Darkened with thin mixture of Burnt Umber and

Blues, yellow and browns were employed to model the waves and water flowing over the rocks, where the thin paint gave a transparent watery look.

Foam and highlights

Flake White, with a minute touch of yellow, was used for the white foam and highlights on the water. It was painted on wherever it seemed to look natural. The single dots were placed with the tip of the brush. Some of the dots needed additional touches of White.

A thickly loaded small brush – White and Naples Yellow.

The sky was still rather patchy, so some medium was rubbed carefully over it to assist adhesion before painting over a blending and smoothing mixture of Cerulean Blue and White with a little Naples Yellow on the horizon.

Summary

The general effect has come out well as the sea and sky colours seem accurate. The distant rock would have been more successful if the modelling had been completed when the first coat was dry, as the wet underlayer interfered. The shine of the medium helps the feeling of wateriness.

PAINTING WITH GLAZES ON A WHITE GROUND

COPY OF TURNER'S "THE FIGHTING TÉMÉRAIRE"

For the building up of a painting in thin layers of paint, almost in the manner of a watercolour, a white ground provides the necessary brilliance to show through the colour. To speed the application of the paint, and to make it more pleasing to apply, coat a commercial canvas with an additional thin layer of Flake White with a little diluted medium and leave it to dry. This will seal the surface, removing the noticeable drag on the brush caused by over-absorbence.

Materials

A medium linen canvas was used, mounted on a panel.

The medium was Liquin, which dries quickly but allows comfortable working time.

The paints were safer modern equivalents of Turner's with the addition of a transparent rich dark red, Golden Barok Red, and Light Brown Ochre as the basis for the warm browns. Turner was happy to use the new colours of his time.

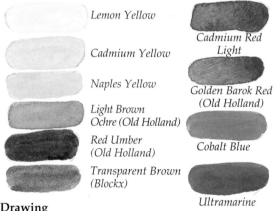

Lemon Yellow

Cadmium Yellow

Naples Yellow

Light Brown Ochre (Old Holland)

Red Umber (Old Holland)

Transparent Brown (Blockx)

Cadmium Red Light

Golden Barok Red (Old Holland)

Cobalt Blue

Ultramarine

Drawing

The ships and general positions of the less defined shapes were indicated with a small sable brush using Raw Umber diluted with White Spirit and medium. A solvent by itself is too harsh and denudes the oil paint.

The drawing just locates the main shapes.

First stage – Glazes

The main colours were mixed up and spread thinly in position with a bristle brush and diluted medium. The colour areas were blended to overlap at the edges, only the ships and sun retaining their outlines clearly.

The sky was developed further with additional mixtures and combinations of the initial colour mixtures plus the introduction of orange made from Chrome Yellow with Cadmium Red Light and Golden Barok Red.

The Ships

The darks, including the smoke, were strengthened with thinned Red Umber, and the lights were carefully placed in position with a mixture of Naples Yellow and White. The orange served for the flames and Light Brown Ochre was added for the warm browns on the ships.

The paint was applied thinly and flatly, as a basis for modelling and further detail once it was dry. It is much easier to build up complexity in stages, rather than rely on complicated manipulation of all the factors – lighting, colour, texture, at the same time.

The Sea

Ready-made mixtures, spread on thinly with diluted Liquin, served for the water and shore. Care was taken to avoid covering the sun's reflection with the browns, leaving a strip of brightness. A blue mixture was added for parts of the sky and water.

The Ships

The dark Transparent Brown strengthened the blacks of the ships and their reflections, pressed thinner with the brush to make less intense darks. White, Naples Yellow and a little of the orange mixture were placed on the lights. Painting with glazes over a coloured under-painting quickly and easily produces rich colouring.

On the scale of this reproduction the thin glazes of the completed first stage seem to have almost completed the picture; the whole area has been laid in using the final colours. The painting was then allowed to dry. The next stage will improve colouring, add the considerable detail and bring out the intensity of colour and tone.

The Sea

The sea was developed by repeating the methods of the first stage, thin glazes and horizontal streaks augmenting and improving the initial coat. The darks were strongly intensified with Transparent Brown to match the ships, and red-browns glazed down the building and shore in the corner.

Second Stage – Glazes and Impasto

The sky colours were made up with some additional white, and applied more opaquely, and the sky colours were blended. Oranges made of Cadmium Yellow and Cadmium Red Light, together with the reds were applied thickly above the sun, darkened with brown and red where necessary. A small painting knife was used on these thickly painted areas. In view of its size and importance, time was taken to work over the sky at some length.

Finishing

Final glazes adjusted tones and colours where necessary; highlights and the masts and rigging were added onto dry paint at the end.

The copy of **The Fighting Téméraire**. *The original painting has considerable brilliance, with the transparency of the colours enhanced by the soft gloss of the oil paint and the well placed intense darks. Oil paint is long-lasting in thin coats, and with care in drying each layer, a number of glazes can be applied. Turner himself developed many of his pictures with numerous glazes.*

PAINTING ON A COLOURED GROUND

COPY OF CONSTABLE'S "THE CORNFIELD"

Sky and trees are regular subjects; trees in particular sometimes cause problems. The painting medium can be thinned to achieve the small detail needed for trees, and the paint can be applied with either sable or synthetic interlon brushes. The colours and tones of the underpainting were broadly similar to the final coats, and show through in many places.

Materials

Linen canvas was stretched over a panel, and given a base coat of Raw Umber with Titanium White, mixed with the medium Liquin and white spirit to give fluidity and assist drying. This made a warm grey tone to paint on. The colours on the left, below, are those available to Constable. On the right, some modern alternatives are compared.

Flake White	*Titanium White*
Genuine Ultramarine	*French Ultramarine*
Prussian Blue	*Cerulean Blue*
Raw Umber	*Burnt Umber*
Burnt Sienna	*Raw Umber*
Raw Sienna	*Mars Orange*
Yellow Ochre	*Mars Yellow*
Vermilion	*Naples Yellow*
Rose Madder	*Cadmium Red*
Ivory Black	*Ruby Lake Deep*
	Ivory Black

Mediums containing a varnish dry quickly and minimize the movement of the drying paint, making earlier overpainting more practical. Roberson's Medium has these ingredients and qualities.

Beginning

The main shapes were carefully drawn in with a sable brush using diluted Raw Umber, with occasional shadings to clarify details. Each area was then painted thinly in its own general colour, using thinned medium, overlapping and blending the edges of the less defined foreground areas. The outside tree edges had been drawn just inside their true edges and were later painted farther out to overlap the sky.

The Sky

The coloured ground was ideal for the clouds; darker shadows were placed first, the ground provided the middle tones, and the whites were placed cleanly in position. The tones were then worked over and blended. A little blue here and there completed this stage.

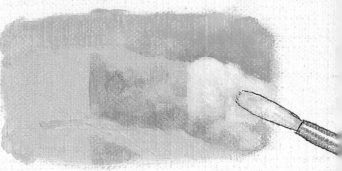

Three stages of the clouds; the coloured ground; the shadows modelled with grey; the whites added last.

The trees

The dark warm colour of the trees was painted over all the trees, slightly thinner over the lights. The method followed was first the laying in of the whole tree in silhouette with thin shadow colour, followed by painting the sunlit bunches of leaves over the dark tree shapes with brighter opaque paint. The shadow colour was a mixture of Roberson's Olive and Golden Greens, sometimes with a little Light Brown Ochre for the warmer parts.

Tree trunks

The dark sides were put in with the dark tree green and some Red Umber.

The cornfield and distance

The darks and middle tones were put in thinly, then the lights dragged across and blended where necessary. The medium corn colour was Chrome Yellow Deep with White. The brilliantly lit parts were overpainted later with White and Cadmium Yellow.

The distant scene is a picture within a picture and the focus of the whole painting. The cornfield has to be kept as brilliant as possible to make the most of the contrast with the surrounding shadows.

The foreground

The foreground was put in initially in broad overlapping areas of colour; a dark mixture of Raw Umber and Cobalt Blue was used for bringing out the detail, low fence boards, sheep dog, some branches and deep shadows.

The first paint layer was put on with diluted medium to keep it lean and avoid too high a gloss. The thinness of the lower paint layers, and the stickiness of the medium as it began to dry, made it possible to add and blend in detail throughout the painting session.

With a medium that begins to dry quickly, a little additional turpentine to the mixtures on the palette will make them more fluid again. The grass, made of Golden Green, a little Cobalt Blue and White, was scumbled across the warm brownish underlayer, and the shadows were achieved by adding more Cobalt Blue to this mixture.

Figures, animals

These were painted in carefully at the end, introducing a bright red for the first time on the boy's sleeveless jacket and the distant scarf.

Finishing

The picture was examined to make sure the overall effect was retained. The sheep were glazed to keep them within the shadow tones, and some parts of the foreground were also glazed down to harmonise them with their surroundings. A few blacks and deep shadows were finally intensified, and small lights added to the water and fence tops.

The copy of **The Cornfield**

A MONOCHROME UNDERPAINTING ON A COLOURED GROUND

The first stage shows the modelling in grey, highlighted with Titanium White, on the flesh and head-dress. The colour of the ground and the drawing are seen in the lower half; they still show through to make the half-tones in the painted parts.

COPY OF "THE VIRGIN AT PRAYER" BY SASSOFERRATO

The superb quality and finish of the Old Master paintings often stands in marked contrast to the difficulties most amateurs experience in simply managing the paint. One reason for the difference is that the older paintings were built up methodically, solving one problem at a time in the simplest way, and with the use of a rich quick-drying medium, which avoided the messiness and delay associated with refined linseed oil. The following example shows a possible reconstruction of one of the methods of the Old Masters, using modern materials.

Materials

A canvas was tinted with a coat of Titanium White and Burnt Umber. This coat provides an immediate middle tone for modelling forms, and also removes the absorbency of the priming, so that the paint moves more pleasantly on the surface. Venetian Medium, from Lefranc and Bourgeois, is a quick drying jelly medium, containing some wax, which reduces the gloss when dry. The medium was thinned with turpentine.

The medium comes in a tube. Squeeze onto the palette.

Drawing

The figure was carefully drawn with a sable brush using Burnt Umber thinned with turpentine and just a little medium. Preliminary shading was put in with the same colour.

Undercoat

A light grey, made of Titanium White and Ivory Black with a little medium, was painted over the lighter parts of the face. At the edges of the shadows, increasing brush pressure pressed the paint out more thinly to let the darker ground show through and make the transitional, or half-tones. They were then smoothed and blended in with a dry brush. Titanium White was applied into the grey to the highlight areas and similarly blended. The stronger shadows and other dark parts were brought out with a darker grey mixture, and finally the reflections were restored with the initial light grey.

The head-dress was painted in the same way; one or two shadows first, then Titanium White applied broadly, pressed more thinly by the brush into the canvas in places, so the ground could show through and create modelling automatically. Blending with a dry brush, to soften transitions, was simple as the medium quickly set to a sticky consistency that was ideal for slightly moving the paint without lifting it off. The darker shadows were strengthened with grey. The greys were all various mixtures of Titanium White and Ivory Black.

Draperies

These were treated in just the same way, but using much lighter versions of their actual colours. The shadows on the red were first put in with very thin Caput Mortuum. The lights were opaquely applied with a mixture of White, Cadmium Yellow and Scheveningen Red Scarlet, while the middle tones were created by spreading the same more thinly so the darker ground could show through. This is a simpler and often more effective process than specially mixing up a range of matching tones and then blending them together.

The blue cloak was given a similar treatment in blues with white highlighting.

Colouring the flesh tones

When the first stage was dry, a light flesh colour made of Naples Yellow, Cadmium Red Light, Titanium White and a little Mars Yellow was painted over the lit side of the face, and a darker version of the same was painted very thinly over the shadows. Some time was spent in smoothing the gradations and edges, using a dry hog's hair brush. Stronger shadows were emphasised with a mixture of Transparent Brown and Red Umber (Burnt Umber is similar to this mixture), and the same mixture restored the features where they were becoming lost.

White and Naples Yellow, added to the original flesh mixture, was painted into the highlights and blended in. The shadows around the eyes and the eyebrows were strengthened with Transparent Brown and Red Umber, and the normal flesh colour brightened the reflections on the right-hand side of the face. The cheeks were reddened by working in a little Cadmium Red Light. The hands received the same treatment.

Colouring the draperies

The red was coloured with Scheveningen Red Scarlet, a little more orange and brighter than Cadmium Red Light. The Old Masters didn't have access to such bright reds, although their genuine Ultramarine was slightly more brilliant than our synthetic versions. The lights of the red dress were produced by pressing the colour thinly into a glaze over the pale modelling below, not by mixing a lighter colour. The shadows were reinforced by adding in a darker red.

The blue was coloured with Ultramarine in the same manner, but the lights had additional modelling with some White and Ultramarine.

The background was given two coats of Transparent Brown with a spot of Ultramarine to darken the lower parts further.

Finishing

The darkest shadows of the ultramarine cloak were still rather flat-looking, so they were separated out by glazing over a little black and then blending in the edges. The flesh shadows were strengthened, and the lights, especially the cheeks, brought to a rosier colour with a glaze of Cadmium Red Light and Mars Yellow. Finally the eyes and eyebrows were sharpened with finer detail.

The flesh and the red dress, more finished, contrast with the underpainting of the blue cloak, which shows the white highlighting painted into the blue.

The copy of **The Virgin at Prayer**, after Sassoferrato. *Relatively few colours were needed, and little mixing. Scumbling the lights over the darker ground, followed by glazing, produce colour gradations only otherwise achievable by laborious mixing.*

The effect of colour over a modelled ground. The depth of colour is varied to suit the underlying tone

237

PASTELS

INTRODUCTION

Pastels are chalk-like sticks of pigments lightly bound together. They are quite dry, with no trace of waxiness or oiliness.

There is less binder in pastels than any other medium, so the colours are unaffected by it. They neither darken nor crack because it is usually the binder that is responsible for deterioration rather than the pigments themselves.

Pastels bridge the gap between drawing and painting. They are held rather like pencils and applied as if for a drawing, but their effect and treatment has more in common with painting.

The overlap with drawing is most apparent with the harder pastels and Conté crayons. The latter have been developed from the few colours used for drawing, and are now produced in a wide range of colours that can be combined with pastels.

Pastels are drawn directly onto the paper and are immediately complete. Depending on the ultimate use of the picture, there need be no alteration of colour if the surface is protected from rubbing by glass. Otherwise, fixatives have a selective darkening effect.

Unlike paints, pastels cannot be mixed on a palette, everything happens on the paper. Colour mixing is not a big part of pastel technique, which depends more on strokes laid side by side. Instead of mixing, the artist should accumulate as large a collection of pastels as possible. A great range of shades and tones are made, and imaginative colour schemes derive from the juxtaposition of your colours, rather than from combining them literally.

Most artists start with a manufacturer's selection in a box; starting up is expensive, but add colours as soon as the opportunity occurs or the need arises, as pastels can be bought singly.

Some of the wide variety of types and makes are shown on these pages; they are all compatible with one another, bearing in mind that there is also a range of softness and hardness which sometimes makes it impractical to draw one colour over another.

Heading Home, by Sally Strand.
An imposing large picture demonstrating the subtle brilliance of colour and tone that can be achieved in pastel. The pastel strokes are carefully placed side by side over a darker ground which is allowed to show through.

Pastel strokes laid on side by side.

Pastels have an immediately attractive appearance of glowing velvety colour that makes some artists reluctant to go in for any rubbing or afterwork. This appearance is easily retained if the colours are handled with confidence and are not re-worked. A picture can comfortably include both rubbed and unrubbed work as long as each is appropriate. Although corrections can be easily made, pastel looks better where the surface is not lost through over-working.

The thickness of pastels compared to brushes and other drawing instruments makes for a broader finish which is suited to larger pictures.

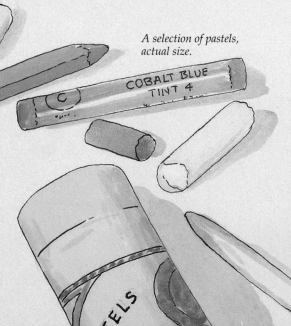

A selection of pastels, actual size.

A Girl with a Kitten, by Jean-Baptiste Perroneau. *This lovely picture shows the ability of pastels to produce smooth gradations and pictures equal in quality and permanence to other media.*

But nothing is impossible, and by sharpening the pastels or using small pieces, a very fine finish can be achieved. Pastels have a tradition of very highly finished work, strongly maintained today. The earliest pastels were developments of the drawing chalks, as the binder was improved and the range of colour enlarged. The flowering of pastel painting was in the early 1700s, the time of the portrait above.

The very softest pastels are liable to crumble if pressed too hard, but with care give the most glowing colours. Each pigment comes in light and dark shades as well as in its natural pure colour. The lighter tints are mixed with increasing amounts of white and the darker with black. Tint 5 is usually the pure colour; some makers label the lightest tint as 0 or 1, others the darkest. The light tints of any colour are generally softer than the dark.

The danger of accidental rubbing and the fragility of the binding agent may cause doubt about the permanence of pastel but they can easily be fixed to prevent accidental rubbing. Behind glass, pastels are as permanent and safe as any medium.

Materials

PAPER

Paper is the natural material for pastel, and specialist makers produce a wide range of shades that are sufficient for every purpose. The paper is usually thinner than watercolour paper as there is usually no need to get it wet. Where there is a need, such as when a watercolour undercoat or tinting is applied first, the paper can be stretched even more easily than watercolour paper.

The sheet-size of pastel paper is also generally smaller than watercolour sheets, but at 51 × 65cm, large enough for most purposes. Fabriano make a larger size called Morilla, and Canson produce rolls about 150cm wide. Where a large size is needed, watercolour paper can also be stretched and then tinted with any water-based medium, such as watercolour, gouache or acrylic. Watercolour paper can also be bought off a roll with a width of 150cm for really big pictures.

The exercise below shows the influence of the paper tint. Unless the pastel is carefully rubbed into the grain, the paper always shows through; on the lighter paper (left), the majority of tones are darker than the paper, with the result that much of the pastel looks heavy against the lighter background. The dark paper (right), shows the pastels as brighter, but the overall tonality is dark. The middle paper matches most colours and intensifies the brilliance of colour. By matching the overall tonality of your paper to suit the subject you can achieve the maximum luminosity from your pastels.

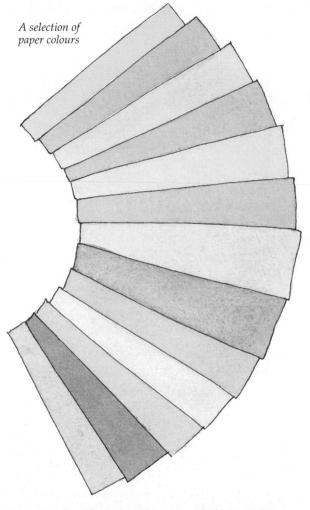

A selection of paper colours

Ingres paper comes in 2 thicknesses.

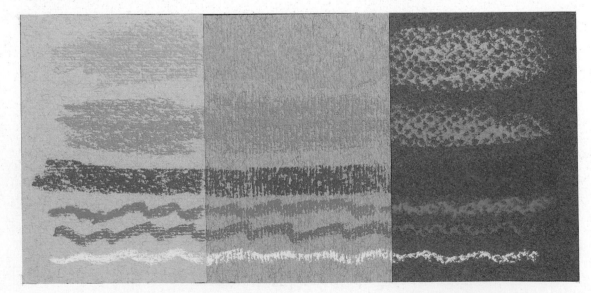

TINTING WATERCOLOUR PAPER

Stretch the paper first (see p. 141), and then mix up a great quantity of colour in a saucer or on a tea plate. Use a large brush, even a house-painter's, and apply the wash evenly (see p. 150), unless you are using it as an underpainting. The "not" surfaces have a moderate grain.

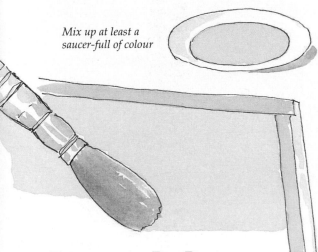

Mix up at least a saucer-full of colour

TINTING WITH DRY PIGMENTS

On stretched watercolour paper, a very pleasing surface can be produced by a mixture of weak size and dry pigments. The pigments can be mixed to your own specification or used pure, but Zinc White as part of the mixture improves the tooth and consistency of all of them. Dissolve 1 part of cooking gelatine in 40 parts of warm water. Add the size to your pigment and stir. Several thin coats will produce an even finish.

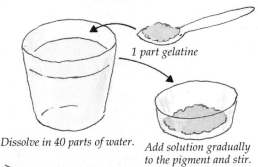

1 part gelatine

Dissolve in 40 parts of water.

Add solution gradually to the pigment and stir.

Hang up the finished paper to dry.

PREPARING A SANDED SURFACE

Paper or board with a stronger tooth can be home-made; acquire some fine grit, such as pumice or carborundum, from a supplier. Test the roughness by painting a brushful onto card, and feeling with your finger-tip when the surface is nearly dry. The mixture is transparent, for use on coloured paper. For white paper, add dry pigment to replace some of the grit, or acrylic paint to replace some gel medium.

■ Dampen the surface of the board thoroughly.

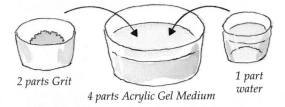

2 parts Grit

4 parts Acrylic Gel Medium

1 part water

■ Mix 2 parts of Grit into 4 parts of Acrylic Gel Medium, then add 1 part of water, and acrylic colouring if required. Mix thoroughly.

■ Paint on three or four coats of the mixture.

■ When the mixture has dried, paint the back with diluted Acrylic Gesso to counteract the tendency to curl.

SANDPAPER

This has frequently been used as a support for pastel pictures, but it is difficult to believe that the backing paper has any real permanence. The method described above is safer because it uses permanent materials.

Gluing the sandpaper onto a board will neutralise its tendency to curl forward. The surface colour can also be improved with one or more coats of opaque oil paint, diluted only with turpentine to avoid any gloss, which would prevent the pastels from sticking to it. Water-based paints will dissolve the glue that holds the sand. The rough tooth enables the artist to apply many layers of pigment to achieve intense colouring.

STRETCHING PAPER

Where paper needs to be stretched, first hold it under a running tap so it is well wetted on both sides, then lay it flat on the drawing board to soak for 5 minutes. Sweep off the surplus water with your hand, but keep the edges damp during this time. Stick down the edges to the board with brown paper tape and leave to dry. A fuller description of this method is shown on p. 141.

THE PASTELS

Each maker makes pastels in their own size and range of hardness. Hardness varies not only according to the maker but also the characteristics of the individual pigments in each one. The illustrations on this page give a rough guide to the average hardness and softness of different makes. Within the range of nearly every maker some are harder than others, but as a rule a dark colour is likely to be harder than a light one. The softer pastels are fragile and have a tendency to crumble, but are very pleasant to use, giving vivid rich tones; the harder ones give thinner lines and are good for detail and the finer drawing.

SOFTER PASTELS

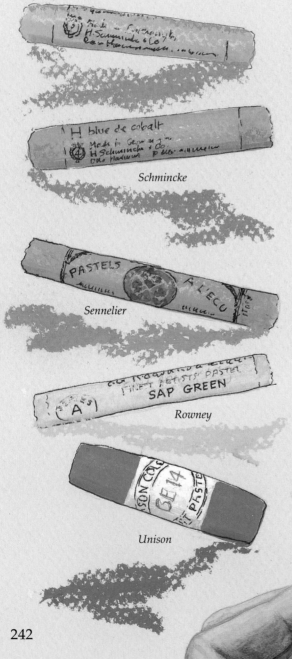

Schmincke

Sennelier

Rowney

Unison

HARDER PASTELS

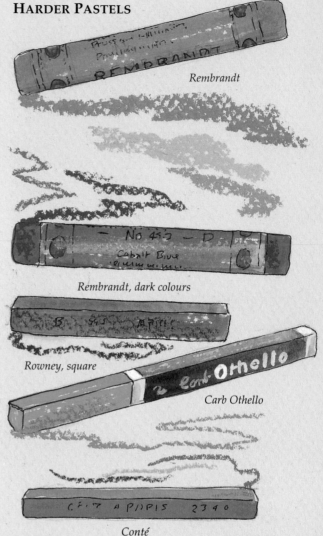

Rembrandt

Rembrandt, dark colours

Rowney, square

Carb Othello

Conté

STUMPS

Stumps are used for rubbing, to spread the colour more smoothly or to blend in adjacent tones. Several are needed so that light bright colours are not contaminated by stumps with dark colour still on them.

WHERE TO KEEP YOUR PASTELS

Their original box is a convenient holder where everything can be seen. Keep a cloth in it and wipe the pastels clean from time to time. Artists who use pastels regularly and buy extra colours, often find that a number of boxes with deeper square compartments are more useful. The pastels become broken with use, and are put into compartments according to colour. This system looks untidy but works very well.

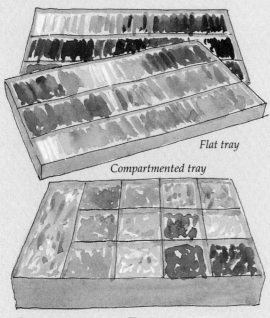

Flat tray

Compartmented tray

FIXATIVE

To prevent accidental rubbing, fixative can be sprayed onto pastel, where it acts as an additional binder, holding the grains to the paper surface. In doing so it inevitably darkens the colours slightly, some more than others, so that the effect is somewhat unpredictable. The main use of fixative is to fix parts of the picture you have worked on, so you can continue to add further colour to them. The new pastel adheres much better to the firmer support, and enables you to work more extensively on building the surface and texture you desire. When you blend by rubbing, some pastel is always lost. By fixing and then blending again in alternate layers you can build up more intense tones and colours. If a picture is complete and is going to be framed there is no need for fixative, as the glass provides a complete protection. Modern fixatives are safer than they were and the smell has been reduced, but are still better used out of doors. Wear a mask indoors.

Spray out of doors if possible.

BE CAREFUL OF THE DUST

Pastels create a lot of dust, some of which you breathe in. If you are doing a large picture, or work regularly with pastels, use the very cheap masks which can be bought from builders merchants or from some art shops.

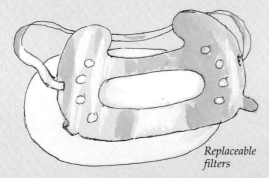

Replaceable filters

A damp cloth is good for cleaning your fingers every so often, and brown parcel paper will cover the table you are working on. Newspaper will do, but is distracting if you keep reading it.

Unfixed

Fixed

The small but significant differences that fixative makes are shown above.

HOW TO MAKE YOUR OWN PASTELS

If it is not convenient or possible to buy commercial pastels, you can make your own. You will need the artists' pigments, gum tragacanth as the binder, and if a preservative is thought necessary, sodium benzoate. Some suppliers who are willing to send through the post are listed on p. 252. Each pigment needs a binder of a matching strength, according to the absorbency of the pigment and its cohesion when bound. Some colours also dry to a harder consistency than others. To accommodate these differing requirements, a basic solution of binder is prepared, from which in turn progressively weaker solutions are made and labelled. 4 solutions should be enough to start with, but you will need to experiment to find a degree of softness or hardness that suits your style of working.

Many of the fine commercial pastels are made with binders unavailable to the public, so you may not be able to match their qualities.

INGREDIENTS

BINDERS

■ Gum tragacanth is the most widely available and works well. It is sold as a powder, which dissolves in warm water.

■ Methyl cellulose is a modern alternative, but harder to find. The powder dissolves in cold water.

WHITE PIGMENTS

■ Precipitated chalk is the whitest form of chalk and makes up a hard pastel. As white is the basis of most pastels, your choice of material is important.

■ Whiting is a slightly softer and less white form of chalk.

■ Lithopone is softer still. It is often used as a filler for tube colours.

■ Titanium White is an excellent white and a base for tints.

COLOURED PIGMENTS

These are seldom needed at full strength, and are mixed in with the white to make the range of tints. With the stronger colours, introduce the coloured pigment gradually into the white you have set aside, otherwise a lot of white can disappear into the mixture before the colour is modified enough to be useful. You can also make up useful colour mixtures to make into pastels.

MEASURING THE INGREDIENTS FOR THE BINDER

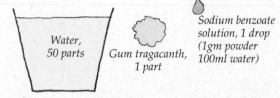

Water, 50 parts *Gum tragacanth, 1 part* *Sodium benzoate solution, 1 drop (1gm powder 100ml water)*

Sprinkle the tragacanth powder into the mildly warm, but not hot, water, and leave overnight to dissolve completely. Add a drop of the preservative, sodium benzoate, if you wish to store the solution for any length of time.

MAKING UP THE SOLUTIONS

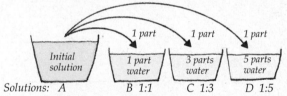

Initial solution *1 part* *1 part water* *1 part* *3 parts water* *1 part* *5 parts water*

Solutions: A *B 1:1* *C 1:3* *D 1:5*

Take some of the initial solution, A, add to it an equal quantity of water and stir it together. This is solution B. Make up solutions C and D in their proportions.

MAKING THE PASTELS

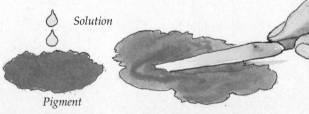

Solution

Pigment

Put out a quantity of pigment on a ground-glass slab or other hard surface, and with a dropper add some solution to the heap; mix together thoroughly with a palette knife to a stiff consistency, like putty. Use as little solution as possible as the gum hardens the pastel.

DRY A PIECE AND TRY IT

Test a piece to see if it is too hard or soft before making the set of pastels.

■ Remove a small piece, dry it with a hair-drier or in the airing cupboard.
■ Try it on some pastel paper to see if it works.

ROLL OUT THE PASTELS

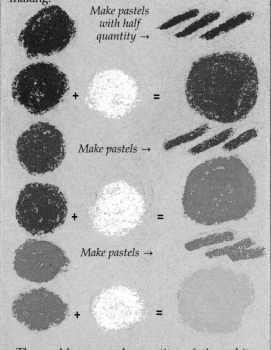

Roll lumps gently at first

Divide into two equal parts, roll one into a ball, then a sausage, and then in some paper to a smooth cylinder. When you have the shape you want, put it aside to dry.

DRY THE PASTELS THOROUGHLY

Dry the pastels overnight in a warm place.

MAKING THE TINTS

Divide the total amount of paste into two equal parts before rolling the pastels to shape. Put one part aside while you roll the pastel you are making.

Make pastels with half quantity →

Make pastels →

Make pastels →

Then add an equal quantity of the white paste for the next tint, and so on for each tint.

BINDING SOLUTION STRENGTHS

Some suggested starting strengths for some common pigments are listed below. Try them experimentally in small mixtures before committing yourself. For mixtures, an intermediate strength should be tried, bearing in mind the proportions of each colour in the mixture. The Phthalocyanine colours need dilution with White right from the start.

Pigments	Solution
Precipitated Chalk	C
Cadmium Yellow *	C
Mars Yellow	A
Yellow Ochre	D
Raw Sienna	D
Cadmium Red *	C
Alizarin Crimson	B
Earth Reds	D
Mars Red	C
Burnt Sienna	C
Raw Umber *	D
Burnt Umber *	B
Mars Violet	D
Ultramarine	B
Cobalt Blue *	B
Cerulean Blue *	C
Phthalo. Blue 1:4 White	D
Phthalo. Green 1:4 White *	D
Oxide of Chromium *	C
Mars Black	B
Ivory Black	D

WARNING

There is increasing concern over the toxicity of some pigments, and mixing your own colours exposes you to them in their most hazardous form as free floating dust particles.
■ Wear a face mask
■ Keep away from food and drink
■ Wash your hands carefully afterwards

The colours derived from metals are the most dangerous if ingested, and are marked above with an asterisk *. Several others are slightly or moderately toxic, but no pigment is safe to eat or breathe in. Where alternative colours are available; test them to find the best solution strength.

Techniques

PASTEL STROKES

The numerous colours of pastels are the same as those for painting, but the way of holding and working with them is closer to drawing. Use an edge or tip where possible to increase precision. The sharpened edges of harder pastels are good for drawing and detail and the sides of broken pieces make a broader mark, good for large areas. The nature of the individual strokes influences the final effect because the grain of the paper clearly shows the texture of the pastel, whether soft and velvety or hard and scratchy.

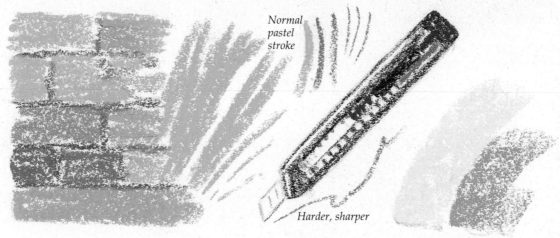

Normal pastel stroke

Harder, sharper

Sideways, broad

The character of the strokes depends on the size and softness of the pastel itself. Try out new pastels on a spare piece of paper. Sharpen them if the ends have become rounded off.

STROKES SIDE-BY-SIDE

Unrubbed pastel, with each stroke set down in place, is the hardest way of achieving a pleasing result, as each stroke has to stand by itself. As an exercise, making a picture this way forces you to think carefully about each colour you employ, and the method is the basis of the more elaborate techniques.

In more normal techniques, where you apply a variety of strokes in connection with some rubbing and blending, the use of strong side-by-side strokes will help to make the foreground seem to advance. Make them in different directions according to the form being created.

246

OVERLAPPING STROKES

Most artists find they need to combine colours and textures, and pastels lend themselves to a light combination of their colours on the paper itself.

As long as there is a tooth for the new layer to grip, and the pastel below is not so slippery or powdery that there is no grip, it is possible to overlay pastels. In combination with light rubbing or blending with the fingertip, this is the nearest pastels come to mixing colours. Even so, they are by no means mixed in the same way as paints, and the results differ considerably. Pastel colours look better if still identifiable, and texturally dull if over-blended.

Cross-hatching of related colours makes for a lively surface where such a texture can be incorporated into a picture. The lower layers can be made firmer, and their tooth increased, by an intermediate spray with fixative. This is the practice of many artists who build up their effects in stages.

SOFT OVER HARD, HARD OVER SOFT

The relative hardness or softness of the underlying layer has a big influence on the behaviour of the strokes over them.

Hard   *Soft*   *Soft*   *Hard*

Soft over hard
This is the easiest way to work. The hard pastels are thin on the paper, leave the grain unclogged, and provide a firm surface for the later applications of softer pastels with their rich texture and vivid colour.

Hard over soft
Light strokes of soft pastel can be blended, and fixed if necessary. Over this prepared ground, harder pastels will still take, and detail can be finally drawn in or strengthened. Very precise detail is possible with this method.

SMOOTH TONES WITH RUBBING

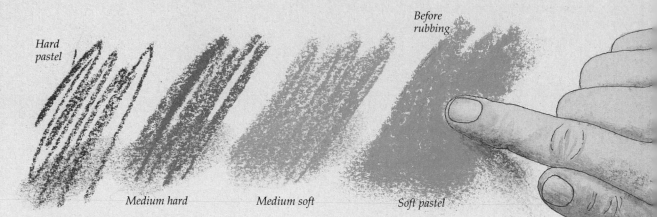

Before rubbing

Hard pastel

Medium hard *Medium soft* *Soft pastel*

Rubbing is more effective with lightly applied soft pastels than with the harder varieties, because the soft pastel spreads evenly, whereas harder pastels only spread partially, giving more of a smeared effect. If you fix the pastel, then it is possible to add another layer and rub again, increasing the soft effect or blending more smoothly.

Unblended side *Blended side*

The sky on the right-hand side shows some of the smoothness characteristic of a sky, and makes a more telling contrast with the foreground detail.

For very small areas use a cotton wool bud

Unrubbed

Rubbed smooth with a cotton wool bud

A stump rubs smaller areas

PASTELS OVER A PREPARED GROUND

The paper colouring does not always suit every part of a picture, but by applying loose watercolour washes to parts of the paper you can give your picture a flying start.

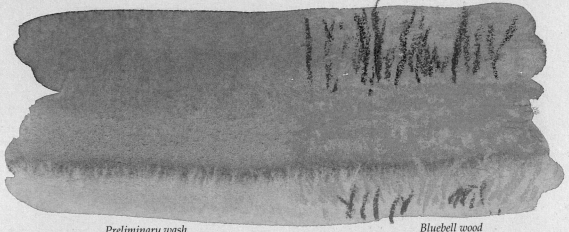

Preliminary wash   *Bluebell wood*

The two tonal areas are painted with colours suited to their different final effects. The grey-brown behind the trees makes for a quick and economical rendering of a complex area. The warmth behind the bluebells gives vibrancy to the blues.

The smooth gradations come readily from the underlying middle tones. Extensive smooth areas need a larger-scale space and treatment for their full effect. ▷

Aeroplane engine

The strong washes save a heavy build-up in the darks, and simplify the work of creating a rich and velvety finish so as to bring the vase and flower textures to life.
▽

Preliminary wash

Preliminary wash   *Bowl of violas*

A PASTEL DEMONSTRATION

SHADED WATERFALL

Pastel seemed the ideal medium to capture the strong contrasts and make most of the brilliant sunlight on the tree and ground. Pastel combines the attributes of both drawing and painting, and with the aid of tinted paper is capable of quick results.

Aims

The texture of the bright soft pastel in the foreground should contrast well with the flatter treatment of the darks, giving a three-dimensional feel to the picture. The colour scheme of the photograph lacked interest, and pastels are ideal for introducing further colours experimentally.

The photograph

This gives a good general impression, and brings back the scene, but shows that the foreground stones have been covered with concrete. Separate shots were taken of the waterfall and background rocks where detail is easily lost.

The drawing was done on dark paper with charcoal, as it is easy to remove if inaccurate, has a controllable blackness, and blends in easily with the darks.

Charcoal was used to suggest the rock strata as an aid to placing the pastel strokes. Following the charcoal guidelines, the dark rock surrounding the waterfall was gradually developed with blue-violets and coloured greys in various combinations. The pastels were very lightly applied. These colours were introduced to move away from the neutral grey and green colours of so many rocky scenes.

The river stones are modelled mainly with light colours, tending towards warm buff and a hint of violet-grey, rubbed slightly with a finger before adding the creamier lights. The paper colour served well for the shadows, into which some deeper violets were introduced. The river-bed takes the eye from the foreground towards the waterfall, so the contrast was gradually reduced to lead the eye away.

The temptation to brighten the waterfall had to be resisted as it would have competed with the contrast of the nearby tree trunks. Blues and violets were stroked on following the direction of the water's flow, with frequent checks to compare the overall effect.

The dark river water is put in with a range of green-blues, care being taken not to stray into the cool greens which would overload the colour scheme by introducing an extraneous colour. Pastels can be picked up and used so easily that there is a constant temptation to introduce attractive new colours into the picture. The darks are confined to shades of blue and brown, and the yellows and some reds are well represented in the lights.

The brighter parts of the foreground rocks are lightly stroked in over the drawing to begin the modelling, which includes some blending and overlaying of colours. The first strokes were rubbed to make a smooth layer for the brighter modelling that followed. On a larger scale, the treatment is the same as for the river stones. Some of the more distant of these were lightened with blue-violet to open up the middle distance.

The trunks were earlier defined with dark brown shadow outlines, and were now now built up with firmer strokes of soft light pastel, going crossways to match the texture of the trunk. The pressure of the pastel was continuously varied to follow the quick changes of tones across the trunks. As few strokes as possible were used to keep the edges sharp, but further bright pale creams were needed to emphasise the sunlit edges. The highlights had to be carefully reinforced to fill the grain and overcome the dark paper showing through.

By thinking of the pastel in your hand as a drawing implement, you automatically make strokes in the right direction and of about the right strength, and there is no real need to do exercises to learn how to make any particular stroke.

Frequent pauses were made to assess whether the picture was still going in the right direction, and further additions to the dark rock wall next to the waterfall were carefully made, using pastels of a tone and colour close to the paper. It was important not to accidentally create a rival centre of interest.

The twigs were drawn in directly without guidelines, then some dark reds that matched the tone of the paper were put in lightly, followed by the sunlit leaves, carefully added with single strokes of brighter pinks and creams. The blue water was spread gradually downwards to avoid an empty look in the lower river bed, also matching the tone of the paper, and finally, just a few dots of pure white at the bottom of the waterfall. The shadowed edges of the trunks were strengthened with a dark violet-brown.

There is a practical limit to the darkness of most pastel pictures because pure black and a few close relations are noticeably darker than most of the other darks and would stand out crudely if not used carefully.

Shaded Waterfall.
The dark paper strongly influences the picture and suggests the strong shadows of the forest. The lights show up well against it, and the dark grain showing through the lights is more natural than the alternative of having lighter spots show through the dark pastels if a lighter paper had been chosen. Cooler colours have been used in the shaded areas and warm colours employed to bring out the lights.

251

SUPPLIERS

All art shops sell either Winsor & Newton or Rowney paints, and some larger shops sell both. This list concentrates on specialist shops who also supply the finest quality but less common makes of materials from the UK or abroad.

L. Cornelissen & Son, 105 Great Russell Street, London WC1B 3RY (0171 636 1045) – Schmincke oils, watercolours, gouache; Roberson oils; Liquitex acrylics; Unison, Schmincke and Sennelier pastels; Winsor & Newton watercolours and brushes; Cornelissen brushes and dry pigments. Oils, resins, waxes etc.

Daler-Rowney, 12 Percy Street, London W1A 2BP (0171 636 8241) – Rowney oils, watercolours, gouache, egg tempera tubes, pastels; Roberson dry pigments.

A.P. Fitzpatrick, 142 Cambridge Heath Road, Bethnal Green, London E1 5QJ (0171 790 0844) – Sax, Old Holland and Di Volo oils, Lascaux acrylics, Kremer dry pigments. Oils, resins, waxes etc.

Green & Stone, 259 King's Road, London SW3 5EL (0171 352 0837) – Blockx oils.

Heffer Art & Graphics, 15-21 King Street, Cambridge CB1 1LH (01223 56849) – Winsor & Newton oils, watercolours; Rowney oils, watercolours, acrylics, pastels: Rembrandt watercolours, oils, pastels; Maimeri watercolours, oils; Sennelier watercolours, pastels.

Frank Herring & Sons, 27 High West Street, Dorchester, Dorset, DT1 1UP (01305 267917) – Winsor & Newton oils and alkyd/oils, acrylics and watercolours; Rowney oils, watercolours, acrylics, egg tempera and pastels; Holbein watercolours; Liquitex acrylics.

T.N. Lawrence & Son, 119 Clerkenwell Road, London EC1R 5BY (0171 242 3534) – Da Vinci oils, watercolours; Old Holland oils; Lukas watercolours; Sennelier pastels; Golden acrylics.

London Graphic Centre, 16-18 Shelton Street, Covent Garden, London WC2H 9JJ (0171 240 0095) – Rembrandt oils, watercolours, gouache, pastels, Roberson oils, dry pigments, Liquitex acrylics.

Russell & Chapple, 23 Monmouth Street, London WC2H 9DE (0171 836 7521) – Old Holland oils and dry pigments, Lukas watercolours, Golden acrylics, Unison pastels. Canvas specialist. Watercolour paper in rolls.

Winsor & Newton, 51-52 Rathbone Place, London W1P 1AB (0171 636 4231) – All Winsor & Newton paints including alkyd oils and dry pigments; some Old Holland oils.

FURTHER READING

The following are only a small selection of the many admirable modern books on painting and drawing.

General	*Developing Ideas in Artwork* by M. Stephen Doherty, Watson-Guptill, 1988. *Perspective for Painters* by Howard Etter and Margit Malmstrom, Watson-Guptill, 1990. *The Science of Art* by Martin Kemp, Yale Univesity Press, 1990. *The Creative Artist* by Nita Leland, North Light, 1990. *Marine Painting* by Susan Rayfield, Watson-Guptill, 1991. *Energise Your Painting with Colour* by Lewis Lehrman, North Light, 1993. *Artist's Guide to Composition* by Frank Webb, David & Charles, 1994. *How to Discover Your Personal Painting Style* by David P. Richards, North Light, 1995. *Painting Birds Step by Step* by Bart Rulon, North Light, 1996.
Technical	*The Artist's Handbook of Materials and Techniques* by Ralph Mayer, Faber and Faber, 1987. *Art Hardware* by Steven L. Saitzyk, Watson-Guptill 1987. *The Materials and Techniques of Painting* by Jonathan Stephenson, Thames & Hudson, 1989.
Drawing	*Drawing Lessons from the Great Masters* by Robert Beverly Hale, Watson-Guptill, 1974. *Draw* by Jeffery Camp, Dorling Kindersley, 1981. *Drawing Nature* by Stanley Maltzman, North Light, 1995. *The Complete Drawing Course* by Stan Smith, Collins & Brown, 1995.
Watercolour	*The Complete Book of Watercolour* by José M Parramon, Phaidon, 1993. *Watercolour Techniques* by Jan Kunz, North Light, 1994. *Texture and Detail in Watercolour* by Richard Bolton, Batsford, 1995. *Basic Flower Painting Techniques in Watercolour* by Rachel Rubin Wolf, North Light, 1996. *Painting Wild Flowers* by Marjorie Blamey, Dorling Kindersley, 1998.
Tempera	*New Techniques in Egg Tempera* by Robert Vickrey and Diane Cochrane, Watson-Guptill, 1973.
Oil Painting	*How to Paint Like the Old Masters* by Joseph Sheppard, Watson-Guptill, 1983. *A Light Touch; Painting Landscapes in Oils* by David Curtis, David & Charles, 1994. *Oil Painting Secrets from a Master* by Linda Cateura, Watson-Guptill, 1995. *Capturing Light in Oils* by Paul Strisik, North Light, 1996.
Pastel	*Creative Painting with Pastel* by Carol Katchen, HarperCollins, 1991. *Capturing the Light in Pastel* by Lionel Aggett, David & Charles, 1995. *Vibrant Flower Painting* by Frances Treanor, David & Charles, 1995.

INDEX